GENDER, PARTICIPATION AND CITIZENSHIP IN THE NETHERLANDS

Gender, Participation and Citizenship in the Netherlands

Edited by
JET BUSSEMAKER
RIAN VOET

LONDON AND NEW YORK

First published 1998 by Ashgate Publishing

Reissued 2018 by Routledge
2 Park Square, Milton Park, Abingdon, Oxon, OX14 4RN
711 Third Avenue, New York, NY 10017, USA

Routledge is an imprint of the Taylor & Francis Group, an informa business

Copyright © J. Bussemaker and R. Voet 1998

All rights reserved. No part of this book may be reprinted or reproduced or utilised in any form or by any electronic, mechanical, or other means, now known or hereafter invented, including photocopying and recording, or in any information storage or retrieval system, without permission in writing from the publishers.

Notice:
Product or corporate names may be trademarks or registered trademarks, and are used only for identification and explanation without intent to infringe.

Publisher's Note
The publisher has gone to great lengths to ensure the quality of this reprint but points out that some imperfections in the original copies may be apparent.

Disclaimer
The publisher has made every effort to trace copyright holders and welcomes correspondence from those they have been unable to contact.

A Library of Congress record exists under LC control number: 97078096

ISBN 13: 978-1-138-31647-8 (hbk)
ISBN 13: 978-1-138-31650-8 (pbk)
ISBN 13: 978-0-429-45563-6 (ebk)

Contents

Figures and tables	vi
List of contributors	vii
Preface	ix
Acknowledgements	x

Introduction
Jet Bussemaker and Rian Voet — 1

1 Citizenship and female participation
 Rian Voet — 11
2 Gender and the separation of spheres in twentieth century Dutch society: pillarisation, welfare state formation and individualisation
 Jet Bussemaker — 25
3 Political participation and social rights. The triumph of the breadwinner in the Netherlands
 Tjitske Akkerman — 38
4 Double lives: labour market participation, citizenship and gender
 Janneke Plantenga — 51
5 Participation through care? The case of the Dutch housewife
 Trudie Knijn — 65
6 Citizenship, participation and the social policy on girls in the Netherlands
 Annemieke van Drenth — 79
7 Political empowerment of women in the Netherlands
 Monique Leijenaar — 91
8 Furthering the 'cause': femocrat strategies in national government
 Joyce Outshoorn — 108
9 Can a woman be just like a man? The representation of women in the corporatist world in the Netherlands
 Jantine Oldersma — 122

Bibliography — 134

Figures and tables

Table 4.1	Female activity rates in the European Member States, 1975-1994	58
Table 4.2	GDP per capita in Belgium, Denmark, France, Germany and the United Kingdom, 1820-1989	61
Table 4.3	Gross Domestic Product per working-hour, 1870-1987	62
Table 5.1	Time spent in hours per week on unpaid care labour within the household	67
Table 6.1	Participation in full-time education for age group and gender (in percentages)	86
Table 7.1	Background characteristics of male and female MPs, 1918-1946	95
Figure 7.1	Percentage of women in Parliament, 1946-1975	96
Figure 7.2	Percentage of women in Parliament, 1977-1994	99
Table 7.2	Women's participation in political decision-making (in percentages)	103
Table 7.3	Women's participation in European Cabinets, European Parliament, Regions and Local Councils (in percentages)	103

List of contributors

Tjitske Akkerman is an Assistant Professor at the Department of Political Science at the University of Amsterdam. She is the author of *Women's Vices, Public Benefits: Women and Commerce in the French Enlightenment* (1992) and co-editor of *Perspectives on Feminist Political Thought in European History* (forthcoming, 1997). She is currently writing a book on democracy. Her current research interests include gender and the history of the Dutch welfare state.

Jet Bussemaker is an Assistant Professor at the Department of Political Science and Public Administration at the Free University in Amsterdam. In 1997, she was a visiting scholar at the Centre for European Studies, Harvard University, Cambridge Mass. Her PhD thesis, published in 1993, received an award from the Dutch Organisation of Political Research. She has written widely on political theory, welfare states, gender and citizenship.

Annemieke van Drenth is an Assistant Professor at the Department of Women's Studies of Leyden University. In recent years she has been a Research Fellow on a grant from the National Science Association for the program 'Gender and Care'. She has published on the history of girls' education and women in social care. She is currently researching the life histories of lone mothers, and related social policy.

Trudie Knijn is an Associate Professor at the Department of General Social Sciences and Managing Director of the Centre for Economic and Social Policy Research of the Social Faculty (both at the University of Utrecht). She has published on a variety of topics in the field of private care relationships. Her current research is on the relationship between public and private care arrangements from a comparative perspective.

Monique Leijenaar is an Associate Professor of Political Science at the University of Nijmegen and a consultant for the Dutch government and several intergovernmental organisations. She has published several articles and books on local politics, election studies, women and politics. Her most recent work is *How to create a gender balance in political decision-making* (for the European Commission).

Jantine Oldersma is currently employed as an Assistant Professor at the Department of Women's Studies in the Social Sciences at Leyden University. She studied political studies at the University of Amsterdam and received her PhD at Leyden University. She has published on women in politics, policies on women, feminism and popular culture, and on feminist detectives.

Joyce Outshoorn is Professor of Women's Studies at Leiden University, the Netherlands, and is Chairperson of the Netherlands Research School for Women's Studies. She studied political science and contemporary history at the University of Amsterdam. Her current research focuses on women's public policy, women's movements, and abortion policy.

Janneke Plantenga is an Assistant Professor at the Economic Institute of the University of Utrecht. She has a PhD in economics from the University of Groningen. Her main fields of interest are the history of women's work, changing working time patterns, and social policy. Together with Geske Dijkstka she edited *Gender and Economics: A European Perspective* (1997).

Rian Voet is an Assistant Professor at the Department of Political Studies of the University of Auckland, New Zealand. She obtained her PhD in political studies at Leyden University and. is the author of *Feminism and Citizenship* (forthcoming 1997). Her teaching and research topics include political theory, women and politics, identity politics, and élite theory.

Preface

Over the last few years many Dutch academics have been working on questions concerning participation, citizenship and gender. This book emerged from a shared conviction that a judicious selection of some of their recent projects should be made accessible to a wider audience by being published in English. All of the chapters in this book appear for the first time in print, in either language. The contributing authors are all recognised Dutch academics in the areas of economics, education, political science, social policy or women's studies.

It is the aim of the editors that this book will prove a useful contribution to international scholarship with regards to the interdependence of definitions of gender, participation and citizenship. While providing details specific to conditions in the Netherlands, the chosen contributors relate their discussions to international and theoretical scholarship.

Distinctive features of the Dutch social and political environment highlight the utility of the chosen country-specific examples to comparative studies and theoretical arguments. Some of the distinctive characteristics covered in this volume are: consociational democracy, the comprehensive welfare state structure, gender-specific policies and subsidies, the combination of feminist ideas and traditional gender division of labour, pillarisation, individualisation, corporatism, the popularity of civic republicanism and communitarianism, and the influence of Christian-Democratic ideas.

This book has been written with both the general reader and specialist in mind and has therefore been kept as jargon-free as possible.

Acknowledgements

In the preparation of this book we have benefited from the supportive environment of the European Network for Research on Women, Welfare State and Citizenship. For various reasons some authors who once were involved, could not be included in the final book. We would like to mention here Odile Verhaar (Free University Amsterdam) as well as Selma Sevenhuijsen (Utrecht University).

A grant from the Foundation for Law and Government (Reob), which is part of the Netherlands Organization for Scientific Research (NWO) created the possibilities for Jet Bussemaker to work on this book. It also created the opportunity, together with the assistance of the Department of Political Science and Public Administration of the Free University in Amsterdam, to work on it while she was a fellow at the Center for European Studies, Harvard University. Also thanks to the University of Auckland who provided Rian Voet with a half-yearly sabbatical and a grant for her stay at the Department of Political Studies at the Catholic University of Leuven (Belgium).

We want to show our gratitude to Paul Stone and Mike Crawshaw: Paul Stone for his help with the assistance of the final language correction; Mike Crawshaw for his assistance in the preparation of the final manuscript.

If not mentioned otherwise, all quotations from originally Dutch publications are the authors'.

Introduction

Jet Bussemaker and Rian Voet

Recently, western societies have been confronted with developments that pose new questions about citizenship, particularly if we consider citizenship to be not only the rights, activities, and virtues of the individual citizen in relation to the state, but also the socio-political relationships that bind citizens to each other (Barbalet 1988; Heater 1990). The restructuring of welfare states has had implications for the status of citizenship (Culpitt 1992; George and Taylor-Gooby 1996; Roche 1992; Twine 1994). Further, societies have become increasingly pluralistic, which has led to new debates on what forms democracy and representation should take and whether or not one should have special rights for special groups of people (Kymlicka 1995; Phillips 1995). Also the consequences of migration have posed new questions about citizenship, nationhood and 'belonging' (Brubaker 1992; Soysal 1993). In addition, the globalisation of the economy and of decision-making in general, as well as the development towards an European Union has led many writers to query whether we should still put citizenship rights and participation within the framework of a (national) state (Guéhenno 1995; Meehan 1994). Finally, the growing individualisation of western societies has called into question the significance of citizen participation in different public and semi-public spheres (Barber 1984).

Feminist scholars have participated in these debates, linking citizenship issues to gender. Several feminist theorists have indicated that most citizenship theories have been built on the model of the male citizen (Elshtain 1981; Fraser 1989; Jones 1990; Lister 1990; Pateman 1988, 1989). Other feminists have laid bare the gender assumptions behind the notions of citizenship developed in particular countries and periods (Bock and James 1992; Einhorn 1993; Rendall 1994; Sullivan and Whitehouse 1996). Most feminist studies focused on the meaning of rights and the status of citizenship for women. Indeed, in most countries, the acquisition of rights has differed considerably for men and for women (e.g. Carter 1988; Frader 1996; Lister 1990; O'Connor 1996; Orloff 1993; Pateman 1989; Pedersen 1993; Schuler 1990; Vogel 1991, 1994; Walby 1994). Recently, scholars have put slightly more emphasis on the meaning of participation for citizenship (cf. Dietz 1985, 1987; Mansbridge 1993; Mouffe 1993; Phillips 1991; Sarvasy and Siim 1994; Siim 1994; Young 1990, 1995).

In this book too, an approach is taken which argues that citizenship is more than just a formal legal status which entitles citizens to civil, political and social (or welfare) rights. It argues that citizenship is also a matter of participation, be it political participation, participation in the labour market, civil society or in another semi-public sphere. Citizenship is something that needs to be enacted and cannot be achieved by just sitting in a chair enjoying one's rights. Such an approach moves beyond the dominant notion of citizenship. It relates the various forms of participation to gender (cf. Schlozman et al. 1995) and questions ideas such as the separation of public and private spheres. It explores the meaning of identity, heterogeneity and difference. It examines the relation between social and political equality, and reflects upon the necessary conditions for the empowerment of women.

This book is about the relationship between citizenship, participation and gender, and how they are currently being rethought. All contributions in this book refer to international discussions on citizenship and gender. However, they also contain a good deal of information on, and detailed analysis of, a particular case study the Netherlands.

The Dutch case

International discussions on gender and citizenship have not had much to say about the Netherlands. This book tries to redress that relative neglect. We would argue that a closer look at the 'Dutch case' raises some interesting questions. How to explain for example, that the Netherlands is distinguished both for being a well-developed, rich country with extensive welfare arrangements, and for having unequal gender relations? Whereas the Netherlands in 1996 ranks number four in the UN Human Development Index, which measures the general well-being of citizens in various (137) countries, it drops to number 11 (UNDP 1996) - and even to number 20 in 1995 (UNDP 1995) - in the Gender Disparity Index, which measures the share of earned income, life expectancy, literacy rates and education between the sexes. The Gender Empowerment Measure, which measures gender inequality in key areas of economic and political participation and decision-making, ranked the Netherlands eighth out of 104 countries (UNDP 1996, pp. 33-35). To explain this difference in ranking, we must look at Dutch gender relations in more detail, and establish their connection to issues of citizenship and participation. In doing so, we touch upon questions that are, we believe, of more general significance.

One reason why the Dutch case is interesting from an international point of view, relates to its historical heritage (Geyl 1963; Israel 1995; Kossmann 1978; Lijphart 1968; Zahn 1984). It could well be, for example, that the distinctively Dutch tradition of strong social and political segregation, developed within a context of pluralism and respect for the difference of other groups, may throw new light on contemporary discussions on difference and pluralism and citizenship. With the Dutch example in mind, one may ask whether, from a feminist point of view, pluralism is always positive and something which we should accept uncritically (Phillips 1993)?

Interestingly, in the Netherlands a revival of the concept of citizenship in both the academic and political world has appeared (Simonis, Hemerijck and Lehning 1992). Citizenship has even been the subject of a large research project of the Scientific Council for Government Policy (Gunsteren 1992), while related notions such as civil society have been studied by governmental research institutions, especially with regard to voluntary work (Dekker 1994). Dutch debates on citizenship pull one of four ways: citizenship is connected with rights, or it is connected with labour market participation, or with political participation, or with care. The popularity of republican notions of citizenship, which emphasise political participation and communitarian notions of citizenship, which emphasise care is remarkable. The popularity of communitarianism seems to be easily explained by the legacy of a strong welfare state and because of the powerful influence exercised by religious interests on Dutch politics for almost a century (Lijphart 1968). To what degree the popularity of republicanism might be explained by the strong democratisation movements of the 1960s and the social movements of the seventies and eighties (Kriesi 1993) or even by the origin of the modern Netherlands in the Batavian Republic which emerged after the war of independence against Spain, is unclear (cf. Gelder 1993; Huizinga 1968; Kossman 1978; Schama 1977). Perhaps this republicanism, which has been so characteristic a feature of Dutch debates over the past 30 years, is surprising in a country that has always been accused of suffering from an 'administrators mentality' (cf. Velde 1993; Zahn 1984).

Several citizenship projects have been developed in response to the needs of various migrant and ethnic groups. The Netherlands has extensive ethnic communities; some of them come from former Dutch colonies (some Indonesians, but especially Surinams and Antillians), others from Southern Europe and the Middle East. Recently, policies have been developed under the umbrella title of 'inburgering programmes' (citizenship examinations for foreigners) to stimulate - and sometimes even force - them to participate in Dutch society, as well as to improve their knowledge of the Dutch language, history and society. The recognition of differences (whether these reside in questions of gender or ethnicity) has influenced political debates on pluralism, group identity and the meaning of shared values for citizenship (Koch and Scheffer 1996).

The Dutch case may also be of more general interest because the relation of gender to citizenship in it has been ambivalent (Sevenhuijsen 1996 pp 152-88). Dutch women have been stereotypically depicted as being very good housewives. As early as the seventeenth century, their tidy, cosy houses were favourite subjects of artists and writers. Nowadays, many women remain housewives, although more and more of them are choosing to participate in the work force as well. Though the labour market participation rates of Dutch women were once very low, their participation has recently increased, even if largely in part-time jobs.

Of the total female population aged 15 to 64, 53 per cent were engaged in paid employment, according to 1990 figures. For 1960, 1970 and 1980 the percentages were respectively 26, 31 and 36 (OECD 1992, p. 29). While in 1980 the number of women in the Dutch work force lagged far behind the other 17 richest countries in the Organization for Economic Cooperation and

Development (OECD) (36 per cent of the female population when the OECD average was 54 per cent), by 1990 this had increased enormously (53 per cent where the OECD average was 61.5 per cent (OECD 1992, p. 29). Yet again, we have to bear in mind that approximately two-thirds of the female labour force works part-time in the mid-nineties: the highest amount of all the countries within the European Union (OECD 1990).

As for political participation, Dutch women got the suffrage relatively early (1919) and until very recently, the percentage of women in parliament exceeded the percentage of women in the work force. In 1981 the percentage of female members of parliament was still 17, but it increased in 1994 to 33. However, the current rather high level of women's participation in parliament is not matched by their involvement in other decision-making institutions. To complicate the story even further, the reproductive rights for women - contraception and abortion - work out rather liberal, even though the Dutch are often supposed to take severely conservative positions on many moral issues. When all these contradictory points are brought together, it is indeed difficult to say whether Dutch women are first-class or second-class citizens. As this book shows, they may be both at the same time, depending on the particular topic one considers and the concept of citizenship one is following.

There is yet another reason why the Dutch case deserves more attention, and that is because of the far-reaching social and cultural transformations that have taken place in recent years. There have been important changes in women's rates of participation and their status as citizens. Women are under new pressure to participate in different social spheres simultaneously. They are now expected to be housewives, workers, politically active citizens and participants in civil society all at the same time. As many articles in this book show, current policies regarding women's participation are far from coherent, and, even when they are not self-contradictory, are shot through with tensions, unresolved dilemmas and ambivalence. Nonetheless, new ideas are also being developed, both inside and outside the government. Some of these ideas, which are discussed in this book, offer interesting alternatives which may eventually contribute to a more balanced and complete model of citizenship that takes proper account of women and men.

In the rest of this introduction, we will put the Dutch situation in a more international comparative perspective, give some general peculiarities of the Netherlands and introduce the different chapters in the book.

The Dutch case in an international perspective

For a long time, the Netherlands was famous for three things: tulips, windmills and cheese. All three can still be found in promotional brochures for tourists. Nowadays, however, many people associate the Netherlands with less picturesque concerns, among them soccer, the red light district, drugs and euthanasia. These phenomena are as much a part of the contemporary Netherlands as the tourist images. The Netherlands seems to be a country of contradictions -- and not only with respect to gender. On the one hand, liberal policies towards prostitution, homosexuality, contraception and abortion; on the other, a political rhetoric that remains in many respects, morally traditional, even severe. It is instructive to see how these opposed points of view are resolved in practice. The use of drugs and euthanasia, for example, is still proscribed under the penal code, but the attitude towards the actual incidence of each has been far more permissive. Rather than being an effect of the well-known notion of 'Dutch tolerance', as is often assumed, permissive liberal policies are a consequence of an over-riding pragmatism. Policies are often directed towards controlling negative side-effects, rather than to enforcing a strict standard of moral and political 'correctness'.

From a comparative perspective, the Netherlands seems to occupy a 'middling' position in rank of European countries. Although small in terms of land mass, the Netherlands is one of the most dense populated countries in the world. From that perspective, and regarded from an European point of view, it is notable larger than, for example, the Scandinavian countries and Switzerland and Austria, but still much smaller than the larger powers such as Germany, France and the United Kingdom. Its size, together with a long tradition of international trade, has made the Dutch economy very open. As Katzenstein (1985) has argued, such an open economy has no choice but to adapt to world market changes, and this the Dutch have done. Within the Netherlands, however, there has been much heated debate on the organisation of the internal labour market. Although potential conflicts were often canalised by institutional ways of deliberation in a well developed system of neocorporatism, some issues - notably, the regulation of women's participation in the labour market - have continued to provoke extensive discussion and disagreement.

An international orientation can also be found in the Dutch welfare system. Due to its position at the crossroads of Europe, and to its relatively late industrialisation, the Netherlands freely 'borrowed' much of its thinking on welfare from different foreign examples. Contemporary practice in the Netherlands reveals some corporatist-conservative notions of insurance schemes, social democratic notions of universal rights, as well as more liberal notions of schemes based on means testing. In the well-known typology of Esping-Andersen (1990), the Netherlands is placed under the Social Democratic regime, although the author shows more than once that it also has a lot in common with the conservative regime. These inconsistencies mean that, in most comparative studies of welfare states, the Dutch case is regarded as atypical. Although some scholars have tried to explain the Dutch system from a comparative or international point of view (cf. Engbersen et al. 1993; Kersbergen 1995; Roebroek 1993; Therborn 1993), their attempts have largely bypassed any considerations of gender.

In our view, it is necessary to incorporate gender if we are to arrive at a proper understanding of how and why the Dutch system of welfare operates as it does (Bussemaker and Kersbergen 1994; Plantenga and Doorne-Huiskes 1992). The Dutch system shares a high level of public expenditures and rather generous welfare entitlements with the Scandinavian regime. However, whereas in the Scandinavian countries state contributions have been used to facilitate women's participation in the labour market, in the Dutch case generous entitlements have been used to keep women out of it. For a long time a breadwinner's income was assumed to be enough to maintain a family (that is, the breadwinner, his wife and their children). That is why scholars on gender and welfare have often characterised the Netherlands as a 'strong breadwinner model', in common with countries as the United Kingdom and Germany (Ostner and Lewis 1995). In comparison with these countries, particularly the United Kingdom, the Netherlands seems to be unusually generous and effective in putting the 'breadwinner' ideology into practice. As a result, and in spite of its image as an open and tolerant society, the Netherlands maintains a rather traditional welfare state, when seen from the point of view of gender. Indeed, it is this combination of a well-developed welfare state and a powerful ideology of gender difference that helps explain why, when the Netherlands was 'ranked' on gender issues (by the United Nations survey, mentioned above), the results should have been so discrepant. Although there have been considerable changes in the past decades, many policies still assume that men are the main breadwinners and women the main care-givers.

Politically, the Dutch system shows less international orientation although an increasing part of its laws now derive from European Union regulations. Of course, it shares some features with other European countries, such as its being a constitutional monarchy, (with, moreover, a female head of state for more than 100 years), and having a representative democracy made up of various political movements, such as Liberals, Social Democrats, and Christian Democrats. However, the Dutch political system is less known for its similarities to those of other countries than for its distinctive peculiarities. Some of these - for instance the notion of 'consociational democracy' (Lijphart 1968) which combines a plurality of identity groups with methods for creating consensus and stability by élite co-operation - have become 'exportable commodities', particularly in situations where political tension is rife between competing social groups, as in South Africa (Lijphart 1985; Tash 1991). Related to consociational democracy, the phenomenon of 'pillarisation' ('verzuiling'), that is a highly segmented but stable society, has attracted a good deal of interest outside the Netherlands (cf. for an extensive study of the Dutch political system Andeweg and Irwin 1993).

Pillarisation can be rightly understood only if we grant that the Netherlands is a country of minority groups. Historically speaking, Protestants dominated the country for a long time. Catholics were still a large, oppressed minority group around 1850, but the establishment of Catholic emancipation movements in the second half of the nineteenth century freed them from Protestant domination, and enabled them to become one of the main political forces this century. Over the same period, in common with the religious groups, socialists and liberals too were developing their own pillars, that is to say, they were setting up their own subcultural networks. The political, as well as the social features of pillarisation, have also had a significant influence on debates on gender and citizenship.

From the point of view of gender, pillarisation is relevant on two counts. First, because the different pillars have variously conceptualised women's citizenship in the light of their own political preoccupations. Second (and often in contrast), the pillars have often agreed on gender and family policies in a bid to create consensus across an otherwise divided society. Moreover, although pillarisation diminished after the sixties, it has recently taken on a renewed relevance. In so far as Dutch society and its political system respond to the demands of oppressed 'minority groups' by acknowledging the need for pluralism (Daalder 1989), they continue some aspects of the pillarisation tradition. In general, since the sixties, the state has readily given financial help to those wishing to set up their own subcultural organisations, whether the initiatives have come from feminists, homosexuals or ethnic minority groups. But it has proved much more difficult to bring the issues raised by these recent subcultures to the attention of 'mainstream' organisations. A good example is the organisation of women's studies at Dutch universities. The Netherlands has a very respectable amount of professors in women's studies; almost every university has, at least, one professor appointed in women's studies. There also exists a rather large Research School on Women's Studies, in which most scholars working on gender participate. However, there are almost no full female professors in the other disciplines. A survey in 1994 found that only 2.3 per cent of full professors were women, and that, of the countries surveyed, only Botswana did worse because they had none (Noordenbos 1995). By 1996, the percentage of full female professors had increased to 4 per cent.

These figures point to an important difference between the 'old' and 'new' forms of pillarisation. Whereas in the 'old' system, various religious and 'quasi-religious' groups were very well represented in the top-level organisation of society - because this was assumed to be the necessary condition for consensus - such is no longer the case. Women, as well as ethnic and other minority groups, are allowed - and sometimes even encouraged - to develop their own organisations and 'group identities' but are largely excluded from top-level positions in decision-making channels and public institutions.

When these facts are borne in mind, it is understandable that Dutch feminist scholars should often experience a sense of *déjà-vu* when they come across contemporary discussions on communitarianism and the meaning of group identities. From the feminist point of view, these notions seem to hark back to traditional forms of pillarisation, as well as to its still existing heritage. Consequently, Dutch feminists treat strategies that strongly focus on group identities with some caution. Something similar might be said about discussions on citizenship and civil society; the emphasis on the role of civil society, particularly by communitarians, remind many Dutch scholars of the old pillarised hierarchical and undemocratic structure of civil society.

The atypical character of the Netherlands again becomes obvious when we look at its norms and values. Much of the country's political history could not be written without reference to the long-term structures of breadwinners and care-givers, the traditional relationships between the sexes and conservative family policies - all of which undoubtedly served at times as so many barriers against harsh developments in the public sphere. Yet simultaneously the Netherlands is often described as quite progressive and morally neutral (Cox 1993). There is a traditional and conservative morality in Dutch politics that, from the 1960s, has coexisted with a considerable freedom of thought on sexual matters, for instance the relative accessibility of abortion (Outshoorn and

Lovenduski 1986) and - partly as a result of this - the low percentage of unwanted pregnancies and teenage mothers.

In general we can say that the Netherlands is quite liberal and feminist as far as attitudes and ideas are concerned, but that actual behaviour and organisational structures lag behind. For instance, it would appear that many people pay lip service to the idea of full participation in the labour market, but that in practice many women still work part-time - more than in other countries - or are not part of the paid work force at all. To give another example, there appears to be broad support for the idea of equal division of care-giving between men and women, but in practice care-giving is still mostly a task for women. Finally, policy makers are full of good intentions as they relate to preparing girls for full citizenship, but have scant regard for the concrete difficulties with which these girls are confronted in their everyday life.

We can put the tension between ideas and behaviour in a broader historical context. The Dutch national character is often said to unite the figures of the preacher and the merchant. That is, in its domestic and even more its foreign politics the Netherlands conjoins the strict morality of the priest with the pragmatism of the merchant. While these metaphors are somewhat too 'masculine' to use in connection to the theme of 'gender, participation and citizenship' they do indicate the special, ambivalent and atypical nature of Dutch society.

Plan of the book

The chapters in this book will elaborate extensively on some of the topics we have mentioned. They will also show why Dutch developments are interesting from a comparative standpoint, empirical as well as theoretical. The first two chapters will give a more general and broad perspective, the chapters thereafter will deal with more detailed studies.

Rian Voet describes and evaluates how women's participation in western societies in general and in the Netherlands in particular would be evaluated by four major citizenship traditions. She does this by summarising the facts of women's participation in the Netherlands, by analysing the internal logic of each of these citizenship traditions and by referring to contemporary Dutch discussions on citizenship. Voet concludes that the dominant citizenship tradition, social liberalism, does not really see participation as an inherent part of citizenship. Alternative citizenship traditions could be drawn upon to emphasise the importance of women's participation: republicanism for political participation, Marxism for participation in the labour market, and communitarianism for participation in public and private care.

In the next chapter, Jet Bussemaker shows how the public and private spheres have been separated in twentieth century Dutch society, and what the implications are for the citizenship status of men and women. She explains in detail the role of pillarisation, paying special attention to the idea of subcultures and the typical Dutch form of civil society (the 'social middle field'). She discusses how some of these notions have been incorporated and altered during the postwar welfare state formation and, more recently, have been linked to notions of individualisation and women's citizenship. Traditional 'pillarised' notions of pluralism, above all the respect for different life styles, Bussemaker argues, have deeply influenced contemporary feminist theories of citizenship in the Netherlands.

In Chapter 3, Tjitske Akkerman examines the first half of the century more closely, charting the history of arguments for and against family allowances and endowment of motherhood. In doing so, she shows what barriers have impeded women's organisations from being successful and how institutional contexts, together with different political beliefs and organisational strategies, have determined women's political participation. Akkerman argues that a deep divide separated Dutch women's organisations, for reasons of religion and (even more) of class, and prevented them from wielding any collective influence on social policy, and thus served to exclude women from participating as active citizens in welfare institutions.

In Chapter 4, Janneke Plantenga describes the pattern of women's participation in the labour market during the twentieth century; she argues that for much of this period citizenship was 'specialised' in the sense that men and women were allocated gender specific social positions, each of which carried a particular set of rights and obligations with regard to paid labour and care. In recent times, however, things have changed rapidly. Plantenga also looks at the extremely low levels of female participation in the labour market, and casts some doubt on the existence of a peculiarly Dutch pattern of norms and values, as well as on the supposedly central role played by pillarisation. In place of these partial answers, she posits explanatory notions of 'productivity' and 'passion'.

Whereas Plantenga focuses primarily on women's lack of participation in the labour market, Trudie Knijn deals with the other side of the story in Chapter 5: women's participation in care, including care for the family, informal care work and activities within the community. She shows how much women contribute to community life and what this means, or should mean, for our attempts to conceptualise civil society. Knijn also examines the relation between care and citizenship. She argues that women's participation in care gives them a second-class citizenship status, while men's participation in paid labour and the resulting position of care dependency, gives them entrance to first-class citizenship. Knijn, furthermore, evaluates some proposals that have been put forward to redress this imbalance.

In Chapter 6 Annemieke van Drenth examines the assumptions about citizenship that underlie the emancipation policy worked out by the Dutch government, especially in its policy towards girls. She argues that these policies are mistaken in so far as they regard the main problem to be girls' choices, considered in isolation, rather than the circumstances in which girls have to make their choices, and the extent to which these choices have been conditioned. As a consequence, van Drenth argues, there is a stark contrast between the implicit assumptions of social policy and the reality of daily life for many Dutch girls. Van Dreth pleads for an alternative concept of citizenship that includes the rights, as well as the duties, of care-giving, thereby allowing girls to participate more readily and more fully in society.

In Chapter 7 Monique Leijenaar surveys women's participation in social and political decision-making in the Netherlands and compares this with other countries of the European Union. According to Leijenaar, there have been four distinct phases in women's access to decision-making bodies in the Netherlands, only in the most recent of which has significant progress been made in getting large numbers of women into political decision-making positions. In contrast, the representation of women in social decision-making bodies is still inadequate. She concludes that women will sooner achieve equality as citizens in political decision-making rather than in social decision-making roles.

Joyce Outshoorn discusses the rise of 'state feminism' in the Netherlands in Chapter 8. She argues that it has opened up significant new routes to women's participation as citizens of modern welfare states. State feminism and its 'femocrats' (feminist bureaucrats) have the potential of enhancing participation in a double sense. They can advance women's political participation not only by pressing for more balanced representation, but also by gendering policy issues, which might give women's advocacy groups further access to government and policy making. Outshoorn concludes that the Dutch 'femocrat' strategy has been relatively successful compared to that adopted in other states, but that its foundation has recently been seriously eroded.

Finally, in Chapter 9 Jantine Oldersma analyses the incorporation of women into advisory bodies of experts and special interest groups. She asks whether the gendering of problems leads to a higher representation of women in Dutch advisory bodies, and decides that this has not been the case. Political actors have heard of 'women's problems', but prefer to think of women as victims, not as political actors in their own right. Furthermore, within advisory bodies the women are different from the men: they have more affiliations with women's organisations and voluntary organisations, they have expertise in women's issues and different views on women's representation. Yet participating 'as women' is precisely what female citizens on advisory bodies are *not* supposed to do.

1 Citizenship and female participation

Rian Voet

Are women in western societies equal citizens or second-sex citizens? It seems to me that those people who speak of women being equal to men and those who speak of their being relegated to a second sex are using arguments from different citizenship traditions (Voet 1995). Some citizenship traditions only refer to citizenship as a formal, legal status, whereas others refer to citizenship as participation. It is my intention here to describe and evaluate how women are placed within the major citizenship traditions in western societies. For this, I will focus on the issue of participation and will use the Netherlands as my case-study.

Citizenship discourses give various meanings to the term 'participation'. Broadly speaking, where participation is considered important for citizenship, it is usually divided into political and social aspects. Political participation might just be taking part in official politics but it could also mean involvement in other decision-making bodies, interest groups or social movements. Its activities can range from decision-making, voting, demonstrating, petitioning and lobbying to debating public affairs. Social participation likewise carries several meanings. It can refer to participation in the labour market, or to volunteer work in civil society or even sometimes to care activities within the family.

As in most other contemporary western societies, women and men in the Netherlands now have approximately the same rights but a very different pattern of participation. In the political arena this difference appears at the top level, rather than at the grass-roots (Leijenaar 1989). Women's level of participation in the upper echelons of official politics is higher than in most western countries but is still markedly lower than the men's. As of 1996 about one third of the members of cabinet, the house of representatives, provincial councils and the delegation to the European parliament consisted of women (Leijenaar in this volume). In other political bodies the percentage of women drops: 22 per cent in local bodies, 23 per cent in the Senate, 20.4 per cent board members of social organisations (cf. Leijenaar in this volume), 16 per cent in advisory bodies (Oldersma in this volume), and 14 per cent of the mayors (European Network WD 1996).

In the bureaucratic decision-making bodies women's participation is lower than in the political ones. In 1994 only 3 per cent of municipal secretaries - the highest administrative post within local authorities - were women. In 1993 30.6 per cent of public servants were female but in higher, academic positions this percentage dropped to 17.3 and at the very top to 5.8. In the judiciary (according to 1993 figures) 33 per cent were women, which is a relatively high figure, but of the 19 presidents of districts and county courts only one was female (Ministerie van SZW 1995).

The economic decision-making positions provide an even gloomier picture: in executive positions only 4 per cent are women, while, out of a pool of 200 companies, only 17 women made it to the Boards of Supervisory Directors (Ministerie van SZW 1995). In the 25 biggest companies (measured by staff numbers) in 1993 not one woman was on the Board of Supervisory Directors. On the Board of Commissioners most of the large companies had no woman at all, 13 had one woman and one company had two women (Tiedemann 1993).

The statistics on women's social participation are hardly more encouraging. Although female participation in the labour market has rapidly increased from its 1975 figure of 21.7 per cent to 47.7 per cent in 1994, 65.9 per cent of these women were working part-time (Plantenga in this volume). There is also a gender inequality amongst those who have their own business: of those applicants who applied for a small business credit in 1990, 83 per cent were men and 17 per cent women (Ministerie van SZW 1995). On the other hand, the participation of women as volunteers in civil society and as prime carers within the family is very high (cf. Knijn in this volume).

Not everyone agrees that these unequal rates of participation in Dutch society between women and men should be a factor in determining the conditions for full citizenship. On this issue, the different citizenship traditions and their feminist variations differ markedly. In the following four sections I will briefly sketch the ideas on (women's) participation developed in the major citizenship traditions of liberalism, Marxism, communitarianism and republicanism, as well as in the feminist variations on each. I will examine both the internal logic of each tradition and current Dutch debates on citizenship. In the final section I will evaluate the citizenship traditions and provide some further thoughts on women's participation and citizenship.

Classical and neoliberalism

Within classical liberalism citizenship is a status that provides equal civil and political rights to all those who are granted the title of citizen. This equal status is supposed to ensure equal protection under the law, equal access for all citizens to educational institutions and open competition for jobs and decision-making positions. According to classical liberals, such open competition ensures that we will get the right person for the right place. Political duties are highly respected but citizenship in the classical-liberal tradition is not based on political participation: participation is rather a choice of career or lifestyle enabled by rights. The only kind of participation required of ordinary citizens is that they should exercise their right to vote every three to four years.

Nor is social participation part of the classical-liberal model of citizenship. Activities in civil society or the family are considered merely choices of lifestyle. Participation in the labour market can be important for some people, but only as a means of gaining citizenship status (should they have no other property). Classical liberals argue that those people whom we expect to be rational should be financially autonomous in order to take their place as intellectually autonomous citizens (cf. James 1992). It was Immanuel Kant who formulated what has become a basic premise of classical liberalism:

> The only qualification required by a citizen (apart, of course, from being an adult male) [sic] is that he must be his *own master (sui iuris)*, and must have some *property*, (which can include any skill, trade, fine art or science) to support himself. In cases where he must earn living from others, he must earn it only by *selling* what is his, and not by allowing others to make use of him; for he must in the true sense of the word *serve* no-one but the common-wealth. (Kant 1991 [1793], p. 78)

As one can see from this quotation, classical liberalism did not allow women to become citizens even if they were financially autonomous. This exclusion was lifted under *social* liberalism, which becomes the dominant citizenship tradition in liberal democracies after the Second World War. Once women have been accepted as equal citizens (or have had this status denied to them), social liberal theory no longer refers to women as such. Social liberalism formulates a different solution to the dependency problem: in order to prevent some citizens becoming too dependent upon others and thus unable to hold independent opinions, the 'welfare' state will protect every citizen against poverty. Citizens should therefore not only be entitled to the same civil and political rights, but also to the same social (or welfare) rights. Social liberals do not indicate that this policy should be any different for women.

Social participation usually functions as a precondition of citizenship rights within the social-liberal tradition rather than as a separate aspect of it. Among the leading social liberals T.H. Marshall is the one who talks most of duties. He argues (1965, p. 129) that the 'duty to work' is of 'paramount importance' to citizenship but even he thinks that it should be considered as a duty to oneself. Whereas he assumes that 'men's' duty to military service can be imposed by the state, he thinks that their duty to work needs to be reconciled with the principle of the free market (1965, p. 131). He also states (1965, p. 78) that all citizens can be expected to participate 'in the full heritage' of a country, but by this he means no more than sharing in material goods.

Social rights are also expected to give people equal opportunities for participation and to allow for genuinely fair competition and merit. For instance, the right to welfare benefits and a minimum wage ought to prevent people from selling their labour for sixteen hours a day. Yet participation is not an essential part of social-liberal citizenship. The social liberal John Rawls says explicitly about political participation:

> The principle of participation applies to institutions. It does not define an ideal of citizenship; nor does it lay down a duty requiring all to take an active part in political affairs. The content of this principle of participation is rather that: all citizens have an equal right to take part in, and to determine the outcome of, the constitutional process that establishes the laws with which they have to comply (Rawls 1971, pp. 227 and 222).

Of late, liberalism has acquired new popularity in the form of neoliberalism. This philosophy pleads for cutting back welfare provisions and social rights and for returning citizenship to its basis in equal civil and political rights (Mead 1986). On the face of it, this would seem to mean going back to classical liberalism since citizens are expected to protect themselves from the threat of poverty. Unlike the classical variant, however, neoliberalism would grant citizenship status almost automatically - including to women. Because they want to root their arguments as much as possible in pure individualism, neoliberals would argue further that the same citizenship rights and duties should apply to both sexes.

Several aspects of the liberal citizenship discourse can be used to say something about women's participation and have indeed been used by feminists - even left-wing feminists (e.g. Okin 1989; Richards 1980). In the Netherlands, the liberal citizenship discourse has been used, for instance, to demand that women be treated as individual citizens and not as members of a specific sex group for whom other rules apply (cf. Smit 1984, p. 359). Social-liberal ideas have been used to demand social rights for all individuals and thus also for married women. This so-called individualisation of the social security system has now been largely set in place in the Netherlands, thanks in part to pressure from the European Union (cf. Bussemaker in this volume). Yet Dutch spouses and partners are considered to be financially responsible for each other, so that, strictly speaking, an individual right to welfare benefits is not guaranteed.

Feminists have also made extensive use of the social-liberal argument that the state should provide equal social rights in order to allow for equal opportunities in social and political participation. They have demanded a right to child-care facilities for all citizens, a right to public and private safety, a right to affordable public transport, and a number of reproductive rights and parental rights. Some feminists have even used this language to demand a basic income for women and men.

At the same time neoliberal discourse is increasingly used to promote women's participation in the Dutch labour market. Working from the neoliberal idea that everyone has financial responsibility for her or his own life, the government has insisted that each citizen has a duty to apply for jobs. In political practice, a major exception has been made for single income earners with children under twelve years old. Yet within the set of policies supported by the Scientific Council for Governmental Policy (WRR 1990, p. 168) participation in the labour market is seen as 'an important condition and form of social participation, integration and individual citizenship' (cf. van Drenth and Plantenga in this volume).

The discourse of liberal citizenship is limited further by its premises regarding women's participation. For, according to modern liberalism, women are already free and equal citizens by definition. This makes it more difficult for feminists to call attention to women's ambiguous citizenship status, and altogether impossible to claim that women are second-sex citizens. After all, participation is not a part of the liberal citizenship model; political participation is not considered important for citizenship and participation in the labour market is seen at most as a condition for citizenship. Anything that goes beyond equal rights is therefore considered a matter of free choice and irrelevant to questions of citizenship. In short, liberal citizenship is a status, not an activity. Social liberalism can therefore not be used to question the unequal rates of social and political participation between the sexes and neoliberalism can only suggest that participation in the labour market should be a duty performed in return for citizenship rights.

Marxism

In most of his work Marx addressed issues arising from participation in the work force, and barely touched upon political participation. He thought that the latter was simply part of the liberation process and would become superfluous once socialism had emerged. Often he seems to have presumed that equal social participation would lead automatically to equal political participation. In one text, however, *The Jewish Question*, he offered a more complex analysis of the relationship between political and social participation.

Here Marx points out that the term 'citizen' historically referred to two different figures: the *bourgeois* and the *citoyen*. Both participate in public life, but in an entirely different manner. The bourgeois participates socially out of self-interest, thinking about his private interests and trying to enrich himself. In contrast, the 'citoyen' participates socially or politically for the common good. According to Marx, capitalism paradoxically required of the same person selfish 'bourgeois' behaviour in the sphere of the economy and altruistic 'citoyen' behaviour in the sphere of politics.

In *The Jewish Question* Marx also notes that political emancipation of citizens can only take place after their social emancipation. One cannot behave as a free citizen in politics, civil society or the public sphere if one is still oppressed within society. Thus some form of social equality is a condition for political equality. In his view the state has to set the material conditions that will make citizens genuinely equal and free citizens. It therefore needs to guarantee not only formal freedom but material freedom too.

Feminists have had recourse to this Marxist discourse of citizenship to express some of their concerns about female citizens and their participation (e.g. Barret 1980; Phillips 1987). Since citizenship for Marx is not only a legal status, but also participation, feminists can use his arguments to reason that women are still second-sex citizens. After all, women have neither participated in official and unofficial politics - as *citoyennes* - nor participated in the work force - as *bourgeoises* - to the same degree that men have done. Besides, one could say with Marx that so long as people - here women - are still oppressed within social life they cannot be considered free citizens. If one accepts Marx's logic here, western women cannot be equal citizens - despite having equal rights - so long as they remain an oppressed group within western society.

In this respect Marx has been a useful ally for the feminist cause, for if equal citizenship is not yet realised, it should be. Women must no longer suffer oppression; they should be socially emancipated; more of them need to enter the public realm, especially the labour market. Moreover, Marxist discourse requires the state to create the material conditions within which these changes can occur. Following Marx, feminists should demand not just formal equality and liberty, but also material equality and liberty for women.

I think that one can see several elements of this discourse at work in recent debates on Dutch citizenship. After all, the citizen-as-worker is prominent in all of these (although Marxists find common ground here with followers of Marshall, feminists and neoliberals). Forty women's organisations have cooperated in one feminist organisation to demand economic independence for women ('Breed Platform voor Economische Zelfstandigheid'). The attempt to get more women into the labour market has been government policy for years (cf. Outshoorn and van Drenth in this volume). Furthermore, the second feminist wave has demanded those material conditions without which equality in citizenship is not possible, namely, the setting up of creches, possibilities for children to have lunch at school, safe streets and workplaces, affordable public transport, and leave arrangements, even though many of these things - in particular creches - have not as yet been realised on a large scale (cf. Bussemaker, Plantega and Knijn in this volume).

In my opinion, however, Marxist discourse does not go far enough on these issues. Marx himself had a limited conception of oppression which overlooked many forms of oppression that women suffer from. For him, oppression was only economic oppression. By contrast, the American feminist Iris Young (1990, pp. 39-65) suggests that individual women may (but not always do) suffer from five different types of oppression: economic exploitation, violence, marginalisation, cultural imperialism and powerlessness. In general, western women have lower-paid jobs than men; they suffer more from sexual violence than do men; housewives and solo mothers are economically marginalised; in the culture of the media, art, education and religion men's voices are much more dominant than women's; and the low representation of women in political, socio-economic, military and bureaucratic decision-making bodies indicates women's residual powerlessness.

Furthermore, Marx's discourse was restricted to the realm of oppositional politics. To gain a feminist perspective, one must extend his argument to include the sphere of the family and to claim that women cannot be free citizens in politics, if they are still oppressed within the private sphere of the family. Another disadvantage in relying too much upon Marx is that feminists may become constrained to centre all notions of citizenship on the state. Although such state-oriented feminism does have its advantages, it also implies that the state should have a large measure of control over citizens' lives and that citizens should expect the state to act for them rather than acting themselves.

Nor does Marx have much to say about the inherent value of political participation for citizenship. He considered political participation by ordinary workers necessary, but only for instrumental purposes. It would only accelarate the necessary course of history if workers could defend their own interests. Within his utopia of socialism political participation has even become superfluous. Moreover, we need to be careful and not assume that women's full social emancipation is needed first before we can ask for their participation in the political realm. History shows us too many oppressed people who did participate in politics for this premise to be credible. Similarly, social emancipation does not necessarily bring about political emancipation. If we look at societies like Japan, France or the United States in which women have a large participation in the labour market but a low incidence of political participation, we may question the assumption that equal rates of participation in the labour market would automatically lead to equal political participation.

Communitarianism

Despite their differences, the next two citizenship philosophies under consideration have a common emphasis on care. The communitarian philosophy is defended by people such as Alistair MacIntyre (1985) and Michael Sandel (1982). It holds citizenship to be the active defence of traditional norms and community practices. It asks citizens to respond assertively against a-social or dissident behaviour and therefore calls for quite a high degree of social control. Yet it also demands solidarity with vulnerable community members. Communitarianism emphasises the value of participation in public and private care. These forms of participation cement society together and show that we are community beings who care for each other rather than just self-interested individuals. Care for children is considered important for citizenship because it encourages citizenship virtues and traditional values to be passed on to the next generation.

The feminist variation of the communitarian citizenship philosophy, advocated by people such as Jean Bethke Elshtain (1981) and Sarah Ruddick (1983), also emphasises care, but argues that citizenship should be redefined from the point of view of the female citizen, rather than (as has conventionally been the case) from that of the male citizen. In their opinion, female citizens are exemplary. By their actions and moral code, women-as-mothers are better able than men to bring notions of care into the public arena. According to maternalist feminists, this is necessary because our public world is too individualistic and too much dominated by war, violence, conflict and egoism. Since women have been more closely involved with the private world of care than have men, they are 'uniquely placed' (Elshtain 1981, p. 349) to bring the ethic of care into the public sphere. Political participation by women is valued in so far as it is done in a compassionate way and does not emphasise the importance of participation in paid labour.

One of the advantages of communitarianism and maternalist feminism is that they go beyond the language of rights and consider participation essential to citizenship. They assert that we are community beings and that civic life has an inherent value. In my view, these are important points to make because otherwise it is next to impossible to conceive a type of citizenship that takes the common good as its goal. Communitarianism and maternal feminism may be the only discourses left which call for solidarity with vulnerable people now that Social Democrats have begun to move in neoliberal directions while other kinds of feminists have embraced strategies of individualisation. Moreover, both citizenship traditions pay attention to the relationships between the private sphere and public sphere, consider some kind of women's participation as important for citizenship and respect women as citizens.

Within the Dutch debate several examples of the communitarian and maternalist feminist discourses can be noted. The organisation of the Dutch welfare state, including its social infrastructure, is already strongly informed by communitarian notions of care (Bussemaker and Knijn in this volume). Yet there has also been a more recent debate on care, initiated by Christian Democrats in search of the 'caring society', but followed eagerly by feminists who have seen in it an opportunity to revalue women's contributions and by some Social Democrats for whom the project promises to revitalise old socialist ideals. In this debate citizens have been asked to take care of their more vulnerable fellow citizens - the elderly, the sick, the handicapped and the young - and to attend to matters of neighbourhood security and environmental conservation (Haan 1992; Sevenhuijsen 1996, pp. 152-187).

Other examples of the communitarian language within Dutch debates can be found in the critique of individualisation processes, in particular of its threat to community feelings and citizenship virtues. Faced with rising crime, some have called for a moral revival or greater social controls. Some have encouraged the growth of community defence organisations to supplement the work of the police. One can hear communitarian and maternalist voices behind the consensus that the duty to participate in the labour market should not extend to those who have sole charge of children under twelve years old (cf. van Drenth in this volume). The Christian Democrat proposal for a Ministry of the Family can also be seen in this light (cf. Bussemaker in this volume). Finally, there is a communitarian 'social renewal' debate in which the government has tried to reintegrate into society those who have been marginalised, in particular the unemployed.

It is easy to see how communitarians and maternalist feminists could agree on several points regarding the grounds of citizenship, yet full agreement between the two philosophies is unlikely. As Ido de Haan (1992) has remarked, communitarian appeals to participation in civil society can easily be used to excuse the government from the need to make (better) policies. It also risks closing down the avenues for opposition and dissidence. This is worrying not only with respect to the idea of democratic citizenship, but also with respect to feminists who try to develop lifestyles different from the traditional family (cf. Frazer and Lacey 1993).

Very often communitarian and maternalist discourses imply that it will be the women in the family, the neighbourhood and in volunteer organisations who will do all the caring (cf. Bussemaker 1994). We might find ourselves brought to the awkward situation in which there is no longer a problem of female citizenship because women have been transformed into model citizens: active in family care and as volunteers in civil society. Even maternalist feminism suggests that there is nothing wrong with the established practice of female participation in western societies, only with the ways in which this practice has been judged. If we start to respect caring work more than we do at present, women will continue doing it. Communitarianism and maternalism can therefore not be used to question the existing participation by men and women in western societies. Rigidly applied, they will only perpetuate traditional sex roles.

This suggests that it may be a mixed blessing to include private care in our theories of social participation and citizenship: if it is included, it will suggest that nothing is wrong with the institution of 'housewives' - indeed 'housewives' become exemplary citizens. Mary Dietz (1985) has pointed out another danger. According to her, private values requiring intimacy and paternalism/maternalism would become confused with public values requiring respect and equality.

Republicanism

There is more than a passing similarity in the attitudes towards participation in the labour market developed by Aristotle in fourth century (B.C.) Greece, as part of his classical civic-republicanism, and those which later emerged in classical liberalism. According to Aristotle, in order to be a citizen one had to be beyond the sphere of necessity (that is providing oneself with food and shelter). The citizen was he who alternated being ruled with ruling, and thus shared in governing or legislative tasks. Citizenship was seen as an activity referring to participation in the *polis* - the public political sphere of the city. Women, slaves and even manual workers had to be excluded from citizenship and political participation because they were still living in the sphere of necessity and focused on the sphere of the *oikos*, the family household. Besides, here as in other republican theories, women's nature already in itself precluded citizenship. Not being a man (*vir*), women were said to be unable to acquire the important citizenship virtues (*virtù*) (Elshtain 1981).

Neorepublicans have somewhat moderated the classical republican position put forward by Aristotle. Women, manual workers and others are now also called up to political participation as citizens. They too need at times to go beyond the sphere of necessity in order to be a good citizen. For instance, Hannah Arendt (1958) argues that there is an important distinction between labour, work and action. Labour is the lowest human activity because it adds nothing new to society. Work is somewhat higher, but still not very highly regarded, because it produces only instrumental rationality. Action is the highest activity, because it is done in freedom and usually in cooperation with other people. Action in the public political sphere is what really distinguishes humans from animals: the ability to build a state according to our will.

Several ideas that are relevant to our discussion of citizenship and participation have remained constant within the republican tradition. First and foremost, the republican tradition states that it is our duty to develop the highest possible human capacities, that is to develop ourselves as political animals. Without this end we might as well be consumers or even mere subjects. For those in the republican tradition, liberty is a good to be acquired through public participation rather than in private isolation. And although social participation is considered irrelevant to citizenship (indeed social participation is almost the opposite of citizenship), it must be admitted that political participation - which *is* valued, of course - includes not only official politics, but other types of public decision-making and debate.

The modern republican framework has been used by feminists to interpret the different participation of western women and men (Dietz 1985; Mouffe 1992). Feminist republicans argue that gender inequality in political participation is far more serious than gender inequality in social participation or paid labour. The highest of human activities is to discuss and to decide together in freedom, not to work according to some kind of instrumental rationality. From the standpoint of civic-republicanism, women's absence from decision-making is a serious matter, reducing women to a state of second-sex citizenship that must be remedied by action or governmental policies. Finally, the republican framework provides arguments on behalf of women's political participation: the value of positive freedom, the need to safeguard democracy and avoidance of a monopoly of power, the need to control existing rulers by public opinion and by preparing oneself to ruling, and finally the need for a plurality of views.

Within the Netherlands the republican discourse is quite popular. Sometimes it has even been embraced by a major government think-tank (cf. Gunsteren 1992). Increasingly participation in debate and decision-making is considered as a citizenship task or virtue. The discourse goes back to the wave of democratisation from the early seventies but it has since been revitalised by several political parties and social movements (Haan 1992; Stokkom 1992).

The current impetus for this debate has been the realisation that mass parties are no longer possible and that it is therefore important to involve people in politics in another way. The debate has thus far centred on issues such as decentralisation, delegation, referenda, consultation, election of mayors, access of ordinary citizens to more public information, live television broadcasts of parliamentary investigative committees, and on new procedures being adopted by the various political parties. Much of the debate has focused on the difficulties caused by institutionalising so many processes of debate and decision-making and on ways in which conflict can occur between a citizen acting as functionary and as an ordinary citizen (Gunsteren 1992). Thus, a policewoman (for example) may in her capacity as state functionary carry out some kind of policy which she as ordinary citizen would consider corrupt. The obligations of citizenship would then compel her to speak out. Safeguards could be built into state institutions to deal with such conflicts (Bovens 1990).

Outside the women's sections of the political parties, the Directorate for the Co-ordination of Equality Policy (DCE) and some women's organisations, this Dutch neorepublican debate on decision-making is not related to women. One reason may be that the problem is simply not recognised as such; another is the growth of open resistance to policies such as the quotas that were adopted to get more women into politics. There seems to be a strong current of opinion that political parties should be autonomous and that the government should not be allowed to impose any system of quotas on them. In the government, in parties and in the unions many now believe that affirmative action in the form of quotas does not work or is 'passé' (cf. Ministerie van SZW 1995), or they assume that political participation should be voluntary and cannot be imposed from without. Positive discrimination, as practised by the women's sections of political parties, is no longer supposed to contribute to 'political renewal' (Goudt and Hartman 1995). Some sense of the changing political climate can be grasped from the 1994 decision to abolish the women's section of the Social Democratic party (PvdA).

If the problem of women's absence from the decision-making process has been conspicuously ignored in much contemporary neorepublican debate, one explanation might be that, in classical republicanism, citizenship was associated with manliness. Another possible cause is that even if a citizenship tradition like republicanism were made gender neutral, the problem would still remain. Gender neutrality is a type of gender blindness in that it leaves the inequalities between men and women in place, unquestioned. As a feminist resource, republicanism is weakened too by its division of the private from the public sphere and private activities from the idea of citizenship, and by its neglect of social participation - above all, participation in the labour market - as an important factor in exercising citizenship.

Evaluation

We can conclude that social liberalism, still the dominant citizenship tradition in western societies, does not say anything about the value of participation and the unequal rates of participation between the sexes. It cannot because it sees citizenship as a legal status and makes rights the cornerstone of citizenship. Given that women in the Netherlands have more or less the same rights as men, in common with most other western countries nowadays, lack of rights as such is not the major problem for women's citizenship. The major problem lies rather in women's low participation in the labour market and in decision-making (women's participation within civil society is high enough). If we want to challenge this disparity from the perspective of citizenship and argue that - regarding participation - women are still second-sex or second-class citizens, then a social-liberal focus on rights is insufficient. Instead we must argue that citizenship is not only a certain legal status, but also an activity. Otherwise, to the degree that most people still tend to think of citizenship in social-liberal terms, the unequal participation between the sexes cannot be discussed by reference to 'citizenship'.

If one wants to argue that the low female participation in the labour market and in decision-making within western societies is problematic and that it turns women into second-sex citizens - their equal rights notwithstanding - one has to take one's support from the other citizenship philosophies. Yet none of the alternatives provides a thoroughly satisfactory approach to issues such as the value of participation in the labour market, decision-making and volunteer participation within civil society. Neoliberalism sees only the instrumental value of participation in the work force and does not rate the other forms of participation as essential for citizenship; republicanism does not regard social participation as important; Marxism ignores the value of political participation; communitarianism and maternalist feminism privilege to the exclusion of all else volunteer participation in civil society and in private care.

All of these blind spots are apparent in contemporary Dutch debates. In their different ways, the growing popularity of neoliberalism, Marshall's insistence on duty, and the exclusive focus of Social Democrats nowadays on labour have led to a widespread acceptance that participation in the labour market is important for full citizenship. Yet none of these traditions nor their current political advocates pay much attention to the material conditions that need to be created before male and female citizens are in a position to make equal contributions in paid (as well as in unpaid) labour. Now that so many Social Democrats have lost their faith in socialism, it is often communitarians, Christian Democrats and maternalist feminists who argue for collective participation by reevaluating the role of care in civil society. Yet the net result of their efforts is to reinforce the stereotype of women as care-givers - indeed, in this capacity, as moral citizens - without giving them the further incentive of entering the labour market. Besides, all these traditions and movements ignore political participation. This is not the case in the civic-republican tradition, now so popular in the Netherlands among the political élite. Yet here - not surprising given the tradition - women's low political participation is neglected.

One can of course try to select the most useful aspects of these different positions in a rather eclectic fashion. This is what has often happened in the Dutch debate on citizenship. A Marxist or sometimes a neoliberal perspective might be used to question women's relatively low participation in paid labour. The language of republicanism is used as a polemical tool to question peoples' lack of political participation (though women's absence from decision-making tends to get overlooked). Finally, a Christian, communitarian vocabulary is used to call for a caring state, in which it is the caring women who are the exemplary citizens.

Nevertheless, one cannot combine these major citizenship traditions without some overarching sense of just where women should belong, and what precisely are their rights and duties. Should women participate in paid labour, in politics and other decision-making bodies, in volunteer work within civil society or in private care? What citizenship status do women currently hold: are they equal or secondary to men? These questions are not simple, but if one accepts that public rather than private participation in citizenship is important, they can be answered by drawing upon some (though not all) of the positions I have outlined above.

In my view public participation is important to citizenship and several of the alternative citizenship traditions provide convincing arguments for this. Without participation there is no point in being a citizen: one might just as well be a subject or a consumer. It is important to realise one's potential for action, to add something new to society and to engage oneself in shaping the contours of our future society. Participation also makes us community beings rather than isolated individuals and ensures that vulnerable citizens will not only be looked after by an anonymous state, but also by caring fellow citizens. It provides an ideal of positive freedom. Participation by ordinary citizens is an important mechanism for maintaining a genuine democracy and preventing a monopoly of power. Public opinion and competition provide a check on those currently in office. High degrees of participation also broaden the competition and give us all a better chance of having a properly qualified political leadership. Providing a plurality of opinions only makes a republic stronger. Participation enriches one's mind, concentrating it on the common good rather than on private interests. The more people are involved in debate and decision-making the more legitimate - and the better safeguarded - becomes the republic's power.

Since these are my arguments for participation, it follows that I do not consider all the forms of participation, which I covered in the introduction to this chapter, to be of equal importance. Political participation is thus more important than social participation; but I accept that mass participation in decision-making is not practicable, nor for that matter desirable because of the pressure it would have on peoples' lives and because, too, not everyone is qualified for it. Yet even within social participation we should make distinctions. Not all forms of participation in the labour market need to yield the above-mentioned advantages. On the other hand, such participation can be defended with a further, instrumental argument: it gives people the financial independence that is necessary to make them autonomous citizens.

Apart from these general arguments for public participation, women have particular reasons to become full political and labour market participants, because throughout the history of citizenship women as a group have not had a share in power. They could improve their own and other women's economic, social and political position by greater participation in the labour market and in politics. They would gain thereby greater degrees of equality and liberty, values considered important even by traditional citizenship theorists. Respect for women would also be enhanced. Because men and women currently hold different social positions, their interests differ. Although female decision-makers will not automatically defend women's interests, women's interests are therefore now more likely to be defended by women than by men.

Private care within the family, however, does not seem compatible with these ideals of citizenship. I would go so far as to define social participation without reference to private care. Some might counter that participation in private care is an indispensable element of citizenship. After all, children can be provided in this way with citizenship virtues and community values. The care-giver gains a feeling of responsibility for the future generation and perhaps for vulnerable people in general so that mass participation in private care may lead to a more caring society - not only in private life but also in public policies. Finally, one might say that whoever (temporarily) takes care of young, the elderly and the sick allows someone else to participate in public life. Thus one might argue: if public participation by women is one goal, then private participation by men, acting as private care-givers, ought to be another.

I do not object to this position. Nevertheless, I would see equal participation of men and women in private care as a precondition of equal citizenship rather than as being itself a type of equal citizenship, for the same reason that I would define citizenship as public participation in decision-making, as volunteer work within civil society and - to a lesser extent - as participation in the labour market. In my view, citizenship implies a reciprocal relation of equals and community beings, not of unequal intimates. Shared private care enables equal citizenship but is not yet shared citizenship activity. It would follow then that, at the present moment, western women meet the formal requirements of equal citizenship, but they are still second-sex citizens in so far as their participation in the labour market and above all in decision-making is concerned.

2 Gender and the separation of spheres in twentieth century Dutch society: pillarisation, welfare state formation and individualisation

Jet Bussemaker

The separation of public and private spheres has been an important issue in feminist scholarship. The concept of separability, and the gender relations assumed, made women second-class citizens and reinforced the belief that women were 'incomplete citizens' or 'citizens *manqué*'. For a long time, men's citizenship depended upon men's participation in public spheres: the military service, the labour market, or politics. Women's citizenship, or its negation, depended first and foremost on their position in the private sphere as wives, mothers and care-givers. This usually meant that women were not entitled to the same rights enjoyed by men. At times, women did participate in one of the institutions of the public world, but not on the same terms as men. To the extent that women have been incorporated into the public sphere, their incorporation has been as 'women', that is, 'as beings whose sexual embodiment prevents them from enjoying the same political standing as men' (Pateman 1989, p. 4). As we shall see, other important dichotomies in relation to both gender and the separation of the public and the private exist, for example: reason and passion, independence and dependence, mind and body, and self-interest and altruism (cf. Coole 1988; Elshtain 1981; Jaggar 1983). These dichotomies are deeply rooted in the development of the modern state.

The concept of separate spheres has been critical to the development of citizenship rights for men and women. T.H. Marshall's famous distinction between civil, political and social rights assumes a strong private-public separation. Marshall's model is restricted to activities related to public spheres (state, labour market, and so forth) and excludes any consideration of the private sphere of the family - and therefore of unpaid care and women's dependency on men. The 'dual model' of citizenship (Pateman 1989) refers directly to a 'public-private split' in social spheres. However, what is viewed as public and what as private has changed over time, as have the boundaries between spheres, and both changes have affected men's and women's entitlements to citizenship rights. Citizenship rights emerged out of a struggle over these boundaries and gender positions. In Dutch history, this struggle has been part of the segregation of denominational interests within the political and social system. This peculiarly Dutch historical phenomenon, called 'pillarisation', its interaction with the formation of the postwar welfare state and modern feminism, and its consequences for women's citizenship in the course of the twentieth century, are the focus of this chapter. The discussion that follows is structured around three central concepts: pillarisation, welfare state formation and individualisation. These concepts represent, to a certain extent, sequential episodes, although they overlap to a considerable degree. Thus, while pillarisation is primarily associated with the first part of the twentieth century, it continued to develop after the Second World War and into the 1950s, at which time it formed some of its chief characteristics. Welfare state formation began, in a slow and fragmented manner, in the late-nineteenth and early-twentieth centuries, but it expanded dramatically after the Second World War. The trend towards individualisation developed mainly in the 1970s and 1980s, but elements of it can be traced back to the late 1950s.

I will discuss each of the central concepts in their historical sequence, and then follow with more general conclusions about citizenship, gender and the separation of social spheres.

Pillarisation

The idea of separate spheres was, generally speaking, shared by most political movements in the late-nineteenth and early-twentieth centuries. But socialists, liberals, Catholics and orthodox Protestants - the main political movements of the time - held somewhat different positions on gender and the separation of spheres (Bussemaker 1993, pp. 83-98). These differences are most apparent in their views on the state's role in relation to society in general, and to gender in particular. Denominational parties tended to hold one set of views, secular parties quite another. Abraham Kuyper, the outspoken leader of the Anti-Revolutionaire Partij (the 'ARP' - an orthodox Protestant political party that rejected the ideals of the French Revolution and the Enlightenment), expressed one of the most intransigent positions. He wrote:

> There are two kinds of human personality, the male and the female, who differ principally as human species in mind as well as in body, and they find themselves in a world wherein their lives split apart in two entire different parts, the one the inside, the other the outside of our society, creating two separate spheres, private and public. Between the two differences in species, the first one between men and women,

the second one between private and public, exists a close connection. What nature has given to women, directs itself to the private sphere, what suits best for men, belongs to the public sphere. (Kuyper 1914, pp. 64-5)

Underlying Kuyper's particular argument was a more broadly-shared acceptance of this separation, as well as the idea that the spheres and all social communities were mutually dependent (cf. Plantenga in this volume). The concept of 'organicism' is crucial here. According to this concept, society was constructed like a human body, wherein all organs (communities) had a fixed and stable position and functioned organically. One could say that organicism assumed a strict distinction of societal spheres. Each community within these spheres had its own place and order, and was assumed to function as one part of an entire 'body', or whole. Because it stressed the multiplicity and inequality of the individual bodily parts, organicism also implied the need for hierarchy, patriarchy, authority and order - in short, for an overriding structure that would be controlled by the 'higher' members of society. The order of the family consisted of a dominant father and willingly subordinate members under his authority, and served as the model for all social relations (Kersbergen 1995, p. 202).

The family, then, played a fundamental part in forming the concept of organicism. In this regard, it was linked to other distinct communities such as corporate business, the church, and the neighbourhood. However, the family was also held to be a very special community, because it was the smallest community one could think of. Moreover, it was assumed not to be separable into the individuals which comprised it, being rather a 'natural' unit in itself.

The concept of organicism has been central to both Catholic and orthodox-Protestant thought. However, these two groups differed on what relationship between state and society on the one hand, and between the state and the family on the other, was implied by the organicist model. This difference in views is expressed in the Catholic notion of 'subsidiarity' and the Protestant notion of 'sovereignty'.

The notion of subsidiarity can be found within Catholic parties and throughout Catholic-dominated European societies (Kersbergen 1995; Ostner 1994). The central tenet of subsidiarity is that the state should not interfere with problems which could be better solved by other, lower-level, communities, such as the family. However, the state also has a 'selective' power with respect to families: although it should not interfere in the natural order of the family, it should guarantee that families can manage their responsibilities by helping them where necessary (Bussemaker 1993). This conception of the state's role allowed for the provision of social welfare to families, to help them avoid 'evil' (for example, divorce), and to sustain them in the development of 'virtues', such as the support of children through child allowances (cf. Akkerman in this volume).

The orthodox Protestant notion of 'sovereignty in one's own circle' assumes the autonomy of 'life circles' and social spheres. The family is understood to have its own sovereignty. However, if particular family relations become in some way 'unnatural' (from a religious point of view), state intervention might be necessary, although charity and help through intermediate organisations are preferred to direct state aid. Orthodox Protestants are therefore less in favour of extensive welfare facilities, including extensive family support, than are Catholics.

But Protestants concur with Catholics in rejecting liberal ideas of 'individualism' which privilege political and social rights for individual men and women over those of the community. For the denominational groups, separate individuals simply do not exist - there exist only 'persons' who are related to each other through kinship, religion and tradition. One consequence of this outlook is that instead of an 'atomistic' and 'individualistic' suffrage, there should be an 'organic houseman's vote' (the expression used by orthodox Protestants) or 'suffrage for the head of the household' (the Catholic version). Both notions assume that the family is to be taken as total entity, which is sufficiently represented by the male head of the household.

Women's suffrage and their participation in the public sphere were not the only points of disagreement between denominational and secular parties. Also at issue was whether private (i.e. religious) schools should receive, as public schools already did, government subsidies. Kuyper (1914) referred to this cleavage between denominational and secular parties as the 'antithesis'.

Some of the main issues which divided political parties in the early twentieth century were solved in what is known as the 'Pacification' of 1917. Pacification refers here to the acceptance of the constitution by all the main political parties, an act which effectively ended the anti-thesis. Constitutional reforms guaranteed equal state funding for public and private (Christian) schools, universal manhood suffrage, and - due to the efforts of a coalition of liberals, socialists and feminists - a provision for female suffrage. Women were finally granted suffrage in 1919 (rather early, comparatively speaking; cf. Leijenaar and Akkerman in this volume).

The 'Pacification' of 1917 has usually been associated with the emergence of the Dutch phenomenon of pillarisation. Pillarisation refers in part to the shift in hegemonic power from the liberal parties (who were dominant in the second part of the nineteenth century) to the denominational parties (who became dominant after 1918). Denominational representatives held control of the government throughout the period 1918 to 1994 (although often in coalition with either liberals or socialists). More generally, pillarisation refers to a highly segmented but stable society in which denominational parties, collectively, had a numerical advantage over secular parties, but never one large enough to enable them to rule alone. This situation provided a strong incentive (or rather, the need) to develop a working consensus across party lines (Lijphart 1968; Kersbergen 1995). Pillarisation thus generated a system of political negotiation that focused on reaching consensus at the top-level of the different pillars. It was assumed that if agreement was reached among the élites of the different pillars, this consensus would slowly permeate down the lower levels. Unity at the top of the pillars thus ensured that plurality at lower levels was maintained in a peaceful manner.

Pillarisation also refers to an institutionalised system of individually integrated, yet at the same time highly segregated, sub-cultural organisations which belong to the different religious (denominational) and quasi-religious (liberal and socialist) groups. Each group was, as Kossmann describes it, 'encouraged and subsidised by the state to create its own world, comprising the entire existence of an individual from nursery school to sporting club, trade union, university, hospital, broadcasting and television corporation, to burial' (Kossmann 1978, p. 304).

Indeed, as Kossmann remarks, pillarisation affected the whole life-course of an individual, from birth to death. As long as everyone remained in their separate social worlds, all was well. But as soon as someone wanted to transgress these segregational lines, problems arose. For example, an orthodox Protestant who read a liberal newspaper was suspect. Or, to become a member of the socialist labour movement, if one were a Catholic, was simply 'not done', and was sometimes even banned by Catholic organisations. This was especially the case in the 1950s, when the segregation of organizational structures was at its most extreme. Hence, pillarised Dutch society possessed both a high degree of (institutionalised) pluralism between pillars, and a great deal of conformity within the social groups that made up the separate pillars.

Pillarisation also influenced discourse on moral issues, especially among the confessional groups. In 1911, a Catholic minister facilitated the passage of legislation which introduced more stringent regulation of such issues as abortion and homosexuality. In the period of 'institutionalised pillarisation' (from around the 1920s to the 1960s), Dutch society was characterised by a rather severe sexual morality. Motherhood was highly valued and the idea of the family as the fundamental unit of social life was accepted by nearly every political group. Liberals and socialists either shared these family values, or thought that family issues were not important enough to argue about (Stuurman 1983).

In conclusion, we can say that at the same time women were granted suffrage and achieved an extension of their political citizenship, their moral and social freedoms were being limited. Pillarised social segregation and its attendant sexual morality ensured that women had few options other than to behave as 'good mothers' and 'good wives', in accordance with the code of whichever pillar they belonged to.

Pillarisation has thus served to complicate the account of women's citizenship in the Netherlands because it introduced additional factors into the public-private dichotomy. To the different public spheres (state, market and intermediate organisations), pillarisation added denominational and social subcultures and group organisations, which intersected the boundaries of private and public spheres.

Welfare state formation

The first welfare provision in the Netherlands dates back to the Children's Act of 1874, which banned child labour. Some additional social regulations were introduced before the Second World War (cf. Akkerman in this volume); however, it was only after 1945 that the Dutch welfare state developed (rapidly) into one of the most generous systems in the world. The first steps in its development had already begun during the German occupation, when the Dutch queen and government were in exile in London. At this time, they became acquainted with the Beveridge plan in Britain. Directly after the war, the van

Rhijn committee presented its plans for state welfare provisions (dubbed the 'Dutch Beveridge report'). Catholics as well as Social Democrats - the most important political actors in the postwar period - supported the committee's proposals to develop a comprehensive system of social security for the entire population.

The Dutch welfare system, which developed mainly between 1946 and 1965, 'borrowed' several of its characteristic notions on welfare organisation from other European countries. The system has usually been described as a two-track system of welfare, based on both insurance and need. This characterisation is certainly not wrong, but neither is it complete. The Dutch social security system is better described as a three-track system. The first track is composed of rather generous social insurance schemes for employees, such as systems of unemployment insurance which reflect the Bismarckian model of employee coverage, and which have traditionally been directed at male breadwinners. The second track is composed of national social insurance schemes, reflecting some of Beveridge's ideas and Scandinavian concepts of welfare. These schemes provide flat-rate state pensions, are not related to past performance in the labour market, and are not means tested. The General Widows and Orphans Act is a clear example of this track, as is the General Disability Act. The third track consists primarily of the General Assistance Act, passed in 1965. This Act is often viewed as the crowning glory of the whole welfare system, and it provides means-tested benefits to those who are not covered by any national insurance scheme. This component of means testing clearly reflects Anglo-Saxon welfare notions.

On analysis, however, this three-track system also reveals a gendered imbalance. Generally speaking, women have been most dependent on either social assistance (especially single mothers), or flat-rate pensions (especially widows); while until recently, they have been least dependent on employment insurance schemes, because of their low and unstable labour market patterns (Bussemaker et al. 1997). The postwar Dutch welfare state was clearly founded on the assumption of the nuclear family, with the husband as the breadwinner, and the wife as a full-time mother (cf. Knijn in this volume). Even while discourses were emerging in response to the dynamic economic changes of the postwar era, family policies were being targeted to ensure stability and restore the pre-war (family) order (cf. for Germany, Ostner 1994). The Dutch government explicitly discouraged married women from entering or remaining in the labour market. The tax system imposed negative incentives on secondary incomes of families, and it rejected services which would aid women's participation in the labour market, such as public child-care facilities (cf. Plantenga and Knijn in this volume). The identification of men with family maintenance meant that the male breadwinner earned a family wage and received a child benefit, and that his wife and children were, by definition, included in his insurance provisions without the need for additional contributions. Until recently, the Netherlands has provided a remarkable array of transfer payments to families (Bussemaker and Kersbergen 1994; Sainsbury 1996, p. 30).

But labour market and social security policies only constitute a portion of the Dutch welfare system. The postwar welfare state has also provided a number of social services, including ones directed at the development of social citizenship (through health care services, for example). Most of these services, however, are intended to support the male-breadwinner family. This direction was expressed as one of the goals of the Ministry of Social Work (established in 1952), and was especially favoured by the Catholic party. One of the main tasks of the Ministry was the 'support and advancement of religious and private social work on behalf of the protection, preservation, restoration and consolidation of the family-community as the constituent and structuring power of society' (in Bussemaker 1993, p. 114).

As a consequence of this policy, many intermediate organisations were financed by the state but, due to pillarisation and the pluralist tradition of respecting different life styles, these were privately governed (cf. Kersbergen 1995, p. 189). Many service organisations were established, including family consultancy agencies, psychotherapy for families, social work and youth welfare (cf. van Drenth in this volume). They reflected the social and denominational segregation of the country and were directed at different religious and 'social worlds'.

The important role played by these intermediate organisations suggests that a sharp distinction between the public and the private is not possible in the Dutch case. The problem with the public-private dichotomy is the way in which one should define such intermediate organisations: as public because they are publicly financed, or as private because the are privately governed? They might best be described as a very specific form of civil society, or, as this sphere has been traditionally called in the Netherlands, 'het maatschappelijke middenveld' (literally 'the social middle field'). These organisations were closely tied to the institutionalised system of denominational segregation characteristic of pillarisation, and therefore reflected the respect felt for different social values and world views. They were also (with a few exceptions in the field of social work) dominated by men.

The fact that the state 'delegated' some of its responsibilities for social welfare towards these intermediate organisations did not mean that there was no state control over people's behaviour. The generous system of social welfare, and especially its focus on specific provisions for male breadwinners and family structures, required an intensive system of social control by the state. Moreover, intermediate organisations in the 'social middle field' had their own systems for controlling their members. One could even say that the institutionalised nature of these organisations enforced social control, because they encompassed the entire existence of individuals. Thus, extensive social control existed in the 1950s through intermediate organisations and within (segregated) communities (cf. Bussemaker 1997).

While it would seem from the picture outlined above that postwar Dutch welfare state formation produced strict segregation by gender and tightly circumscribed family policies, significant alternatives were also emerging. Over the same period that gender differences were included in social security rights, women - particularly married women - acquired some important civil rights. In 1947, joint parental control of children was formally legalised. In 1955 and 1956, respectively, a recently introduced marriage-bar to women's employment in the civil service, and a law which did not officially recognise married women in legal contracts, were both withdrawn. Additionally, women's political rights were slowly becoming realised (cf. Leijenaar in this volume). For all these reasons, the idea of a 'completed emancipation' was settled by the political parties (Akkerman 1985; Bussemaker 1997).

How are the contradictory (yet simultaneous) trends of gender-segregated family policies and ideas of 'completed emancipation', to be explained? It is important to emphasise that differences between men and women in social security entitlements were not regarded as pointing to any 'natural' inequality between the sexes, but rather as recognising natural differences in abilities, talents and tasks. The relationship between men and women was conceived of as 'equal dignity in difference', which meant that men and women had complementary tasks with respect to the public good, even though men's roles were more public than women's.

To summarise, the postwar formation of the Dutch welfare state shows a rapid extension of rather generous social welfare provisions, all of which assumed a strong division between male breadwinners and female care-givers (cf. Knijn in this volume). The generosity of postwar social security benefits can only be understood if we appreciate that these benefits were designed to replace a family income (Bussemaker and Kersbergen 1994). The emphasis on stable families and particular gender relations was reflected in most of the services offered.

In terms of citizenship, this has meant that society remained structured along a strict division of 'segregated' citizenship for men and women, despite the notion of a 'completed emancipation'. Moreover, new distinctions were made, particularly with respect to social security and social services. As a result of both extensive social welfare provisions and a clear division in gender roles, the Netherlands showed a low level of stratification in terms of families, although it showed (and still shows) much more stratification in terms of gender.

Postwar welfare state formation also complicates the concept of different and exclusive social spheres. The intermediate organisations in the social middle-field (now subsidised by the state, although still privately governed) exerted a powerful force over private and communal life. Belonging to different pillars, they appear to recognise pluralism with regard to lifestyles (between different religious and quasi-religious groups), but not with regard to differences within the 'social worlds' of these groups.

Individualisation

As in many other European countries, a strong women's movement emerged in the Netherlands in the 1970s and 1980s. The Dutch typically locate the starting point of the so-called 'second-wave' of feminism in 1967, when Joke Smit published (under the name of Kool-Smit) her article 'The Discomfort of Women' (Smit 1989, pp. 15-42).

Smit turned the vocabulary of 'completed emancipation' into a guidebook for women's liberation. She focused on the problems of middle-class women, who should be happy but were not, whose existence extended no further than their house, and who had only tenuous contact with the outside world. According to her, women must become more like men. To do this, women must learn to think in terms and concepts that, traditionally, have been reserved for men: 'It is really time that women permit themselves the healthy egoism that has been taken for granted among men since time immemorial' (Smit 1984, p. 36). With this argument, Smit challenged the received notion of the separate spheres and women's customary place in them. In fact, she criticised the altruism and self-sacrifice that the welfare state presumed women to have. She strongly disagreed with the ideas of 'completed emancipation' and a 'generous welfare state', as far as these concerned the position of women. According to Smit, the family was not a working-community of equal citizens, but she saw it as the last vestige of 'institutionalised feudalism' (Smit 1984, pp. 380-1; cf. Bussemaker 1997 and Plantenga in this volume).

Smit's attempt to encourage enlightened self-interest among women might be seen as a logical outcome of the Dutch welfare state, which promised greater well-being, self-development and full citizenship rights for everyone, but in practice denied women's needs. Feminism tended to follow the logic of the welfare state as far as equal rights and the general good were concerned, but, simultaneously, it called for a radical change in the 'unit' of welfare and justice from the traditional family to the individual; that is, to single men and women.

One of the demands put forth by Smit (later to become one of the main issues within the women's movement) was for equal social rights with respect to income, labour, social security and social provisions. What in the 1950s had been imagined to be a just and accurate recognition of natural gender differences, was now regarded as perpetuating inequality, discrimination and injustice to women.

A focus on individual rights has become popular since the seventies. As in many European countries, due in part to the influence of European directives on gender equality in labour and social security (cf. Ostner and Lewis 1995), anti-discrimination policies have been implemented in the Netherlands. Women's participation in the labour market has been growing rapidly, while traditional male breadwinner models are often abandoned in favour of those which accord equal significance to men's and women's work. For example, a Dual-Wage Earners Act was passed in 1984, and in 1985, married women in employment were included in old-age pensions (Sainsbury 1996, p. 184). All the same, important conditions for women's labour market participation, such as public child-care and parental leave, are still lacking for the most part.

But views have been slowly changing since the late eighties, when women's participation in the labour market became regarded as the solution for participatory citizenship of women (cf. Plantenga in this volume). When Hedy d'Ancona (one of the initiators of the women's movement in the sixties along with Joke Smit), became a Minister of State in the late eighties, she introduced a policy to expand public child-care facilities. Her efforts resulted in an expansion of public child-care facilities from two per cent for children nought to three years-old in 1988, to eight per cent in 1993 (European Network on CCP 1996, pp. 3, 91).

Changes in gender relations and social policy are often summed up in one word: individualisation. Indeed, individualisation refers to the increase of women's participation in the labour market, and to changes in legislation which make the individual the unit of entitlements and obligations, rather than the family or household (cf. for interpretation, Sainsbury 1996). It refers also to demographic developments which have contributed to the break-up of families (such as the increase in divorce and single-parent households), and to a whole complex of changes which have steadily chipped away at the notion of the unified social community and at any absolute distinction between the public and the private. These changes began to develop slowly in some subcultures in the late fifties, but became more pronounced from the late sixties. Individualisation, then, is a concept used to describe an array of political, social and moral developments which have resulted in the breakdown of pillarisation.

On the political front, new parties and movements arose in the sixties which criticised the élitist and 'top-down' manner of decision-making in the pillarised structure; democracy - particularly, participatory democracy - was presented as the alternative. The breakdown of the social aspects of pillarisation became visible in the disintegration of solid social communities based on denominational segregation, and in the erosion of organisations of the 'social middle-field'. Finally, moral and religious values and attitudes had changed, as indicated by the increase of secularisation, and of more liberal attitudes towards sexuality and contraception (cf. Knijn in this volume). In short, these trends signalled the emergence of a more permissive society.

As a consequence of these abrupt changes, many of the policies implemented from the 1970s exhibit a contradictory combination of 'old' and 'new' discourses on social regulation and notions of family and gender relations. Thus, in the eighties, some legislation has taken the individual instead of the family as the basis of entitlements, while some elements of traditional family policies have not as yet been eliminated. For example, the importance of paid labour for women's independence has been emphasised since the eighties, but there has not been a corresponding provision for public child-care and parental leave. A contradiction exists in child-care policies themselves: on the one hand, child-care policies emphasise the concept of family and responsibility and do not facilitate the combination of motherhood and employment; on the other hand, maternity benefits are only available to working mothers (Sainsbury 1996). In short, fragmentation and contested individualisation, rather than linearity and integration, characterise existing social policies (Bussemaker 1993).

What these contradictory developments mean for the citizenship status of women is well-illustrated by the case of single mothers who are dependent on social assistance. In this instance, clearly, the consequences of individualisation vary according to the particular sphere in question. For while single mothers are confronted with individualisation in different spheres (the state, the market, the family and the 'social middle field'), they are also confronted with three different meanings of the concept. In terms of the private sphere, individualisation primarily translates into an increase in moral and sexual freedom which makes it easier to enter into, and to break out of, sexual relationships. Concerning the labour market, however, individualisation fosters the notion that it is one's own responsibility to earn an income, thus countering the idea of income redistribution. The obligation, therefore, to find a job becomes more important for individual citizens, and at the same time, caring for one's children is no longer an acceptable reason for not participating in the work force.

On the level of the state, individualisation translates into a focus on individual social rights and obligations, but this has ambiguous consequences. For example, obligations based on the General Assistance Act (which has a predominantly female clientele composed mainly of single and divorced mothers) have been individualised, but not the right of entitlement; instead, there has been a shift towards means-tested benefits (Bussemaker 1993, p. 194; Sainsbury 1996, p. 215). Moreover, organisations in the 'social middle field' no longer provide the supports to women that they once did.

The differences in the meanings of individualisation in these different spheres has resulted in contradictions in the position of women, particularly for single mothers. Their decreased dependence within the private sphere has shifted to an increased dependence on welfare provisions, where cuts and new restrictions have been made in the last decade. Women have also become more dependent on the labour market, which has not adapted to the double role women play as both wage-earners and mothers (Knijn 1994).

What began as a feminist strategy to criticise the focus on male breadwinner provisions and oppressive familial dependence, has become a powerful rhetorical argument for cutbacks, and a call for more individual responsibility along liberal ideological lines. Nevertheless, single women in the Netherlands are still better off than women in many other countries due to a long-standing tradition of redistributive social policies (Hobson 1994; Bussemaker et al. 1997). However, as we saw before, these effects did not so much arise from explicitly 'woman-friendly policies', but rather, from traditionally generous family policies.

As we can see, there have been many changes in social policy and society in recent decades. In terms of citizenship, women have certainly attained greater economic independence and entitlement to social rights, mainly as a result of their increased labour market participation. But strategies for individualisation are, at best, ambiguous; women have gained more individual entitlements, but the net result is not always an improvement, compared with the financial security they may have had through their male partner.

Some of these developments are related to changes in and between social spheres. Pillarisation has eroded, and social cohesion needs to be secured by other means, but just how this will be achieved is the subject of ongoing discussions. In 1995, the Christian Democratic Party (the former Catholic and orthodox Protestant party merged, together with a smaller Christian party, into one party in the mid-seventies) opened a discussion about the need for a Ministry of Family Affairs. The attention they are currently giving to family issues is strongly linked to the history of pillarisation. For they are afraid, more than other political groups, to lose the specific freedom to create separate social worlds; particularly in terms of the traditional (or even modernised) version of the male breadwinner-family, in which care is provided in the home or through community organisations in the civil society (the 'social middle field'), and not by the state or the market. The tradition of tolerance towards different denominations and their ideas is still used as an argument to criticise state intervention in issues of gender.

Political rhetoric today tends towards either a more conservative plea for 'family policies', or towards a more liberal discourse, in which autonomous individuals are assumed to be alive and well. This situation limits possibilities for alternative options (Bussemaker 1991).

Conclusion

The Dutch case enables us to draw some general conclusions about gender and citizenship, pluralism in society, and the distinction between public and private spheres. To begin with, the sequence of citizenship rights outlined by Marshall (1965), might be appropriate for men in the United Kingdom, but it does not hold for many other European countries, and certainly not for women. As many scholars have shown (Frader 1996; Lister 1990; Pateman 1989; O'Connor 1996; Orloff 1993; Pedersen 1993; Walby 1994), the development and experience of rights has differed considerably for men and for women. In the Netherlands, women gained some measure of social rights within the labour market at the end of the nineteenth century, and achieved political rights in 1919. Married women, however, had to wait until the 1950s for full entitlement to civil rights; at the same time, they were excluded from many postwar social rights, because they were assumed to be protected through their husbands. It was not until the 1980s that women, due to the legal individualisation of social rights, could apply for most social entitlements. But the problem of how to participate on equal terms with men in the work force or in the political realm - and simultaneously run a household and care for dependents - has not as yet been solved.

The typical Dutch characteristics which frame the relation between gender and citizenship can be found in the history of pillarisation and the pluralism of lifestyles that went along with it. The histories of pillarisation and welfare state formation are characterised by substantial interventions into family life, either directly or indirectly. However, these interventions were first and foremost a means to guarantee various denominational and religious world views, and were not primarily intended to provide protection from the effects of the market.

Feminists, in so far as they criticised these provisions, had difficulty breaking through the broad consensus on these matters. Moreover, the tolerance towards denominational world views made it difficult to formulate effective feminist positions concerning citizenship. It was easy for critics to counter feminist demands for state intervention to secure women's independence, with arguments tied to respect for pluralism and different lifestyles. Pluralism, after all, did not refer to women.

The principle of tolerance and respect for other groups, however, acquired a different meaning when pillarisation as a social and political system disintegrated in the late sixties, and other movements came to the forefront. The feminist movement was one of these, but the argument can be extended to other groups. The tradition of pluralism and respect for different life styles led, from the mid-seventies, to a rapid adoption of feminist demands, especially if those demands concentrated on self-development, consciousness-raising or autonomous self-help organisations. It was not difficult for feminist organisations addressing these issues to obtain state subsidies. This strategy worked not only for feminists, but also for other groups. Ethnic minority groups have, comparatively speaking, little difficulty in establishing their own cultural and social organisations, which are often subsidised by the state. And for homosexuals, the effect might even be more pronounced. In fact, one Dutch scholar speaks in this context of 'the pillarisation of the gay movement' (Duyvendak 1994).

The history of pillarisation, and its impact on social segregation and citizenship rights, has implications beyond the Dutch context. The Dutch situation demonstrates some of the benefits as well as some of the risks that go with a strong emphasis on group identities and a respect for a plurality of lifestyles - important topics today in discussions about multiculturalism and communitarianism. The benefits at this time might include the (positive) recognition of various identities, of different lifestyles and histories. The risks lie in increased societal segregation which may provide an easy means to avoid public debates about meanings of 'the good life' and of the 'common interest'.

Finally, Dutch history also reveals something about the separation of spheres. Many of the phenomena described thus far cannot be properly understood within the simple dichotomy of the public and the private. Even a distinction between the three spheres (state, market and the family) is not sufficient to understand the history of gender and citizenship in the Netherlands. To these, we should consider adding the sphere of the civil society, and more specifically, the history of the 'social middle field', in order to understand the profound configuration of gender, citizenship and social policy.

Women's citizenship concerns more than the integration of public and private life (which today is often conceptualised as a combination of both paid work and family responsibilities). It also concerns women's participation in different spheres, combined with the necessary conditions to bring this about. As Nancy Fraser has expressed it, women's citizenship is about imagining a 'social world in which citizens' lives integrate wage-earning, care-giving, community activism, political participation, and involvement in the associational life of civil society - while also leaving time for some fun' (Fraser 1994, p. 613).

Fraser's 'social world' is rather different from the Dutch pillarised social worlds described here. However, her idea of the interrelation, as well as the complexity between social spheres, is an important element in any discussion of women's citizenship. For genuine citizenship is about the right to participate simultaneously in different spheres, and on an equal basis. This is what we might call a 'universal' and 'pluralist' notion of citizenship - in the full sense of the words.

3 Political participation and social rights. The triumph of the breadwinner in the Netherlands[1]

Tjitske Akkerman

Participation is usually understood to be an activity engaged in by citizens with a view to influencing government. Research into such activity often focuses on conventional electoral politics, but I would like to argue that participation has to be understood in a broader, historical context. The ways in which citizens aim to influence government vary and change over time, as do the local and national political institutions which are crucial to participation. In this article I will focus on the rise of the welfare state around 1900, a period in which the opportunities for political participation by women changed in fundamental respects. Moreover, I will argue that apart from the institutional context, we also have to extend an analysis of participation to the political beliefs and strategies of organisations and movements. In other words, a contextual and historical analysis of women's participation needs to take account both of institutions and of ideas (Orloff 1996).

In the Netherlands research into women's participation has moved toward a broad approach, but this development applies for the most part only to the very recent history of the women's movement. This research has, for instance, included non-governmental feminist movements, 'state feminism' and 'women's policy machinery' (cf. Outshoorn, Oldersma and Leijenaar in this volume). Yet, with respect to earlier periods, a broader approach is still lacking. Research on political participation has mainly focused on the period after 1919, the year women got the vote. This is also the period in which women's organisations affiliated to political parties emerged (Velde 1994). Implicitly, this focus on electoral politics has encouraged the view that women's *political* participation only began after the First World War. That is not to say that the history of the women's movement before the First World War has been neglected. On the contrary, this history is fortunately relatively well documented. The problem, however, is that there still seems to be a wide gap between the history of the women's movement prior to 1919 and the history of women's political participation from 1919 on.

Strong and weak movements

What politics amounts to has always changed over time; around 1900, however, it changed rather dramatically. Certainly, with the rise of the first welfare states, women's social participation in community associations and voluntary organisations took on a new political meaning. Focusing on these acts of social participation may help us to clarify the ways in which the boundaries between the political and the social spheres were redrawn. The importance of women's participation in social work for instance has been well documented. Participation in social work, at least when women succeeded in taking leading positions, functioned as an important springboard for positions in boards, councils and government committees. Even without the vote, social work became an important gateway to political influence. Extending the notion of participation to the field of social policy, some scholars have raised new questions with respect to the influence women had. In fact, this perspective has more or less upset the established views of women's movements in various countries. Sonya Michel and Seth Koven (1993) for instance, pointed to the inverse relation between strong women's movements and women's influence in social legislation. According to their thesis, in countries where the women's movement was strong, like the United States and Britain, social legislation hardly reflected the interests of women as housewives and mothers. In contrast, social legislation in Germany and France - countries with a relatively weak women's movement - appeared to be favourable to mothers, and in the case of France also to female workers to some extent (Bock and Thane 1990; Lewis 1993; Michel and Koven 1993; Skocpol 1992). When we look at the Netherlands, the paradoxical situation of a moderately strong women's movement on the one hand, and social legislation modelled on the male breadwinner on the other hand, also presents itself.

What are strong movements? Numbers have been regarded as an important criterion to distinguish between strong and weak movements. Accordingly, British and American women's movements of the nineteenth and beginning of the twentieth century have been regarded as strong (Evans 1977; Rendall 1985). More generally, it has been argued that those countries that had a democratic tradition and a Protestant culture saw the most spectacular growth of women's movements (Akkerman and Stuurman 1997). If we take the degree of organisation as an indication of strength, the women's movement in the Netherlands probably belonged to a group of moderately strong movements (cf. Borkus et al. 1994, p. 197; Jansz 1983, p. 209). Another indicator that has been used to rank strong and weak movements, is the winning of the vote. In this respect the Netherlands was not among the 'avant-garde', but belonged to the main group of countries that introduced female suffrage directly after the First World War (cf. Leijenaar in this volume).

In contrast, when we look at social participation and social rights as indicators of women's influence, the picture in the Netherlands is far less promising. First, the participation of women in social work did not provide many opportunities for political influence. On the whole women were strongly underrepresented in positions of authority in charity organisations. Charity in the Netherlands was still dominated by religious authorities. Till far into the twentieth century the denominational institutions had substantial autonomy and the state continued to have a complementary role with regard to poor relief. As Berteke Waaldijk (1996) has argued, this state of affairs forced women to play relatively marginal roles in positions of authority, such as on the boards of social work organisations. In 1909 there were about 500 poor relief boards with thousands of male members, but there were only 22 female members (Waaldijk 1996, p. 102; cf. Bervoets 1994). As research in other countries has convincingly shown, such positions were often the means by which women could begin to gain influence in social policy (Cott 1987; Hollis 1987; Lewis 1991).

Secondly, the social legislation that was introduced in the Netherlands during the first decades of the century seems to confirm the impression that women's organisations did not have much influence in social policy. Social legislation hardly reflected the interests of women as housewives and mothers, but was almost completely focused on the (male) worker. Most insurance schemes focused on (male) workers, such as the Industrial Injuries Insurance Act (1901), the Invalidity and Old Age Insurance Act (1913, into effect in 1919) and the Sickness Insurance Act (1913, into effect in 1930). The Child Allowance Act came into effect 1939.

On the whole then, women's influence in the slowly emerging Dutch welfare state of the early twentieth century, seems to have been marginal, and yet, the Dutch women's movement seems to have been moderately strong. In order to explain this paradox, at least two aspects need to be reconsidered. On the one hand, the established notions of strong and weak movements should be refined. On the other hand, the accepted notion of women's interests may be too crude.

First, on the matter of strong and weak movements, the example of the vote indicates that strength is not only a matter of sheer numbers. It may even have been more difficult for an extensive women's movement to win the vote, as the very size of the movement may have strengthened the opposition of the political elite to female suffrage. In the Netherlands the women's movement was strong enough to put the issue on the political agenda and to gain the support of Social Democrats and Liberals, but on the whole not so strong that the denominational parties feared that the suffrage law of 1919 would fundamentally change the political balance of power. In other words, as long as a substantial share of the potential female voters was not organised, the opposition of the denominational parties to female suffrage was less rigorous, and female suffrage might be granted relatively early (Spoormans 1988). This illustrates the more general fact that the political influence of women's movements is also dependent on the strength of their respective opponents and allies.

Secondly, if we are to test the notion of women's interests, it is essential to know more about the actual goals women's organisations had. In other words, an analysis of the strength of women's movements should be extended to an analysis of their political beliefs and strategies in various countries.

Even though women's organisations in this period may have generally supported a so-called maternalist ideology - that is to say, almost all women's organisations valued motherhood highly and were devoted to the cause of social rights for mothers - this general commitment could imply widely divergent agendas. For instance, a commitment to social rights for mothers might sometimes conflict with other important goals of women's organisations. Even if among Dutch women's organisations a consensus about the priority of motherhood existed - which is doubtful - there could be fundamental conflicts about the political implications of this position. For instance, the question of what the role of the state should be and what kind of social rights mothers should claim were issues about which women's organisations might disagree fundamentally. With regard to the ranking of strong and weak movements, the most interesting question is why in some countries women's movements succeeded in developing broad support for a political program on motherhood, while in other countries they did not.

Endowment of motherhood

Probably the most important issues of social policy to occupy women's organisations before the Second World War were 'endowment of motherhood' and family allowances. The demand for endowment of motherhood was raised by women's movements in many countries as an alternative to family allowances paid to the breadwinner. In this way women's movements claimed that motherhood was an important contribution to society which should be acknowledged by a benefit paid in cash or as a 'wage'.

In Britain, for instance, feminists managed in the 1920s to turn the debate about family allowances toward the principle of endowment of motherhood. The idea of pensions for poor mothers had already gained credence at the beginning of the century among feminists, socialist women, and new liberals (Akkerman 1997; Pedersen 1993). These groups accepted the duty of the state to pay for 'the civic service' of motherhood, and often also stressed the reciprocal duty of the mother to abstain from industrial work and devote herself to the care of her children. As the idea of pensions for poor mothers was defended as a public remuneration for an important service it could easily be extended to the general idea of payment to all mothers.

Although, in the case of Britain, the campaign for endowment resulted 'only' in a provision in the Child Allowance Act of 1945 that the allowance should be paid to the mother, this was more than the Dutch legislation on family income provided. The main legislation in the period before the Second World War was a Child Allowance Act, which after many years of preparation was finally passed in 1939. This act was based on the paternalistic principle that the legitimate father had the disposal of the allowance, even where the mother was in fact the breadwinner. (In 1951 the Act was extended to unmarried mothers and in 1963 the maintenance principle replaced the conferment on the father altogether.)

The explanation usually given for the development of a strong breadwinner model is the dominance of the denominational parties in the Netherlands (cf. Bussemaker in this volume; Sainsbury 1994). In the 1920s and 1930s the Catholic party, in particular, endorsed a social policy that privileged the male breadwinner (cf. Plantenga in this volume). However, when we look at the policy of women's organisations, it is striking that they were not able to formulate a coherent program to counter this policy. Moreover, in the first decades of the century, when the confessional parties did not yet have a stable majority, women's organisations still failed to make a breakthrough. In general, the conflict between secular and denominational parties dominated the 'social question' in this time, and paralysed the development of social legislation.

Yet, there were moments, directly before and after the First World War, when a coalition of socialists and liberals might have broken the political deadlock on the social question. At these moments women's organisations did not succeed in seizing the advantage. The most favourable moment for a strong line of action was probably directly after the war. In 1919, with female suffrage becoming a reality, the Dutch women's organisations that had been working towards that goal were discussing which major issues might now deserve their attention. Social policy, and in particular maternity care, was welcomed by Social Democratic women and feminists alike as a major new issue (Jacobs 1922/23, pp. 60-73; *Proletarische Vrouw* 17 April 1920; Wijnaendts Francken-Dijserinck 1924, p. 5).

There was a general revival of activity and debate on social legislation after the war. Although the political climate initially seemed favourable, by the early 1920s the tide had already turned, and new social initiatives were opposed. In this political constellation, the women's movement found it very difficult to redirect its energies to the social question.

As far as women's organisations were able to develop initiatives, they did so merely in opposition to the prevailing policy of family allowances. From 1920 to 1928 a 'Committee of Action against the Family Wage' was active, but, as the name indicates, it was a defensive committee which did not develop an alternative program.

Allowances and the family wage

In the Netherlands the idea of endowment of motherhood never gained much popularity. Family allowances became an important issue after the First World War, and there was broad opposition among women's organisations to higher wages for breadwinners with large families. However, the campaign to set up endowment of motherhood as an alternative did not gain much support. Only in the first years after the war was it considered as a serious, albeit long term option; but with the political climate turning at the beginning of the twenties, endowment of motherhood disappeared from the agenda.

Family allowances as part of the family wage had been and remained the dominant issue. Allowances were introduced for the first time in 1906 by the city of Amsterdam as part of a wage policy and this remained the predominant context. The principle of a family wage had been part of the wage policy of the labour movement since the end of the nineteenth century, and had become widely accepted (Damsma 1994, pp. 169-183).

Indeed, until the war few in any political group contested the idea of a family wage. Socialists and new liberals saw it as a 'living wage' or a minimum wage, Catholics introduced the term 'absolute wage'. Feminists supported the principle of a family wage too, using both the terms minimum wage and absolute wage (Polak 1917, p. 408; Polak 1920). Even though these terms were endorsed by such different ideological movements, they matched in some crucial respects. Feminists could agree, for instance, that wages were not only based on merit but also on needs, as long as this principle meant that wages were based on a mean standard, like that of a family with three children. As long as this standard was applied equally to all, married and unmarried, male and female workers, they could go along with the principle of a family wage (Polak 1925, pp. 358-383; cf. Naber 1920).

The introduction of allowances in 1906 by the city of Amsterdam, followed by the introduction by the government of allowances for the Postal Service and for teachers in 1912, implied a new development (cf. Plantenga in this volume). In fact, a step had been made on the way to a so-called relative wage, that is, a wage dependent on the size of the family the breadwinner had to provide for. After the war the idea of a relative wage gained ground, especially in confessional circles (Dijsselbloem 1937, p. 62; Jager 1988, p. 44; Stolk 1921; Gosker 1970, p. 82). In 1918 in parliament a Catholic resolution was accepted in which the government was asked to consider the size of families in setting the salaries of civil servants. Although employers argued that the state should take the main burden of responsibility for child allowances, private funds to support large families were nonetheless growing (Dijsselbloem 1937, p. 142; Commissie RKCRB 1920). Finally, the Catholic Minister of Labour Aalberse announced a plan to establish a fund for child allowances (the 'Rijkskinderfonds') in 1920 (Wittert van Hoogland 1940, p. 422).

Liberal feminists and endowment of motherhood

In response to the developing policy to introduce allowances based on a 'relative wage' feminists took the initiative to establish a 'Committee of Action against the Family Wage' in 1920. The committee was supported by about ten organisations. It was dominated by Liberal feminists; the Social Democratic women did not cooperate, even though they supported the aims of the committee (Verslag 1922, p. 85). They followed the policy of the Social Democratic Union (NVV) in this; the union also expressed its sympathy, but would not join. The union organised its own conference against family allowances in 1921.

The main activities of the committee were to publish pamphlets and to send addresses to the government. Its president, Mrs. Boissevain-Pijnappel, spoke against family allowances on several occasions. As she was a member of the Provincial States of Northern Holland for the moderate Liberal party (the 'Vrijheidsbond'), this gave her the opportunity to raise the subject at meetings. On these occasions she argued that the supporters of higher wages for large families were ignoring the right of the mother to a part of the wage. A more equal division of resources within the family was central to her arguments against family allowances. On another occasion Boissevain-Pijnappel was not afraid to confront an audience of council officials with the alternative of endowment of motherhood. She saw endowment as a recognition by society of the great work done by the mothers. A wage for mothers was still an undeveloped idea, she acknowledged. Yet, she made it clear that the example of Great Britain, where allowances were paid to the mother, should be followed (*Algemeen Handelsblad* 9 October 1921; Boissevain-Pijnappel 1921, pp. 159-169; *Gemeente-ambtenaar* 20 June 1920, pp. 145-154; Stolk 1921, p. 106).

Apart from Boissevain-Pijnappel, other feminists who played an important role in influencing public opinion in favour of the committee were Anna Polak, president of the National Bureau for Women's Labour, Johanna Naber, president of the National Women's Council (1917-1922), and Welmoet Wijnaendts Francken-Dijserinck. The women mentioned were all active members of the liberal 'Vrijheidsbond', the rather conservative wing of the liberal movement. In the course of the twenties the 'Vrijheidsbond' became a strong advocate of cutting budgets and a steady opponent of new social spending legislation. This may certainly have affected the policy of its affiliated women's organisation; it became much harder to endorse endowment of motherhood. However, the committee had been divided about endowment of motherhood from the beginning. Boissevain-Pijnappel excepted, only Wijnaendts Francken-Dijserinck advocated endowment of motherhood over a number of years. Anna Polak and Johanna Naber never endorsed this solution. They opposed family allowances primarily because it implied a wage discrimination against unmarried women (Naber 1920; Polak 1921, pp. 108-126).

Anna Polak was too much of a classical liberal to endorse the idea of the state subsidising motherhood. She was afraid, Polak (1925) wrote in a review of Rathbone's *The Disinherited Family*, that society would acquire the right to regulate the number and quality of children, and to control children's care and education. She was one of the few feminists to come up with economic arguments against a relative family wage; her arguments that this would lead to economic decline were based on the theory of a wage fund or capital that would diminish because of the rise in wages. Hence, investment would decline and unemployment grow. Although she did not discuss the economic aspects of endowment of motherhood, she probably would have had similar concerns with respect to its consequences.

Her alternative for the married woman was that she should strive for economic independence through free access to the labour market and through a reform of marriage law which would give her the legal right to a part of her husband's income (Polak 1925, pp. 358-383).

The only outright defender of endowment of motherhood was Wijnaendts Francken-Dijserinck. She was propagating the idea of endowment for mothers around 1920. Until 1917 she was a member of the radical liberal party (VDB), and in 1921 she changed to the more conservative liberal wing ('Vrijheidsbond'), where she became president of the newly established Women's Group. From then on, she moderated her views and gave up her former ideas with respect to endowment. In contrast to most liberal feminists, who stressed the dangers of state control, Wijnaendts Francken-Dijserinck initially valued the community and the role of the state highly. Before the war, for instance, she propagated the idea of a compulsory social service for young women (Kortbeek 1995, p. 60).

Motherhood was in her view a social service to the community (Wijnaendts Francken-Dijserinck 1920, p. 5). She wrote that endowment should only be given to mothers who did not work for a wage, and that it should be restricted to those with young children. Moreover, in the interest of the state, endowment might be restricted to those with four or more children (Vereeniging 1922, p. 63). A few years later, when she discarded the principle of endowment, she appeared to be much more wary of state interference, expressing the concern that the state might try to control the number and quality of births. Her view concerning maternity benefits was now largely in accordance with the more classical-liberal view of feminists like Anna Polak (Wijnaendts Francken-Dijserinck 1924).

These feminists all pointed out that in England allowances were paid to the mother. However, this did not induce them to make payment to the mother part of their strategy. Wijnaendts Francken-Dijserinck remarked that such an idea would cause a storm of indignation in the Netherlands (Wijnaendts Francken-Dijserinck 1924, p. 25). When one takes into account how little feminists had yet gained with respect to the reform of marriage law, this pessimistic tone seems well justified. Dutch feminists were well aware that the marital power of the husband had strong roots in their country.

While liberal feminists certainly hoped for a more equal division of resources within the household, they hardly ever translated this policy into a demand for endowment of motherhood. It remained predominantly an issue to be discussed within the context of the reform of marriage law. In contrast to British marriage law, Dutch law gave the husband, as the legal head of the family, almost full control of goods. Apart from gaining control of their own wages in 1907, married women had not gained much financial independence, and reform of the marriage law remained an important demand of the women's movement throughout the inter-war years.

Social Democratic women and endowment of motherhood

Before the war the Social Democratic women had been the only group who continuously argued in favour of maternity care. This isolated position was not restricted to the issue of maternity care, but was fairly general. Their arguments in favour of extending labour protection for women and restricting women's labour hours, for example, never gained much influence in the Netherlands.

It took a long time before the Social Democratic taboo on co-operation with feminist organisations disappeared. The first time that the federation of Social Democratic women's clubs worked together with feminist organisations was in 1924 (!), when they joined the committee that protested against the government policy of dismissing married female civil servants. Earlier protests against bans on married women's labour had not been joined by the federation, although sometimes individual Social Democratic women had participated (Braun 1992; Eijl 1994, pp. 265, 344; Outshoorn 1973, p. 55).

The suffrage issue, however, fared a little better in terms of co-operation between the Social Democratic societies and feminist organisations. In 1914 the socialist women conditionally supported a petition organised by the main feminist organisation for female suffrage ('Vereniging voor Vrouwenkiesrecht'), but in 1916, when the Labour Party decided to work together with the feminist organisations, the socialist women were against this party initiative (Jansz 1990). However, in the suffrage struggle an alliance - albeit a cautious one - between socialists, feminists and liberals did come about around 1913. It was this alliance that led to the 'pacification' of 1917 and finally to the vote for women in 1919 (cf. Bussemaker in this volume).

Endowment of motherhood did not find much support among Social Democratic women, but for reasons quite different from those put forward by liberals. The idea of a more just division of resources within the family for instance was problematic in Social Democratic circles. The class based solidarity between husband and wife was often regarded as more important than individual rights. Therefore, Social Democratic women were rather ambivalent about marriage reform, and therefore, about endowment of motherhood. The demand for reform was at its best regarded as a bourgeois demand which deserved some support (Braun 1992, pp. 142-145). Even though Social Democratic women were strong advocates of the idea that motherhood was work which had great value for the community, they were reluctant to translate such an acknowledgment into the idea of housewives and mothers having a right to a part of the man's wage. Marriage should not be made into such 'a cold agreement', it was argued in the journal *De Proletarische Vrouw* (The Proletarian Woman) (1 February 1909 and 13 November 1920).

While a discussion about the unity of the family wage was not on the Social Democratic agenda, higher wages for breadwinners with large families were rejected for various reasons. The main arguments against family allowances were that they would lead to lower wages, and that they would diminish the unity of organised workers. Remarkably, the Social Democratic member of parliament Suze Groeneweg used the argument that such allowances were 'anti-feminist', because they implied that only the husband could maintain the family (*De Proletarische Vrouw* 13 November 1920). The predominant view among Social Democratic women was that the social value of motherhood had to be acknowledged by establishing and extending community services such as maternity hospitals, crèches, and communal kitchens.

The idea of endowment of motherhood was however not completely without support within the Social Democratic women's societies. Its most enthusiastic advocate was W. Mansholt-Andraea, who defended the idea steadily from 1908 in the journal *De Proletarische Vrouw*. In 1918 the debate about endowment of motherhood was regarded as important enough to be published in the journal of the Labour Party, the *Socialistische Gids*. Manholt-Andraea's opponent in the debate was Mathilde Wibaut, founder of the Social Democratic

Women's Societies. The latter opposed endowment of motherhood for two reasons. First, such a measure implied an 'individualistic' view of the family. It would mean consigning the important task of raising children to the private sphere of the family. In this respect, endowment was incompatible with the socialist aim of socialising the functions of the family. Secondly, Wibaut was opposed to the idea of endowment because she feared that it would deprive mothers of the opportunity to work. For most Social Democratic women, paid work was of the utmost value. In their journal *De Proletarische Vrouw* it was argued that work would raise women's class-consciousness and that it was the most important way to develop oneself. These arguments lost much of their Social Democratic support during the thirties, but Mathilde Wibaut never wavered and remained committed to the aims of 'socialising' the family and to the principle of full access for women to the work force.

Mansholt-Andraea's defence of endowment was based on the view that motherhood was the highest duty and much more important than professional labour; she accepted the idea that acceptance of endowment implied a ban on work for mothers (*De Socialistische Gids* 1919, pp. 149-152). Her view that motherhood was more important than professional work was not without support in the Social Democratic movement; there was a substantial minority who supported this idea. Yet, the logical consequence that mothers should be paid by the state for carrying out this important duty, was probably far less accepted. Henriette van der Mey was one of the few Social Democratic women who supported Mansholt-Andraea in this. She wrote that she had sympathy for the idea of endowment of motherhood, as it was based on the idea that the mother ought to be at home with her children, but she also stressed that it was no more than faint music of the future (*De Sociale Verzekeringsgids* 1 August 1920).

Mansholt-Andraea's ideas were characterised as 'individualistic' by her opponents, but this criticism was only justified in so far as far as she did not envision a future in which the family would have been 'socialised'. Yet, her view of motherhood was collectivistic too, as she stressed the duty of the state to acknowledge the communal service of mothers and to compensate them in cash. She was well aware that her view was hardly popular in the Social Democratic movement as a whole:

> I do no flatter myself with the idea that I will take the party by storm for the demand of wages for mothers, but I derive comfort from the conviction that once my demand will find response in the working-class, thus blessing mother and child (*De Socialistische Gids* 1918, p. 464)

Her scepticism about the party accepting endowment of motherhood appeared to be justified; state-compensation in kind - like creches, maternity hospitals and communal kitchens - rather than in cash was the prevailing goal of Social Democratic policy during the twenties.

Feminists and state-interference

The main antagonists, then, in the debate about family allowances, the Social Democratic women and the moderate liberal feminists, were divided over the idea of endowment of motherhood. For the Social Democratic opponents, the idea was too individualistic with respect to the family; for the liberal opponents it was too collectivistic as it granted too much power to the state. Fear of the state controlling the number and quality of births in particular inspired the liberal opposition to endowment. This was an issue that hardly concerned Social Democratic women, whose opposition to payment of mothers in cash was primarily driven by their wariness of the 'individualisation' and 'commodification' of family-relations; the state, they believed, should rather provide compensation in kind.

The wariness of liberal feminists about state interference was shared by several other women's organisations. An intermediate position was taken by the main suffrage society, which had changed its name to the 'Society for Female Citizens' in 1919. State pensions for poor mothers were, for instance, accepted by a majority of the committee of the Society (*Maandblad Nederlandse Vereeniging voor Staatsburgeressen* 15 January 1920 and 15 November 1920). The radical-liberal feminist Aletta Jacobs, prominent member of this Society (and formerly president of the Women's Suffrage Society), also acknowledged the need for some degree of state responsibility, so far as this responsibility could be restricted to communal services like maternity homes, clinics and schools for midwives. She was fervently against any form of cash benefit for mothers on the eugenic grounds such benefits might raise the birth rate in poor families and eventually lower the quality of the race (*Maandblad Nederlandse Vereeniging voor Staatsburgeressen* 15 April 1922). In line with her view, the journal of the Society condemned the example of Wales, where the state provided a child allowance paid to mothers, as an example of 'state socialism' (*Maandblad Nederlandse Vereeniging voor Staatsburgeressen* 15 December 1919).

The 'General Dutch Women's Organisation' (ANVO), a women's party established in 1919 that joined the committee against the family wage, published a report by Catharine van Tusschenbroek and other feminists on maternity care. Pensions for mothers were suspect, they argued, not only for eugenic reasons, but also because it was dangerous in itself to turn motherhood into an affair of state. This would undermine personal responsibility. Financial help should only be given in the form of a dole, and for the rest they advocated the principle of insurance as it would leave personal responsibility intact (Commissie ANVO 1921, pp. 8-11).

The influential 'National Women's Council', which represented more than 40 organisations, also rejected almost all forms of state interference. They held that the state should have no responsibility other than subsidising private initiatives. Their report on maternal care stressed the responsibility of women themselves, and rejected the idea of state-pensions for mothers (Commissie ANVO 1925, pp. 9-10).

Finally, the confessional women's organisations, which had also voiced their opinions in the report of the National Women's Council, in the main supported private forms of maternity care. Their view was that the main role of the state was to subsidise private initiatives.

There was, among women's organisations, a widespread wariness of making motherhood an affair of state by paying women in cash. Eugenic concerns, in particular, inspired this general opposition to benefits in cash. With the exception of the Society of Female Citizens, there was even a widespread opposition to almost any form of state-responsibility for motherhood. A substantial number of women's organisations stressed the priority of 'self-help' and personal responsibility or encouraged the protection of private initiatives, and these convictions precluded support for even moderate forms of maternity care.

Conclusion

It appears that alternatives to a social security system geared to the male breadwinner were most viable in the first decades of the century. In the 1930s Social Democrats came to accept the idea of family allowances for the breadwinner. The only principled opposition to the Child Allowance Act at the time came from Liberal members of parliament. Social Democratic ideas about family policy had changed rather fundamentally by then. As early as the late twenties there seemed to be little support left for the policy of 'socialising' the family and demanding community services (Arons 1981, pp. 111-137). Moreover, the aim, espoused by Social Democratic women, of realising economic independence through participation in the labour market became increasingly remote during the thirties. The principle of benefits geared to the breadwinner had become accepted by both the confessional and the Social Democratic parties. After all, then, it was not just the dominance of the denominational parties that brought about the 'breadwinner model'. The revision of the Social Democratic views of the family freed the way for a rapprochement of Social Democrats and Catholics in the thirties.

The crucial question, however, is what women's organisations contributed to this development of social policy. Looking back at the first decades of the century, it appears that the women's movement did not have much success in using its strength to influence social policy. The political deadlock with respect to the social question in the first decades, and the confessional dominance after the twenties made it very hard for the women's movement to develop promising initiatives in this field.

We should also take into account the important barriers which divided the various women's organisations from each other and which weakened the possibility of joint action. Not only was there a deep religious division, but there was also a division in the secular camp between Social Democratic women and (liberal) feminists. Compared to Britain and the United States for instance, the Dutch women's movement was weakened from within by class divisions. In the United States the alternative of strong working-class organisations was simply absent. In Britain the threat of such a cleavage was real, but feminists, socialists and new liberals succeeded in developing a more or less successful alliance in the suffrage struggle and in social policy (Akkerman 1997; Holton 1986; Skocpol and

Ritter 1991). In Britain, the existence of a radical and populist liberal tradition, invigorated by a strong new liberal movement around the turn of the century, made such coalitions easier (Akkerman 1997; Biagini and Reid 1991; Collini 1992; Harris 1992). In the Netherlands, by contrast, the divide between liberal individualism and socialist collectivism appeared to be more tenacious.

One reason for this deeper divide between liberalism and socialism may have been that the Dutch liberal tradition was overall more élitist than the British. Although new liberals did take initiatives around the turn of the century to develop more populist policies, in the Netherlands they did not succeed so well in allying with the socialist movement (Rooy 1987; Stuurman 1992; Velde 1992). On the other hand, the Dutch Social Democratic movement organised far more autonomously. Although there was certainly some cooperation with liberals and feminists - the suffrage coalition is an example - in the field of social policy these initiatives remained weak.

The ideological divide between Liberals and Social Democrats was reflected in the widely diverging notions women's organisations had about the role of the state and of the family. It is striking that, with the exception of Social Democratic women, wariness about state intervention was widespread among women's organisations. This fear was to a large extent inspired by the belief that the confessional parties were trying to use family allowances to enhance control of population policies. Ironically, when the Child Allowance Act was finally introduced in 1939, the predominant Catholic aim was to combat inflation and poverty, rather than to act because of concerns over population policy (Noordman 1989).

Women's participation, then, depended partly on the institutional context in which opportunities to influence social policies were circumscribed. In the Netherlands, there were important institutional barriers which may explain why women's organisations did not gain a strong foothold in social policy, such as the relatively strong position of the churches in poor relief, and the absence of (local) female suffrage. Yet, ideological divides appeared no less crucial in obstructing cooperation. While religion was obviously a main cleavage, the divide between Social Democratic 'collectivism' and liberal 'individualism' likewise worked against collective action across the different women's organisations.

Acknowledgement

1. I would like to thank my collegue Dirk Damsma for his valuable suggestions about the subject of the family-wage.

4 Double lives: labour market participation, citizenship and gender

Janneke Plantenga

> There is a double life. A life in the family, with the children, that has a more private aspect. And then there is another life, almost totally divorced from the first, a life of councils and states, of navies and armies, that has a more public character. This double kind of life demands extremely distinct gifts and talents, and history - and today's empirical data - teaches us that these double kinds of gifts and talents, at least most often, appear to coincide with the differences in kind between man and woman. Private and public life are two distinct spheres, each with its own way of existence, with their own task whose fulfilment calls for a specific kind of qualities and talents. This is the harmony of life and human nature (Kuyper 1914, p. 47).

This is how the Calvinist theologian and politician Abraham Kuyper in 1914 formulated his view of society and the natural position of the sexes therein, in a book entitled The Honourary Position of Women. According to Kuyper, men and women were 'not of the same kind' and were thus destined for different activities. The Woman was defined primarily through her ability to bear children and hence her destiny was within the home, in marriage, where she was housewife, spouse and mother. In contrast, the Man was defined by the outside world, a world Kuyper described in very masculine terms as a place of councils and states, navies and armies. The differing positions of men and women were not therefore intended to depreciate the one group at the expense of the other, but to serve as social translations of natural differences. Kuyper: 'And I base my premise on this state of affairs, which we did not create, but which was imposed upon us by God, that the Woman is not equal to the Man in public life' (ibid; cf. Bussemaker in this volume).

The thinking propounded by Kuyper here is not in itself specifically Dutch; similar notions were current in many countries at the turn of the century. Industrialisation, the rise of large-scale wage work and encroaching urbanisation all threatened the natural gender order, and resulted in a search for new grounds on which it might be justified (Hausen 1976; Rang 1986). What is specifically Dutch is the success of the practical application of this thinking, resulting in a gendered division of labour and care. From the end of the nineteenth century until the 1970s, married women rarely worked outside the home and the full-time housewife was a generally accepted norm (cf. Knijn in this volume). In this respect, the Netherlands appears to have had a 'specialised citizenship' for quite some time in the sense that its men and women had each been allocated their own gender-specific social position with a matching package of rights and obligations. The moral status of both positions was considered at least equal; Kuyper does not use the title 'the honorary position of women' lightly. In practice, however, the gender-specific separation of breadwinner and care-giver meant that social and economic rights were allocated to the male breadwinner, while the Woman enjoyed no more status than that of dependent.

In this article I will explore the relationships between labour market participation, citizenship and gender. The first section focuses on the period up to the Second World War and looks at how the 'harmony of life and human nature' was institutionalised. Then I provide an overview of how in the post-war period the gendered division of labour and care no longer seemed self-evident and became the subject of debate and resistance. This description is followed by an analysis, focusing on the backgrounds of this specific Dutch pattern. In the final section, I sum up the current situation, and outline some potential future developments.

1890-1940: in search of a natural order

In the first decade of this century around 25 per cent of female Dutch labour was active in the work force. The vast majority were young, unmarried women; married women's participation levels were no more than around 10 per cent in this period (cf. Plantenga 1993, p. 52). Compared to other countries, these figures are strikingly low. In Germany, for example, women's labour market participation in the same period was around 45 per cent. In France and the United Kingdom too considerably more (married) women were active in the labour market (cf. Plantenga 1993, p. 53; Eijl 1994, p. 55). This difference was also noted by contemporary authors. Labour inspector de Vooys, for example, concluded in 1910 that 'only in the United States is the percentage of women in paid work lower than in the Netherlands' (in Dorp 1910, p. 67). Almost 30 years later, in 1938, Posthumus-van der Goot arrived at the same conclusion: 'Compared to foreign countries, married women in paid work occurs only sporadically in the Netherlands' (Posthumus-van der Goot 1938, p. 139).

The low rate of participation by married women in the labour market was a priority policy issue. The general consensus was that to have married women working outside the home would be detrimental to healthy family relations. A full-time housewife was not only a major safeguard against miscarriages and infant mortality, she was also seen as a weapon against alcohol abuse and could play a positive role in the fight against anti-social behaviour in the broadest sense. Thus, a woman's role was primarily to create a cosy and comfortable home. Van Dorp, one of the first female lawyers in the Netherlands, spoke enthusiastically of the benefits that could be expected from a (full-time) housewife: 'a woman's work in the home is like a large square which provides light and fresh air, sunshine and joy in a working-class quarter of drudges inhabiting narrow streets of sombre houses. Poverty is closing in, but the square must remain open, because once closed, then the labourer is denied his final zest for life' (Dorp 1910, p. 181).

Nonetheless, it is no easy task to bring such a 'square' under full legal protection; the effort demanded vision, determination and time. The first measures towards achieving this were taken in the Labour Act of 5 May 1889. This Act determined that the maximum working day for women (and for young people to the age of 16) was 11 hours. It further determined that night work and work on Sundays were prohibited to women who were also not allowed to work within four weeks of a confinement. Adult males did not fall under the Act's provisions. The first limitations to male working hours would make their entrance only 30 years later when the 1919 Labour Act imposed an eight hour day on all employees. So, after 1919 men and women had the same working hours, but it remained easier for men to acquire a permit for overtime, work on Sundays or night work. In addition, there was also a whole range of regulations relating to the (physical and moral) safety of women and young people, whereas these were generally lacking for men (Eijl 1994, p. 208).

The separate labour protection for women and young people introduced in 1889 was a direct consequence of a labour survey carried out two years earlier, in 1887. This survey was designed to inform politicians about conditions in factories and workplaces (cf. Giele 1981). The picture that emerges from these reports is shocking. Low wages, (extremely) long working hours and major health risks were the order of the day. However, this did apply to all workers; from the evidence of the survey, it does not appear that women's working conditions were any worse than those of their male counterparts. Yet, the committee to whom the report was made nonetheless recommended that the working hours of women (and young people) be limited; a recommendation which, as we have seen, was followed in 1889. The discrepancy between the survey's goal and its findings on the one hand and the recommendations and legislation on the other is striking, but becomes more comprehensible when we consider the perspective of the legislator who saw women not so much as employees, but as (potential) mothers and wives (Jansz 1991). This is also apparent in the way in which the relevant minister, Ruys van Beerenbroek, defended separate labour protection for women in 1889: 'The undersigned has no hesitation in stating plainly that the objective of the proposed measures relating to the labour of women is primarily to promote family life and household interests' (in Eijl 1994, p. 214). The measures are not, therefore, defended on the grounds of labour conditions. Nor are these separate arrangements for women a first step towards general protection for all adult workers. Rather, they are designed to bring about a distinction between men and women and to support the allocation of a specific social position for both parties.

An absolute prohibition against married women working outside the home would of course have been the most far-reaching step in this process of specialization. But this step was never taken for factory work. An unwillingness to encroach further into the domain of the entrepreneurs probably played a part here. The government was far more active when it came to its own female employees, that is, female civil servants and teachers. In 1904, for example, it was decided that the Post and Telegraph Services could henceforth only employ unmarried females and that women who married would receive 'honourable' discharges. This decision marks the start of a series of (more or less successful) legal measures relating to married women's work and to female civil servants and teachers (Eijl 1994, p. 256). Arguments here were primarily pragmatic. Supposedly, it was in the interests of the service to keep married female civil servants out, while a pregnant teacher was considered contrary to proper morals. In addition and more generally, the idea that the employer should set a good example and did not want to connive in practices which were condemned by other employers was probably also pertinent. One of the few occasions that the pragmatic course was deserted and wage work for all married women was condemned on a matter of principle came in Romme's draft Bill, presented in the 1937 Queen's Speech (cf. Bosmans 1991, p. 305; Plantenga 1993, p. 21; Schoot Uiterkamp 1978).

At that time, the Netherlands had extensive unemployment and the Catholic politician Romme, who had been Minister of Social Affairs since early 1937, was attempting to make (un)employment a cornerstone of cabinet policy. In this context, a broad raft of measures was proposed, varying from emigration to the reduction of working hours. A prohibition against married women's work fitted neatly into this package. However, employment considerations were not decisive here. They could not have been, considering that in the mid-1930s only around 12,000 married women were active in waged labour, as against 400,000 unemployed. So, in the memorandum to the Bill the principle on which the case rests is put as follows: 'According to the natural order, man should be the breadwinner for the family and the woman's task is the care of the family. In general it would be an evil thing if the woman were to evade this task and search out a different work terrain. The family is such a valuable element in society that, where possible, action should be taken against unhealthy family relations' (in Vries-Bruins 1938, p. 69). This quotation again expresses the major significance attached to 'healthy' family relations and the special meaning attributed to the full-time housewife (cf. Knijn in this volume). A quarter of a century earlier, Kuyper had still linked the social division of labour with the biological order. Now, Romme was not arguing from the biological constitution of woman, but rather from the social task with which she was charged. Romme: 'Government should openly join those who believe that, purely by virtue of her married state, the married woman's life's work is the family and that the family should be protected wherever possible against the performance of paid work by the married woman' (in Bosmans 1991, p. 307). In the general debate, advocates of the draft Bill responded in similar terms when they argued that marriage imposes a certain voluntary limitation on a women in relation to paid work.

The draft Bill was well received in Catholics circles and the response from the orthodox Protestant Party was positive too (ARP). But there were some opponents. The Committee for the Defence of the Freedom to Work for Women (CVVAV) came into action immediately after the Queen's Speech and organised a series of activities, including a postcard shower and a national protest in Amsterdam. Resistance was aimed primarily against regulatory activity by the government in what was perceived as a purely private matter and against the inconsistent nature of Romme's proposed Bill. It included exceptive clauses for agriculture and allowed companies to bring in married women for peak seasons. Moreover, the regulation was not seen as applying to household services because this group, according to Romme, was almost impossible to monitor and the nature of the work did not prompt state intervention. Resistance to the Bill also came from the High Council for Labour, which was sent the draft in December 1937. The Council rejected the draft by a large majority and urged the minister to do some proper research on the actual extent of the phenomenon and on the motives of working married women. This research, however, failed to materialise. Romme's ambitious plans to combat unemployment brought him into conflict with the more conservative minister of finance, de Wilde, and the cabinet fell in June 1939.

A common element in these pre-war debates is the perceived contradiction between the paid labour of married women on the one hand, and the interests of the family - and ensuing social welfare - on the other. Given this contradiction, the package of social rights and obligations has a clear gender bias which discourages women from engaging in paid work. It can even be put more strongly: the debates around the Bill are permeated with the realisation that women should have actual access to an exemption. Even opponents of government intervention - probably with the exception of a small group of liberal feminists - are in favour of the full-time housewife (cf. Akkerman in this volume). At issue for them is the fact that women sometimes need to work outside the home *in the interests of the family*, as for example when the man's income is inadequate or too uncertain. The gender specific division of labour between breadwinner and care-giver, however, never became a discussion of principle.

1945-1990: reorientation

After the Second World War, attempts by the government to intervene into (married) women's work outside the home did not cease (Plantenga 1992). In 1947, the Catholic minister Beel produced a paper in which ministers were asked to reduce to a minimum future employment of married female staff. In the 1947 budget debate, Mrs Tendeloo (a member of the Social Democratic Party) protested against this guideline, but without success. But the Catholic Minister of Internal Affairs, van Maarseveen, did establish the Ubink Commission in 1949 whose task it was to study the number of female civil servants in state employment and subsequently to make recommendations to the minister. The

Commission went about its business with great thoroughness and submitted an extensive report in 1952 entitled *The Question of the Married Female Civil Servant* (Commissie Bi.Z 1952). The report comes down to a compromise proposal, namely that when female civil servants marry, they should be dismissed, but that this rule should not apply to women over 30, to women who have been in the service of the state for ten years or longer without interruption; or to women who have reached a higher position. It would be 1955 before the Tendeloo motion was passed - by the narrow margin of 46 to 44 - which stated that 'except when abuse is apparent, it is not in the State's remit to prohibit the work of married women'. That the motion achieved a majority at all owes much to the fact that all female members of parliament - including those from Protestant and Catholic parties - voted for it (Bosmans 1989).

After all the attempts by government to limit or prohibit the paid work of married women, this was an important milestone. From this time on government would remain on the side lines and no longer offer any explicit opposition to married women working outside the home. The decision was, as it were, decentralised; it was assumed that the family would make a responsible choice on the most desirable division of labour. However, this does not mean that those who chose to work outside the home would be actively supported by government policy. Individual choices had to be made in a society whose policy and regulatory point of departure was the family. In (socio-economic) practice, this meant that a stated aim such as full employment was translated into one paid job per family and wage structures were based on a breadwinner with a dependent partner.

During the course of the 1960s and 1970s, the influence of the second feminist wave cast more and more doubt on the natural character of this strict division of labour and care. An article published by Joke Smit in *De Gids* in 1967 acted as a catalyst (in Smit 1984, pp. 15-42). According to Smit, women had an unclear relationship with society. For Man, marriage and fatherhood were social incidents. However, Woman, through her marriage, opted for a way of life and at a certain social level; her home, her financial position and social status were determined to a great extent by her husband. Social alienation through caring for small children and household tensions which emerge because men and women live such very different lives, could be resolved, Smit claimed, if men and women's lives came to resemble each other more closely. Work outside the home should no longer be seen as a kind of leisure activity, as one of the many idiocyncracies that make women what they are, but as a normal and integral part of a woman's life. For this reason, political pressure should be exerted in, for example, the area of fiscal legislation, career policy and work-time reduction (cf. Bussemaker in this volume).

These were ground-breaking proposals. Smit's objective remarks on motherhood and her plea for an equal division of labour and care between men and women opened up, for the first time, the possibility of non-specialised roles for both sexes. From Smit's argument it can also be concluded that the significance attributed to concepts like 'family' and 'society' had changed considerably. In the world view of Kuyper and Romme, the family was still central to society; it buttressed the whole structure. In that context, paid employment for married women was seen as a necessary evil; an evil from which women had to be delivered so that they would be free to carry out their 'natural' task. In Smit, the family is outside society and motherhood leads to social alienation. Society is the world outside the family; the world of paid work, of development, independence, influence and power.

Smit's article, the numerous reactions it evoked and the movement it inspired, did not leave government untouched (cf. Bussemaker, Handelingen, van Drenth and Outshoorn in this volume). In 1977, the first government memorandum on women's equality was published, *Emancipation; Process of Change and Growth* (1976/1977). In this memorandum equality polices are described as a process aimed at increasing opportunities for men and women. The latter are expected to gain parity in terms of rights, level of education and social participation, while men are tackled on their shortcomings in the 'personal sphere' (ibid, p. 10). The aim here is also to revalue those characteristics and activities traditionally associated with women on the premise that this would expand freedom of choice for both sexes. In later policy papers the perspective has narrowed considerably. Equality policies refer increasingly to the world of paid work and policy is increasingly aimed only at women. Paid work outside the home is seen more and more as an activity in which every citizen - male and female - should participate (cf. van Drenth in this volume; Keuzenkamp and Teunissen 1990).

The real breakthrough came in 1990 when the Scientific Council for Government Policy (WRR) published its report '*A working perspective*'. With the aid of both cultural and economic arguments, this report pointed out the necessity of increasing participation levels in the Netherlands. The economic argument is based primarily on the costs incurred by low level participation levels, referring to the unproductive use of human capital. The report also stresses the negative consequences for the Netherlands' competitive position as low participation tends to be translated into a greater tax and premium burden. The cultural argument refers to the importance of paid work as a form of social integration. Especially at a time when other integrative options are shrinking (organised religion and the family), participation in the labour process becomes important for social cohesion. The welfare state, according to this argument, does no more than create collective dependence rather than make, as it should, 'independent citizens'; in contrast, formal work is considered a major dimension of full citizenship.

The contrast with the prewar debates is very marked. Citizenship is no longer described in terms of motherhood and care. Quite the contrary: full citizenship is equated to participation in the labour market, assuming more or less explicitly the equality of men and women. The problem here is, of course, how to achieve this kind of full citizenship in a society where care responsibilities are for the most part still defined as private, family-related activities. The solution appears to be sought in a combination strategy: women seek a paid job in so far as family responsibilities permit (cf. Knijn in this volume). In practice, this has meant that the majority of women are opting for part-time jobs: in the mid-1990s around two thirds of the female labour force was employed part-time. This also means that from the late 1980s the 'deviant' Dutch pattern is no longer a statistical given, and that the levels of female participation in the labour market are on par with those customary in other European countries. If 'deviation' still exists, it is rather qualitative than quantitive: no other country within the EU has as many part-time workers as the Netherlands (cf. Table 4.1).

Table 4.1.
Female activity rates in the European Member States, 1975-1994*

	1975	1981	1985	1990	1994	% part-time in 1994
Belgium	30.7	35.0	35.9	36.0	40.2	28.3
Denmark	45.4	53.3	58.7	60.8	58.3	34.4
Germany (W)	35.5	37.2	40.6	44.9	47.8	33.1
Greece		29.0	34.2	34.9	35.0	8.0
Spain			27.4	31.9	35.0	15.2
France	39.7	43.4	45.7	46.0	47.9	27.8
Ireland	27.4	29.0	32.6	34.5	39.5	21.8
Italy	22.5	26.9	32.4	34.5	33.7	12.4
Luxembourg	26.8	n.a.	34.4	33.6	38.4	19.7
Netherlands	21.7	26.8	34.1	43.3	47.7	65.9
Portugal			42.8	46.8	49.6	12.1
UK	43.4	41.4	47.9	51.7	52.5	44.3
EUR 9	34.5	40.1				
EUR10		36.4	40.9	43.7		
EUR 12			39.4	42.4	44.2	30.7

Source: Eurostat, Labour Force Survey, 1975, 1981, 1985, 1990, 1994.
* Due to changes in definitions, data for 1975 and 1981 are not fully comparable with data from later years

Backgrounds: passion and productivity

What is the background to this specific Dutch pattern? Why was the division of labour so rigid and why was married women's work outside the home so problematic for so long? Detailed research on these questions is surprisingly scarce. In discussions on the subject, references to stiff Protestants and strict Catholics abound, without revealing much about the exact backgrounds. The *Woman's Social Atlas*, for example, states that 'the mixed Catholic-Protestant composition of the population in the first half of this century brought about a particular Dutch pattern of norms and values relating to the position of the married woman in the family and that the church 'for longer than elsewhere' determined the division of tasks within the family' (Hooghiemstra and Niphuis-Nell 1993, p. 27). This explanation certainly accords with rich Dutch anecdotal evidence on the role of the church, but on further examination proves unsatisfactory. One must first ask whether the Dutch pattern of norms and values was really so very deviant. There are enough indications in international literature that the Netherlands was in no way unique in this respect. At the turn of the century, politicians and civil reform movements in Germany and England also emphasised the great social value of the full-time housewife and warned against the destructive consequences of (factory) work for women (Brinkler-Gabler 1979; Lewis 1984; Walby 1986). Moreover, it is doubtful whether the family ideal is Christian in origin. The emphasis on the full-time housewife and the importance attached to healthy family relations is also and especially part of a bourgeois ideology in which the family as source of love, happiness and peace is set against a hostile outside world (cf. Hausen 1976). In this respect, it could be argued that the role of the church was limited to the sanction of an essentially bourgeois morality (Damsma 1988, p. 218). There are indications that the church in the Netherlands certainly fulfilled this role with alacrity, but that is a very different proposition from stating that it inspired a specifically Dutch pattern of norms and values.

It would appear more likely that the low numbers of women in the labour market should be attributed to two very different factors, namely passion and productivity. Passion here refers primarily to the specific quality of Dutch religion which has been formed by the mixture of Catholic and Protestant faith in its population. Productivity concerns mainly the Netherlands' economic history and its degree of relative prosperity.

The passion is well documented in two articles on Dutch Catholicism by the Leiden-based sociologist van Heek, first published in the 1950s. According to van Heek, there is a so-called 'front mentality' in Dutch Catholicism which can be found primarily in a pattern of intense and theologically normative experiences (Heek 1973). Part of van Heek's explanation for this front mentality is that Dutch Catholics were in the minority for a long time and were actually oppressed in the Dutch Republic of the seventeenth and eighteenth centuries. They were forbidden to hold public office and Catholic schools were prohibited. At the same time, the front mentality owes something to the stricter forms of Protestantism. The Catholic community is said to have absorbed the Calvinist experience of norms, prompted by a combination of admiration and awe. This *pénétration calviniste* is believed to lie primarily in the area of moral theology, that is, in the degree to which certain mores or customs were condemned as sinful. No lusty, carnival celebrating Catholics here, but puritans who tend to be rather morose and who take everything much more seriously than their Burgundian neighbours to the south.

Important indicators of this front mentality are, according to van Heek, Sunday observance, which was much more regular in the Netherlands than elsewhere; the Dutch prohibition against mixed-faith trade unions; and a greater exclusivism with regard to non-Catholic international organisations. As regards this latter point, van Heek offers the useful example of the Rotary Club. Membership of this club was classified as undesirable for bishops and clergy by Rome in 1929. However, the Netherlands subscribed to a stricter interpretation and both clergy and laity were absolutely forbidden to join. Further significant indicators are the 'greater rigour of the Dutch clergy against the use of means to impede conception' and the 'high value placed on a large family'.

The use of contraception was for a long time vigorously condemned by the Dutch Catholic church. It was even hesitant to accept the rhythm method - a method approved by the Vatican itself in certain circumstances. The conservatism of the Dutch position is also apparent in the great aversion shown to the neo-Malthusians who, it was said, degraded men to 'monsters of egoism'. On this point, van Heek quotes a well-known speech against neo-Malthusianism given by Father de Greeve during the Roman Catholic National Congress of 1929. In the course of this speech, de Greeve blamed the disunity of the modern family on the use of contraception. Raising a neo-Malthusian family of only two children was doomed to failure because the children would become 'spoilt tyrants, difficult characters, spoilt brats, old before their time'. By way of contrast, de Greeve extolled the happiness of the large family whose 'patriarch', when celebrating his silver wedding anniversary, looks back wistfully on his 'scamps and scallywags' and on his wife who 'became more lovely with each child' (Heek 1973, p. 246). The large family was and remained for some time the preferred Catholic norm. Even in the 1950s, a clear majority (71 per cent) of those Catholic engaged to be married wanted three or more children. The percentage was 44 per cent among Protestants and only 31 per cent among non-churchgoers.

Reasoning from this front mentality, the strict division of labour could be explained by the intensity with which norms were experienced. To be precise, it was not a consequence of the norms and values as such, but rather of the passion and rigour with which they were expressed. In all probability, pillarisation was extremely conducive too in this respect (cf. Bussemaker in this volume). After all, it was these structures - the pillars - which offered channels for communicating attitudes from above, by imposing them forcefully on the whole population. Local level research, especially, makes clear how fine-meshed and interwoven were the relationships between clergy, manufacturers and social institutions, and with how much force the bourgeois ideal of the woman as full-time housewife, spouse and mother was put into practice by means of prohibitions, mutual agreements and continual debate (Plantenga 1993, p. 122).

However, it seems unlikely that passion alone would have sufficed; if they are to be held, wishes must also have at least some possibility for fulfilment.

This brings us to the second major reason for the deviant Dutch pattern - the relative prosperity of the Netherlands. Although international comparative data on wages earned are lacking, there are indications that, from the end of the last century until well into the twentieth, the Netherlands achieved a relatively high wage level due to its very productive economy. Some data to support this premise are given in Tables 4.2 and 4.3.

Table 4.2 provides information on the per capita gross national product of five European countries (Netherlands equals one hundred). From a comparison of the results, it appears that in the period up to the Second World War, Dutch per capita GNP was well above that of Germany, France and Denmark. Differences with neighbouring Belgium are smaller, while the figure for the United Kingdom clearly demonstrate its former economic power; until the Second World War, British per capita income was well above that of the Netherlands.

Table 4.2.
GDP per capita in Belgium, Denmark, France, Germany and the United Kingdom, 1820-1989*

	B	DK	F	G	UK
1820	74	78	80	70	111
1870	101	75	76	61	131
1890	103	75	75	65	131
1913	103	95	86	80	131
1929	88	88	83	64	97
1938	91	108	85	92	120
1950	90	111	88	71	120
1973	92	103	101	98	92
1989	101	106	109	109	101

* (The Netherlands=100)
Source: own calculations based on Madison 1991 (Tables A.2., B.7 and C.10)

If productivity per working hour is compared (see Table 4.3), then the differences naturally increase, owing to the relatively small labour force in the Netherlands; in the period between the wars, only the United Kingdom had a higher productivity per hour. Such data must, of course, be interpreted with care. Differences in income distribution, for example, are not taken into account. If the assumption is nevertheless that a certain relationship exists between productivity and wage levels, then, based on the evidence collected in Tables 4.2 and 4.3, we can conclude that socio-economic conditions were relatively favourable for a strict division of labour between men and women; Dutch women were not under as much pressure to take paid work as their counterparts in, for example, Germany or France (Plantenga 1993; Pott-Buter 1993).

Table 4.3.
Gross Domestic Product per working-hour, 1870-1987*

	B	DK	F	G	UK
1870	92	66	63	57	118
1890	92	111	61	61	115
1913	88	84	70	72	112
1929	75	80	65	57	90
1938	83	84	84	71	99
1950	92	94	88	65	124
1960	83	85	91	84	104
1973	92	82	92	84	87
1987	93	73	102	86	87

* The Netherlands
Source: Own calculations based on Maddison 1991 (Tables A.2, B.7 and C.10)

This argument - that women in the Netherlands were less active outside the home as a result of relative national prosperity - can be found frequently in older publications. In 1938, for example, Posthumus-van der Goot attributed the low rates of labour market participation among married women to 'the relatively very high prosperity in the Netherlands' (Posthumus-van der Goot 1938, p. 139). Heinen, too, who was with the National Bureau for Women's Labour for many years and was certainly well informed on socio-economic relations, mentioned relative prosperity and 'the dutiful nature of the Dutch man' in 1938 (in Eijl 1994, p. 64). Likewise, just after the Second World War, the Social Democrat Banning suggested that the limited labour market participation was linked to 'the generally high level of prosperity in the Dutch population' (ibid). Surprisingly enough, this argument disappeared almost entirely from later publications. In its place the authorities referred to the lack of demand for female workers. The family sociologist Damsma, for example, explains the low level of participation by a fairly consistent shortfall in demand over a longer period of time (Damsma 1988, p. 234). In a widely-read and often quoted book on women's work and the sociology of labour, de Bruijn (1989) also states that emerging Dutch industry was initially able to get by with cheap, unskilled male workers. This explanation, however, is adequate only if we assume that women were in fact available for the labour market. Given socio-economic relations, this would appear an untenable premise for the Netherlands. Rather, the reverse obtained: in general, (married) women were not available for the labour market.

To summarise, then, low level participation by women in the labour market is not a consequence of a specific Dutch pattern of norms and values. What is specifically Dutch is the intense way in which those norms were experienced and the rigour with which they were expressed. That the Dutch were successful in this respect should be attributed primarily to the country's state of relative prosperity. It is precisely this relative prosperity and the comparatively small number of married women working outside the home which made possible the ideal and indeed reinforced it. This is also why Romme's draft Bill - despite all the principles - is only imaginable in a world where married women's paid labour was a relatively marginal phenomenon. The bottom line is that principles should not (or rather, cannot) be too expensive.

This specific constellation of passion and productivity remained intact until at least the mid-1950s. From that time on, however, the structure began to show cracks. Married women's work outside the home was associated less by poverty and need, and more with personal development, rights and independence. At the same time (in the 1950s and 1960s) pressure from a tight labour market led to increases in the social cost of non-participation. Both factors put their own pressure on the traditional division of labour, and in the end sharply drove up the numbers of married women participating in the labour market. However, there remains a certain 'unease' in the sense that the socio-economic order is badly tailored to the specific situation of working mothers. Part-time jobs are one answer and at the close of the millennium the once strict division of labour appears to have been transformed into an one-and-a-half-income model, with women emphatically in the role of secondary earner.

To conclude: beyond specialisation

The question now is how the Dutch model will develop in the near future. The one-and-a-half income model is not unattractive. The lives of men and women - as Smit hoped - have come to look more alike, while the importance of unpaid labour is still widely accepted (cf. Knijn in this volume). It could be argued that the one-and-a-half income model provides some space for qualities, activities and responsibilities historically associated with women and facilitates the combination of work and care in an acceptable manner. At the same time, this model also carries some risks. Female employees working part-time are and always remain first and foremost 'women', that is, workers with other 'more important' nonpaid commitments. In this way they are clearly differentiated from their full-time (male) colleagues. The one-and-a-half income model therefore goes hand in hand with an enduring inequality in the labour market, when questions of income, responsibility and power are concerned. To complicate matters further, this one-and-a-half income model has been linked to a growing inequality between families. If the changing levels of participation by women in the labour market are examined in detail, it would appear that it is women with higher education who are the principle beneficiaries. The changes for less well-educated women have been less great, partly because breadwinner facilities limit the net return on the labour market participation, especially at that level.

These old and new forms of inequality give rise to differing responses. On the one hand, a 'democratisation of the one-and-a-half income model' has been advocated recently to remedy the polarisation between families with one (or no) job at the bottom end of the labour market and those families with one-and-a-half (or two) jobs at the top end. On the other hand, the one-and-a-half income model itself is under pressure on account of the unequal division of paid and unpaid work. The proposed alternative could be called the 'twice-three-quarter model', a model whose characteristic element is the lack of any form of specialisation. Both men and women are supposed to participate in the labour market for approximately thirty hours a week and to share the responsibility for unpaid work (Emancipatieraad 1996). In this context, full citizenship is not equal to labour market participation, but implies participating in both paid and unpaid labour. It is this equitable division of paid and unpaid work which forms the unique, but also vulnerable aspect of the twice three-quarter model. In most other countries, rising rates of female participation in the labour market have tended to go hand in glove with the externalisation and commercialisation of care. This is considered less appropriate in the Netherlands and adjustments in the organisation of labour are sought that will facilitate and make accessible the combination of work and care in every citizen's life. The twice-three-quarter model not only requires adjustments in the organisation of labour, however. It also implies a shift in perspective. It is no longer about - to use Kuyper's terminology - whether women in public life 'are equal to men', but also and particularly about whether men in private life 'are equal to women'.

5 Participation through care? The case of the Dutch housewife

Trudie Knijn

This article is about a typical Dutch phenomenon: the housewife. This is not to claim that only the Netherlands has housewives, but to emphasise that almost no other western industrialised society has so many housewives among its female population as the Netherlands does. Moreover, it can be stated without exaggeration that no other country is so confused about the status of housewives. On the one hand it must be admitted that exempting so many women from employment, as the Netherlands does, is a luxury only very affluent societies can afford. Nor can it be denied that the longevity of Dutch women is the highest (average of 80 years compared to 74 years for Dutch men Uitterhoeve 1990, p. 39) in the world, an empirical fact which is not seldom associated with the 'good life' housewives are supposed to lead. On the other hand, the restructuring of the Dutch welfare state demands a higher participation of all its citizens in the labour market, including mothers.

Dutch social policies in the 1990s are characterised by a kind of bewilderment about how to deal with this situation: should policies focus on protecting the housewives' specific contribution to family life, the care for children, other relatives and to the community, or is society and are women themselves better served by an increase in the rate of women's participation in the labour market and therefore also by the redistribution or institutionalisation of caring labour? Dutch society is confronted with contradictory political messages, arrangements and analyses in which the valuation of care, women's identity and the meaning of social participation itself are at stake.

In this chapter I will analyse the caring labour of the Dutch housewife from a perspective which takes into account such factors as gender, participation and citizenship. I will likewise analyse her activities in the social domains outside the work force, especially her work for her family, her participation in informal care-giving work and her activities within the community. I will consider the meaning of these activities in the context of civil society, suggesting how the traditional gender position of housewives relates to their citizenship status and rights and what the implications are for movements towards gender equality. Finally, I will touch on two problems raised by care-giving: the one concerning the combination of paid work and care-giving, the other concerning the balance of formal and informal care.

What are Dutch women doing when they are not employed?

Recent national surveys on what Dutch people do besides paid work and leisure-time pursuits can be grouped into four distinct categories: housekeeping, caring for children and others in the immediate family, Do-It-Yourself activities and informal care for relatives and non-relatives. The overall term used for these activities is 'unpaid care labour' (Commissie Toekomstscenario's 1995, p. 12). Besides these activities within the household, people are performing all kinds of community care, which I will discuss later in this article. According to figures from 1990, the average Dutch male (over 12 years old) spends about 16 hours and the average Dutch female (same age range) spends about 32 hours in these kinds of unpaid care labour, the most substantial in terms of time being housekeeping (Hart 1995). Table 5.1 shows that some categories of women in particular do much unpaid care labour within the household. The most extreme category is, not surprisingly, unemployed mothers with children under 14 years old. These mothers spend more than 50 hours a week to unpaid care labour.

Apart from unpaid care labour within the household, people also undertake activities within the community at large: about 30 per cent of Dutch men and women participate in all kinds of community activities and spend on average five hours a week doing so (men: six hours, women: four hours). And again, housewives - and the unemployed - have the highest participation rates in voluntary work (41 per cent and 36 per cent respectively) (SCR 1996, p. 546).

Unpaid care labour and activities within the community are not necessarily inversely proportional to the rates of participation in the labour market. But for mothers of young children they are. Whereas most men, and a minority of women, combine employment with a certain amount of unpaid care labour and community work, most mothers of young children are unable to do so because these are mutually exclusive activities for them. Although the labour participation rates of mothers show an increase in the 1980s and 1990s, the majority of mothers with children under 12 are still housewives, and if they are employed, only a very small minority of them is working full-time (cf. Plantenga in this volume).

Table 5.1
Time spent in hours per week on unpaid care labour within the household

			Men	Women
Single	<40 years	- no paid work	15.0	23.2
		- 0-19 hours	14.8	19.3
		- >20 hours	11.8	14.8
	40-64 years	- no paid work	28	38
		- 0-19 hours	19.9	34.7
		- >20 hours	13.9	24
	> 65 years		28.7	34.5
Partners without children	<40 years	- single income	11.4	35.5
		- one-and-a-half incomes	10.1	33.7
		- double incomes	13.1	20.6
		- no wage earners	22.8	35.7
		- other combinations	21.8	23.4
	40-64 years	- single incomes	9.9	44.1
		- one-and-a-half incomes	10.2	41.3
		- double incomes	12.1	27.0
		- no wage earners	26.9	42.2
		- other combinations	21.1	36.6
	>65 years		23.2	39.8
Partners with children	youngest child <6 years	- single income	15.6	55.9
		- one-and-a-half incomes	15.1	49.6
		- double incomes	16.9	35.0
		- no wage earners	36.6	53.1
		- other combinations	33.0	47.4
	youngest child 6-14 years	- single incomes	11.8	50.0
		- one-and-a-half incomes	11.9	43.5
		- double incomes	14.7	30.5
		- no wage earners	25.9	49.2
		- other combinations	22.4	39.9
	youngest child >14 years	- single income	11.4	48.8
		- one-and-a-half incomes	11.3	39.0
		- double incomes	15.5	26.5
		- no wage earners	20.1	41.9
		- other combinations	20.6	44.7
Solo parents		fathers	25.1	
		mothers		
		- no paid work		45.5
		- 0-19 hours		37.6
		- >20 hours		27.2
Children		12-18 years	6.2	9.7
		19-25 years	8.9	14.8

Source: Commissie Toekomstscenario's 1995 pp. 198-199/SCP, TBO 1975, 1980, 1985, 1990.

When we narrow our definition of housewives to women who are not employed at all, 70 per cent of all mothers with children under five, 49 per cent of all mothers with children of 6-14 years old, and 52 per cent of all mothers with children younger than 14 years old were housewives in 1990. When we also include women who work less than 20 hours a week, these percentages rise to 91 per cent, 82 per cent and 78 per cent respectively (Hart 1995, p. 79). These figures refer only to married and cohabiting mothers. If we also included solo mothers, the percentage of housewives would certainly increase, although the average working hours of solo mothers in employment are much higher than those of employed married mothers (Niphuis-Nell 1997).

The causes of this Dutch phenomenon are complex. They can be found in several pre-Second World War developments, such as the social and political structure of pillarisation (cf. Bussemaker in this volume), as well as in economic trends, notably a rather high labour productivity by male breadwinners (cf. Plantenga in this volume), reinforced by ideological assumptions about motherhood and housewives. The pre-war belief that a woman's place was 'in the home', was in one sense reinvigorated by the post-war extension of the welfare state. The government in particular propagated the ideology of 'modern motherhood' as an instrument of social and cultural renewal (Gastelaars 1985, p. 181).

However, family values were upheld throughout the population. Until 1964, birth rates increased to the rate of 3.1 per woman. At that time, seven out of every ten adults said that the ideal family should have at least three children (Uitterhoeve 1990, pp. 37 and 73). Women were supposed to be 'essentially mother and housewife', and they were not seldom praised for their pivotal role in the family (Knijn and Verheijen 1983; Knijn 1994a). They were encouraged to devote all their energy to housekeeping and taking care of the children. The lack of labour saving devices and the large size of many families - many families included five to ten children - was seen as a challenge for housewives to run their familial domain in a disciplined and energetic way. And that is what they did; Dutch housewives worked on average 62 hours a week in their homes and were so busy with housekeeping and raising their children that none of them even thought about seeking employment.

Moreover, local migration was exceptional and social control overwhelming in the immediate post-war period. Most mothers lived in the same neighbourhood as their female relatives who supported each other in taking care of their families. Such a close social network, however, also meant that opportunities to change customs or life styles were minimal. Mothers followed their common sense when it came to care-giving (Knijn 1994a). In her study of those few mothers who had a paid job, Marjolein Morée concludes that: 'working was considered to be so outrageous for mothers of young children that coping strategies were concentrated on justifying their situation' (Morée, 1992, p. 251). These mothers thought they must conceal from their children that they were doing paid labour.

During the second half of the 1960s, changes took place which called into question the women's traditional position in the family. General wealth increased and labour saving devices - such as central heating, showers and washing machines were introduced on a large scale; the use of the new contraceptives decreased family size; local migration and women's education reduced the influence of social networks and religion; and the feminist movement tried to alter the position of the housewife because she had been excluded from social and labour participation and too dependent on the husband-cum-breadwinner.

Since that time the number of full-time housewives, particularly among mothers with children above 12, has steadily decreased. Currently, most full-time housewives either have young children or are over 45 themselves. This slow increase of integration into the work force is, however, only one aspect of changing relationships between men and women. Another remarkable change concerned living arrangements, lifestyles and public behaviour (cf. Bussemaker in this volume). From the end of the 1960s, tolerance of all kinds of lifestyles has become a striking feature of Dutch society. Cohabitation - not only before, but also in place of marriage - is commonly accepted, as is the choice made by some couples to have children out of wedlock. Contraceptives and abortion are now accessible to every woman - no matter what age she is. Moreover, the free expression of homosexuality, and, more recently, the de-tabooing of lesbian and homosexual parenthood, and the liberal policy towards AIDS are not exactly indications of a rigid gender categorisation. Also, the opinion polls on attitudes to gender suggest that the Dutch population is among the most progressive of the industrialised countries (SCP 1996, pp. 510-525).

Nevertheless, the primacy of the housewife seemed to be more entrenched in the Netherlands than in most Western countries. That is why the Dutch situation is so strange and complex: a variety in lifestyles goes hand in hand with a strong division of gender roles within the family. A high level of tolerance, together with a strong division of household tasks and child care coexists with a severe lack of child-care facilities and a low rate of female participation in the labour market. And finally, while the majority of the adult population seems to accept that a woman has the right to choose whether or not she wants a child, the predominant practice remains full-time motherhood.

Gender, participation and civil citizenship

What are the characteristics of housewives' participation in terms of social cohesion and the link between public and private life? What is their contribution to informal care and the community? In other words, is there any reason to believe that housewives are now full participants in civil society? The common definition of civil society holds that it includes these activities which are performed on a voluntary basis on behalf of fellow citizens in particular, or of society in general (Dekker 1994). This would imply that of the several caring activities that housewives perform - i.e. her work for her family, her participation in informal care and her activities within the community - only informal care and activities within the community belong to the domain of civil society.

Recent figures (from 1995) show - probably not entirely by coincidence - that the highest percentage of volunteers can be found among housewives. While

32 per cent of the population at large participate in volunteer work, this percentage rises to 41 per cent in the case of housewives, who spend on average more than four hours a week on guiding, supervising, managing and supporting cultural and leisure activities, sporting clubs, child care and religious activities as well as on political participation and interest groups. Significantly perhaps, housewives' participation in voluntary work has increased enormously - from 30 per cent to 41 per cent - since 1980, whereas, among employed persons (both men and women), it has decreased from 34 per cent to 28 per cent (SCP 1996, p. 546). It is not easy to account for these results. One can hardly argue that housewives have more free time than those in paid employment, when one recalls the amount of time housewives must spend daily on chores within the home.

The most plausible reason might be that housewives have more flexible time to invest in activities that take place while other people are involved in paid labour (Luykx and Versloot 1994). Furthermore, it can be said that the increased participation of housewives in this kind of voluntary work, shows that they see these activities within the community as an alternative to participation within the paid labour market. By taking part in these activities, their needs for social contacts, self-development and social commitment can be satisfied.

Nevertheless, and despite the increased participation of housewives in voluntary work, van Daal (1993) concludes that fewer care-related activities are being undertaken in the general community. Probably organised - informal - care contributes less to those needs than all other kind of activities which offer more social bonding, such as sporting and cultural festivities. Housewives, however, still perform much of what is being done. In 1991, 15 per cent of all Dutch women and 7 per cent of all Dutch men over 16 years of age took care of 'significant others' on a regular basis. Not surprisingly, housewives - and lower-educated persons - are over represented among the informal caregivers who address the needs of half the number of people in need of care (de Boer et al. 1994, pp. 121-126).

A recent report on patterns of informal care predicts that the supply of informal care-givers will not change, despite the growing rates of female participation in the work force, because it assumes that most women work part-time and will do so in the future (Boer 1994). However, the demand for informal care will increase rapidly over the coming decade, especially because of the growth of the number of frail elderly. The authors also conclude that 'feelings of solidarity with relatives and friends appear to be very strong in the Netherlands, probably because solidarity is not forced upon us as it is in some other countries. It is also possible for people to put their feelings of solidarity into practice because the official care system is generally adequate. In countries which are debating payment for care and care leave, the level of benefit payments is generally lower than in this country' (Boer 1994, p. 261).

The report rightly indicates that the bulk of informal care is provided by housewives and women working part-time. However, its conclusion that these care-giving tasks are not forced upon them but taken up voluntarily as a supplement to adequate professional care is debatable. I will examine this argument in more detail later. For the time being, suffice to say that informal care contributes to social coherence, is based upon feelings of solidarity and, like voluntary work, is done in the main by those women who can be relatively flexible with their time because they are not (completely) involved in paid work. That is not to say that informal care-givers are satisfied with their lot; in particular, those who must take care of relatives often complain that they are compelled by moral obligations to act as they do. They stress that the workload and the mental burdens are too high and that even those receiving the care experience the care relationship as too demanding. A quarter of the informal caregivers would prefer not to be obliged to give this kind of help (Daal 1990).

Taking care of one's own children and housekeeping are not easily classified within the usual terms of civil society, since they are activities belonging to private life, and hence seem to fall outside the public domain. Yet it is important that some attempt be made to rethink this division. After all, Dutch women spend an inordinate amount of time on housekeeping: while men spend on average 9 hours per week on housekeeping, women spend on average 34 hours per week on this work (Hart 1995). Although housewives are mainly performing their activities in the home, the social consequences of their work in terms of social peace, prosperity and community upgrading are nevertheless becoming more and more visible.

In an article on the consequences of unemployment among unskilled men even *The Economist* recently stated:

> consider for a moment a neighbourhood in which most working-age women are not in paid jobs. This may conjure up a picture of tidy homes, children at play and gossip. Now think of a neighbourhood in which most men are jobless. The picture is more sinister. Areas of male idleness are considered, and often are, places of deterioration, disorder and danger. Non-working women are mothers; non-working men, a blight.
> (*The Economist*, 28 September 1996)

This quotation seems to recognise the immense contribution that women as housewives make to their community. It underlines their contribution to the overall quality of life. But does this recognition justify us in including women's housekeeping activities as a necessary contribution to civil society? To extend our notion of civil society so far would be too extreme. First, because housekeeping is by definition domestic and so not a field of public debate in terms of solidarity, justice and commitment. Second, because the primary purpose of housekeeping is to attend to the well-being of the family and not the community as a whole. Moreover, a plea for maintaining women's caring role as a cornerstone of civil society can enforce the assumed self-sacrifice of women and confirm inequitable gender relationships (cf. Bussemaker 1994).

If we examine some of the current assumptions in the field of child care, we can see that such cautions may be well founded. As public child care for children under five years old (the age at which children enter compulsory education) is hardly developed in the Netherlands, most mothers of young children have their children at home full-time. In 1989, public child care only involved 20,000 children. In 1991, the government agreed - after years of protests by parents - to extend child care facilities. This move raised the number of child care places available to 70,000, but much remains to be done. In 1993 only eight per cent of all children under four years old were covered (Handelingen 1993-1994). About 28,000 children, a third of the total capacity, are still on the waiting lists.

When children reach the age of five, mothers are not less involved in care-giving. This is because the Dutch school regime is characterised by two peculiarities: its time schedules and a tendency to mobilise mothers as volunteers for all kind of activities. An average Dutch primary school starts at 9 a.m.; children go home during lunchtime - between 12 and 1 p.m. - and again at 3 p.m. Ten years ago the government enacted a new law which states that schools are obliged to make a room available for children having lunch at school, but often that is the only service the school provides and supervision must be provided by the mothers. Lunchtime supervision is only one of the many structural activities performed by mothers (and sometimes fathers) at the schools. Most primary schools expect parents to assist teachers in education. For instance, mothers are helping teachers in reading and physical education, in guiding children to swimming lessons, and in preparing for all kind of festivities. How important this kind of assistance is to schools became clear recently when teachers complained in the national newspapers about what they called 'the growing egoism among parents'. They were especially concerned by those 'selfish' mothers who preferred paid work to helping their children at school.

It can be argued that housewives participate - at least to a certain extent - in civil society, precisely *because* they are housewives. This role facilitates their contribution to activities within the community on a voluntary basis and to informal care. Housewives can participate in these domains of civil society because their time tends to be flexible and they choose to do so because it satisfies their needs for social contacts and commitment.

As we have seen, the term civil society is commonly used to describe the social domain that lies between the state, the market and the family, and not the activities performed on behalf of the private domain of the family itself. Feminists have questioned this rigid conceptualisation of civil society on several grounds: it separates social domains which actually are strongly related and interdependent; it makes women's activities in and especially between several social domains invisible; and finally it hides the social importance, and cohesive force, of many activities performed by women in order to improve their own life and that of their family members (Pateman 1989, pp. 132-133; Bussemaker 1994, p. 179). Some authors state that the conceptual distinction between civil society and private family life leads to a situation in which women as housewives and caregivers are locked up in the private domain.

We can conclude that the distinction between private life and the community is not sustainable. The housewife spends the bulk of her time on housekeeping, which may contribute to the well-being of her family, to the maintenance of the current and future work force and to her own and her family's quality of life, but this cannot be interpreted as a contribution to civil society in general. Her activities within the community, whether it be in informal care or in sporting, political and cultural activities do contribute to civil society in general. Yet they are directly related to her work for her family, in particular her activities within schools and the various voluntary work she undertakes on behalf of her children. Her community work is indirectly related to her position as a housewife; she contributes to these domains of civil society simply because she has more time flexibility than the average employee has and because she experiences such activities as a form of social integration.

Does care participation give entrance to citizenship?

Care-giving and housekeeping, the main duties of housewives, have been neglected in terms of civil society, and have been overlooked in discussions of citizenship. These activities are seldom recognised as part of the citizens' basic needs. Even in T.H. Marshall's very influential conceptualisation of citizenship, care was only recognised so far as it concerned medical health care (Marshall 1965). In his description of social citizenship he included the right to housing, education, employment and income, but not the right to receive or give care. Marshall's notion of care does not stand up to close scrutiny; care was simply viewed as a communitarian duty, to be provided by women as members of the family or social networks; it was domesticated and so stood outside the public domain; it certainly did not enter into any account of the state's responsibility towards its citizens.

This domestication of care, and as a consequence of women too, de-individualised women as citizens and still determines women's position as caregivers. It does so in several ways. First, participation in this kind of care work does not give rights in itself. Income, social security or insurance cannot be derived from giving care. Social citizenship rights can only be obtained by participation in the labour market. People whose main activity consists of care-giving can only obtain mediated rights and therefore depend on somebody else financially. So most women, by giving care informally, remain dependent on men for their income, for insurance and for pensions. This implies that participation in care gives many women a second-class citizenship status, while men's participation in paid labour and the resulting care-dependency, gives entrance to first-class citizenship. Women's financial dependence enforces this position, because it makes clear that they are not only second-rate citizens *vis-à-vis* the state, but also dependent on their fellow citizens: their husbands.

The consequences of this continued dependence are unfortunate. Women remain dependent on the goodwill of their husbands in all aspects of modern life and citizenship. In such matters as buying a house, going to school or taking courses, participating in organisations, sports, having a holiday, or possessing a car, they have to make use of their husbands' money and not seldom ask him for permission. It goes without saying that this inevitably leads to unequal relationships and, occasionally, also to misuses of male power. In an influential study, AafkeKomter (1985) shows that financial resources influence the definition of rights and duties in relationships. She concludes that it is hard for women who have no resources of their own to realise desired changes in the relationship, whether it concerns the allocation of household tasks, sexual arrangements or the education of children.

On the other hand, the imbalance of relationships can be reduced when women have the option of an 'exit', as Barbara Hobson (1990) calls it. If women have the possibility of leaving their marriage through access to an income of their own or to a subsistence level of social assistance, the power relationships in marriage will alter. Until recently, Dutch housewives could count on such an exit in the form of social assistance (Bussemaker et al. 1997; cf. Bussemaker in this volume; Knijn 1994b).

This exit option not only reduces the impact of financial dependency within marriage, but also well-illustrates the Dutch welfare state's ambivalent attitude towards care. In assuming that a mother's first priority is to take care of her children, the state did not overlook the difficult case of solo mothers, and indeed was rather generous in its treatment of solo mothers during the 1970s and the 1980s. Although it was never intended to cover so many as eventually received it, this benefit was nonetheless given to approximately 60 per cent of all solo mothers. Under the terms of the legislation, solo mothers were exempted from the obligation to work, and implicitly accepted that they had the right to care for their children full-time until their youngest child reached the age of 16 (Bussemaker et al. forthcoming, 1997; Knijn 1994b; Kremer 1994).

Considered from the point of view of citizenship rights, however, the terms of the benefit implied that the rights of married women engaged in caring labour were still mediated through their husbands, whereas solo mothers received citizenship rights of their own (though these were not spelled out as such and were always means tested) because they took care of children. Recently, in an effort to increase female participation in the labour market, the Dutch government has targeted the current levels of social assistance, and one casualty might very well be these autonomous solo mother households (Orloff 1993). Interestingly enough, this new policy clearly and undeniably reveals the Achilles' heel of the Dutch gender regime: its valuation of care as a matter of private responsibility.

Dilemmas in the Dutch welfare state

If we consider current tendencies in the transformation of the Dutch welfare state we may conclude that its policies concerning citizenship, care and gender are at least open to question, if not downright problematic. On the one hand the Dutch government tries to improve labour participation in general, and women's labour participation in particular. On the other hand, this same government stresses the need for care within - and by - the community in order to cut back the growing costs of formal professionalised care. These policies are self-contradictory and lead to confusion in a society in which family-life, community-life and informal care are still strongly reliant on women's unpaid work. Attempts to raise the number of women in the labour market are further called into question when one recognises that many women, especially mothers of young and school-age children and older women, do not want to work full-time or -in the case of women over 45 who lack permanent employment - no longer meet the criteria for skilled work. Because of their heavy demands of care-giving duties, most Dutch women generally do not have a continuous employment career.

Incentives to stimulate women's participation in the labour market which overlook this specific position of women in the welfare state may prove self-defeating. Moreover, they may lead to gender struggle. In the corporatist welfare state, Taylor-Gooby (1991) expects a gender struggle between higher educated employed women and lower educated housewives; in the social democratic welfare states, he expects a gender struggle between the public service sector and the private economic sector; and in the liberal welfare states he predicts a gender struggle between men and women within the realm of the family. It is no exaggeration to say that the three types of gender struggle educed by Taylor-Gooby occur in the Netherlands simultaneously.

The conditions for corporatist gender struggle in the Netherlands are the following. Because increasing numbers of well educated women, particularly in the younger generation, are choosing to combine motherhood and employment, and also as a result of the government's efforts to encourage more women to enter the labour market, policies are changing. There is a noticeable trend towards individualisation in matters of income tax, social assistance, and insurance schemes. The effect on traditional single-income families can be unfortunate, especially for housewives who are put under extra pressure to find paid employment.

There is also a social democratic gender struggle in the Netherlands. The increase in the number of women in the labour market tends to undermine the informal care system for children and the elderly. Women, especially housewives, are going to lack time, proximity and willingness to carry out all the informal care-giving tasks they did before their entry into the labour market. As a result the quantity as well as the quality of informal care starts to fall to levels that are lower than ever. An increase in public care provisions, child care and care for the elderly, would therefore seem inevitable. Yet despite this apparent need to extend public care, current policies seem determined to cut back on public expenditures and remove the government further from the domain of care. With the (only partial) exception of public child care, politicians now routinely aim to reduce all institutional care services. Interestingly enough, however, opinion polls indicate that among the population there is a growing plea for extending, not cutting, public services (SCP 1996). Moreover, by being opened up to market forces, the quality of care provision has becomes unpredictable and causes much uncertainty among those receiving it.

Finally, there is a liberal gender struggle. The traditional gender structure of the Dutch family is under pressure due to the lack of sufficient public care and the increasing demands placed upon women to keep their jobs when they become mothers. More and more women want to share housekeeping and child-rearing duties with their male partners. The need to stay employed, however, is not only occasioned by the lack of public care currently available, but also by new attachments to private care, formed over the last few decades. As the traditional motherhood ideology is slowly transformed into a ideology of parenthood, not only mothers but increasingly also fathers now prefer to take care of their children themselves, at least for some days a week. That is why most Dutch children attending public child care (eight per cent of the children under five) do so for only a few days a week. The parenthood ideology puts an increasing claim on fathers to take their share in care-giving. How radical these changes have been is another matter. It is true that the Netherlands have the highest rates of men working part-time, but this is only a possibility for a small minority of fathers of young children, and limited to a few men working in the public sector or in particular branches of industry (Mozes and Wester 1993). Most companies and professions do not permit men to reduce their working hours.

Given this rather complicated relationship between, on the one hand, incentives to increase labour market participation and, on the other hand, a renewed emphasis on care within the community together with commitments to private care made by the Dutch welfare state, it might not be surprising that all kinds of proposals are being put forward to enable part-time work among both men and women (cf. Plantenga in this volume). For many, the possibility of part-time work combines the best of both worlds. That is why the Ministry of Social Affairs in particular is involved in developing strategies, judicial measures and laws which facilitate the combination of work and care within the family.

One of the Ministry's initiatives has been to set up a 'Commissie Toekomstscenario's' (Committee for Future Scenarios) that would advise the government about future relationships between paid and unpaid work. After outlining four possible lines of development, the Committee recommended what it called the 'Combination Scenario', because this one would seem best able to meet the five necessary conditions for any changes in work and care policy, namely, the changing attitudes of Dutch men and women towards the division of labour, the attachment to private and informal care, the employers' acceptance of employees who also want to take care of their children, the development of employment, and the possibility to maintain the level of familial incomes (Commissie Toekomstscenario's 1995, p. 131). This scenario assumes an increase of public and institutionalised care in combination with a reduction of men's working hours and an increase in women's working hours.

Its ideal is a working week of about 29-32 hours for both parents of young children. It aims to reach this redivision of paid and unpaid work by changes through the fiscal and social insurance system, by extending public care provisions and by giving employees a right to part-time and flexible working weeks. At the same time the Ministry made several proposals for changes in legislation: an Act on the right to work part-time (i.e. 32 hours a week) has already been passed by Parliament and is now being discussed in the Upper House; a proposal for new work-leave arrangements has been developed which allows employees to 'save' time for emergencies, including care and education. Last year, the Ministry financially encouraged the extension of child-care centres, particularly for solo mothers with young children intending to find a job or to improve their education in preparation for finding a job. This latter initiative is rather remarkable, since it implies a shift of child-care subsidies from the Ministry of Welfare and Health care towards the Ministry of Labour. This shift illustrates the priority given to women's participation in the work force as well as the willingness of the Dutch government to support women who wish to combine motherhood and paid work. However, it also illustrates the Dutch policy of 'incidents' in the case of care. Since a general and comprehensive policy with regard to gender relationships and social, labour market and care participation is lacking, all kinds of incidental - and sometimes accidental - arrangements can be introduced.

Conclusion

In matters of gender equality the Netherlands has been a slow developer. A generation ago it seemed as if the Netherlands was plunged into a long, deep sleep while women in other countries claimed or were forced to claim their rights. Labour participation was seen as a luxury for those better educated women who were dissatisfied with being only a housewife or mother. Now the Sleeping Beauty is waking up and when she looks around and sees the price women all over the world pay for full-time employment, with little leisure time and almost no time to take care of the ones they care about, she may say: 'this is not what I want'.

Would the strategy of part-time work and part-time involvement in care improve equal participation in terms of civil society and gender equality in terms of citizenship? In theory a gender-neutral combination of part-time work with part-time care-giving would seem to give a strong impetus to a de-gendered inclusive citizenship (Knijn and Kremer 1997). It would implicitly recognise care as an aspect of social citizenship, and accept as a given the interdependency of work and care, not to mention the mutual dependency of workers and care-givers. Besides, it would change thinking on economic and social issues because both domains (i.e. the economic and the social) would have to take account of each other's particular dynamics. Thereby it would challenge too the dominant image of the individualised masculine human being, who depends on receiving care, but is never supposed to give care.

This strategy also implies a change of the foundations of social security, patterns of labour law and fiscal systems, all of which up till now have presupposed a complementary family. In other words, this combination of work and care by men as well as women, would be a powerful tool to improve the citizen status and rights of those citizens who are currently deprived precisely on account of their role as care-givers. It would offer them new rights and a new status, not at the expense of care, but through recognising care as an important aspect of social citizenship. Again, theoretically speaking, it would imply a radical revision of women's and men's participation in civil society and within the family.

It would also inevitably lead to new approaches to care-giving and voluntary work, as well as to new arrangements for co-operation between professional and informal care-givers. While at the moment much caring labour, community care and volunteer work has to be done instead of, or in the margins of paid labour, new arrangements will develop when people increasingly have to combine this kind of care with paid work. Admittedly a new attitude and approach to the relationship that exists between professional, institutionalised care provisions and informal caregivers will be required. Several experiments, for instance in the extension of the opening hours of hospitals and youth health care or the improvement of adjusting paid and unpaid home care, have already shown that a great deal can be gained from such reforms.

However, for the moment, while several Ministries, political parties and women's associations are very busy in drawing up blue-prints, women are voting with their feet. The age at which Dutch women are having babies has risen to an average of 29, one of the highest in Europe, and a growing number of women are choosing not to have any children at all. This may indicate that being a full-time housewife is no longer such an attractive a career option to many young Dutch women. Many prefer to combine a part-time job with taking care of their own children, being active within the community and assisting in informal care for friends and relatives in need of care. But since these women recognise that neither their male partners, nor the welfare state and the labour market are very willing to share their care-giving responsibilities, they are delaying their decision. The Dutch welfare state is still far from offering the chance to combine work and care and hence the further possibility of enjoying full citizenship with an active membership of civil society remains distant too.

6 Citizenship, participation and the social policy on girls in the Netherlands[1]

Annemieke van Drenth

The Dutch welfare state is often thought to be highly gendered (cf. the introduction to this volume). Gendered welfare arrangements certainly affect the participation of women (and men) as citizens. Men, being the bread-winner citizens, not only participate more than women do in the labour market, but in public life and politics as well. If we agree with Voet (cf. Voet in this volume) in her account of citizenship as the ability, based on certain rights, to participate in paid labour, in social life and in politics, we are forced to conclude that the Netherlands have assigned a second-rate citizenship to the female sex. However, should citizenship only be seen as a certain status that is determined by particular rights? Should not citizenship also be seen as carrying with it a commitment to particular duties? An idea of citizenship conceived in terms of both rights and duties, especially the duties of care-giving, can already be found in the 'gynocentric' feminist tradition (Voet 1995, p. 246). In this tradition the social importance of the 'caring function', mainly fulfilled by women, is very prominent. In the light of this fact, Knijn and Kremer (1997) have recently argued for an extension of the traditional notion of citizenship. They want to set up a new norm of 'inclusive citizenship', which subsumes the 'right to time for care' (that is, to give as well as to receive care). Thus, every citizen has the right to participate in caring activities in the private life, regardless of whether he or she participates directly in the labour market.

What, however, are the consequences of this new 'inclusive' citizenship formulated in terms of rights? In my opinion, basing our notion of citizenship on rights alone implies a certain inequality between women and men, because men will acquire rights (to receive care) without necessarily sharing the responsibilities (to give care) that women have. I would argue that it is precisely when we take into account both the right to be cared for and the duty to care for others that our understanding of citizenship can be usefully modified. Voet's notion (1995, p. 263) of 'feminist participatory citizenship', by which she means the participation of all citizens in economical and social (cultural/political) activity, could also gain from taking into account the duty to care. What Knijn and Kremer (1997) see as the process of 'ungendering care' requires more than the mere right of participation, both economically and privately. If we fail to work the duty to care into the concept of citizenship, it will simply be taken for granted that women are, self-evidently, responsible for this duty. Indeed, outside the private world of care, women are still severely short-changed in the opportunities afforded them in the public world, notably in politics. Thus the gendered presumption remains that female citizens have to take care for others, while male citizens are the ones who are taken care of. It is this presumption that often hinders women in their full participation as citizens.

In this article my focus will lie on the prevailing notion of citizenship in the emancipation policy pursued by the Dutch government, especially as it is directed to girls. I intend to argue that this policy has rather emphasised the idea of femininity being synonymous with care-giving, instead of contributing to the deconstruction of the male-breadwinner stereotype. I will start with a closer examination of the often implicit notion of citizenship present in government policies on girls, and will explain how the central problem is seen as girls' choices. A brief sketch of the social construction of girlhood in Dutch society, which is characterised by pillarisation, is therefore necessary. In order to shed more light on the friction between the social policy on girls and the reality of daily life for many of them, I will also discuss some recent research on the situation of girls in the Netherlands and the attempts that have been made to change gender relations. Lastly the issue of citizenship and participation will be addressed. What does the notion of citizenship, which implies rights and duties for both sexes and is aimed at both economical and social participation, mean for the social policy on girls, or better yet, on youngsters in general?

Citizenship in Dutch social policy on women and girls

Although the welfare regime in the Netherlands has been profoundly influenced by an ideology of the family, political opposition to certain inequalities between the sexes has also emerged since the 1970s. This opposition, mainly to be found in the political ideas of Social Democrats and Liberals, has had its impact on the state machinery. Under the pressure of the women's liberation movement initiatives were taken to develop policies aimed at creating equal opportunities for men and women to participate in society. The state policy on 'emancipation' that resulted from these initiatives was supervised by a special advisory board, the Emancipation Council. This council was a first sign of the process of institutionalisation of 'state feminism' in the Netherlands. In the course of time it was followed by the foundation of a special state subdepartment, called DCE ('Directie Coördinatie Emancipatie Zaken' or, Directorate for the Co-ordination of Equality Policy). This department became responsible for co-ordinating the various equality policies from different parts of the state machinery.

Research on the aims of emancipation policies and the ideas of the so-called 'femocrats' (civil servants at the DCE) has revealed that their main goal is to integrate women more fully into the labour market (Keuzenkamp and Outshoorn 1992; Keuzenkamp and Teunissen 1990; Outshoorn 1994; cf. Outhoorn in this volume). Their guiding idea is that women, like men, must be held responsible for their economic participation. The economic independence that results from this, it is argued, will provide women with the same rights male breadwinners already have, and will, moreover, enable them to participate better as citizens. Not included in this equality policy, however, is any attempt to give men the responsibilities and duties of care-givers. As a consequence, the social policy on women practised by the Dutch government has allowed a gendered form of citizenship. However 'equal' men and women may seem in respect of the 'equal rights' they enjoy in the labour market, inequality in care responsibility still remains. Whenever the duty to care for others in the private sphere is not taken into account, women's 'double burden' is ignored and no compensation is given.

Besides a policy on women's emancipation, the Dutch government has also initiated a special social policy aimed at girls. Such a policy is unique in Europe (Hoogeveen and van der Zande 1995). In 1988 the Dutch government presented to parliament a memorandum on the *Social position of girls and young women* (henceforth referred to as the Girls' Memo), which included intentions and proposals for a set of policies (Handelingen 1988). Different advisory bodies, like the Emancipation Council (Emancipatie Raad 1987), the Socio-Economic Council (SER 1988) and the Council for Youth Policies (RJB 1988) were consulted by the government before the Girls' Memo was written. All these councils have underlined the centrality of economic independence. The Socio-Economic Council concentrates exclusively on education and labour, because of the need to increase female employment in the near future when the proportion of young people in the Dutch population will decline sharply. But the Emancipation Council and the Council for Youth Policies have also pointed out the negative consequences of segregation and stereotyping for the participation of girls in leisure activities, sports and politics. In addition, they have paid attention to the problematic position of specific categories of girls who were considered to be in need of social and psychological assistance, for example in cases of sexual abuse.

Before we examine further the notion of citizenship implied in the social policy on girls, an immediate cause of this policy, the so-called '1990 Measure', needs to be discussed. When this measure was accepted by Parliament, the majority of the members had assumed the duty of (young) women to participate in the labour market. The '1990 Measure' is a provision of the so-called Supplementary Benefits Act, which is a safety-net for certain employee-insurance schemes. Under this act breadwinners whose income falls below a fixed minimum due to illness or unemployment qualify for benefits. Article 3, however, states: 'From 1990, a married person whose spouse was born after 31 December 1971 has no entitlement to supplements unless his [sic] household comprises an own child, a step or foster-child younger than 12 years' (Hoogeveen and Zande 1995, p. 69). Consequently, partners (in most cases women) born after 1971 are not entitled to supplementary benefits and have to be available for the labour market, unless she (or he) has to take care of children under the age of 12. If she (he) is unable to find work, the family income can be supplemented up to the legal minimum level, but only by means of a social security payment, which is based on the needs of the family as a whole. This means that partners, mostly women, on whom an obligation to participate in paid work has been imposed, are not at the same time entitled as individuals to benefits in case of unemployment. Here again the family ideology dominates, even if now the individual responsibility of women to participate in paid labour could have paved the way for giving women access to benefits of their own.

Although one might imagine that the '1990 Measure' would much assist young women who were preparing to enter the work force, in reality this regulation has only had limited effect. The number of women that experience and will experience any consequences of the '1990 Measure' is small, and is largely confined to partners of the small group of lowest paid breadwinners. Of the total number of women working at home in the next ten years only 0.2 per cent will be affected (Jansweijer 1989, p. 366). From this one may conclude that the '1990 Measure' in fact mainly functions as symbolic legislation, promoting the idea that economic independence is important for women, and encouraging them to prepare for paid employment (Morée and Vliet 1989). The female Social Democrats who proposed the '1990 Measure' in parliament seem to have intended to help girls plan their lives, including entry into the labour market. The '1990 Measure' would also serve to put political pressure on the Dutch government to bring about an effective social policy for girls (van Drenth 1992). In fact the central target of the policy in the Girls' Memo is more broadly formulated as the aim 'to advance the development of girls and young women toward independence in a process of participation and integration in society'. According to the Girls' Memo, independence has to do with both socio-cultural and socio-economic matters, whereas 'participation and integration' refer to the current status as a youth as well as to future adulthood (p. 7). Despite these broad parameters, issues of education and employment were given priority. The Girls' Memo thus implicitly emphasised a notion of citizenship pertaining to the rights of an adult who is a full participant in society, by which the memo primarily meant a participant in the work force.

In view of this emphasis, one would expect the proposed policies to push for concrete changes in the socio-economic system. A closer examination of the Girls' Memo shows, however, that the opposite is the case. The government does not pay any attention to the economic structure and the opportunities that are provided. Girls and young women are seen as problematic precisely because they lack proper education and have had faulty vocational guidance. The resulting weakness in the labour market is seen as the girls' own fault. They themselves are responsible for having made the choices that diminish their opportunities to get jobs with high wages and good prospects. The policy expressed in the Girls' Memo can therefore be said to have arisen from the conviction that girls were being raised and educated in the wrong way. The unfortunate subtext that lurks beneath the rhetoric of economic independence and labour market participation is that the victims - the girls themselves - are to blame. The majority of policies proposed in the memorandum concern the upbringing of girls, their education and their entrance into the work force. The aim of the policy is limited to altering certain misleading preconceptions held by girls, and, to a lesser extent, by their parents and educators. The education of girls should become less stereotyped. At school girls should be encouraged to choose 'boys' subjects' like mathematics, and to develop an ambition for 'men's work', in particular in technical areas. A substantial part of the policies in the Memo concerns the promotion of what are considered the 'right choices'. In a significant and expensive move, these choices were widely espoused by media campaigns, in particular on television, in the years following 1988, yet the success of these campaigns was only limited.

Another striking characteristic of the Dutch state policy on girls is the tendency to focus on specific categories of girls, i.e. those who are considered to be especially vulnerable and therefore need special attention. These 'target groups' consist of girls with little or no schooling, unemployed girls and girls from ethnic minorities. They are considered to be in danger of becoming trapped in dead-end jobs. Furthermore, according to the Girls' Memo, the culture the girls experience at home clashes with the idea of equality between the sexes and the notions of feminine identity that predominate in Dutch culture. Being more vulnerable, these girls need extra encouragement to continue their education, and to follow adequate vocational guidance programs. In addition to the specific policies of the Girls' Memo, research is planned in order to keep the government informed about the target groups and about (improvements in) their situations. As easily understood as this focus may be from the perspective of, say, ethnic emancipation, the impact on the *general* policy is negative. First, because an emphasis on isolated segments of the total young female population inevitably raises the idea that the main issue here is the advancement of girls in the most disadvantaged positions, and not the emancipation of girls in general. Second, the effect of focusing on girls from ethnic minorities underlines the problems of ethnic groups as if they were not effects produced by social relations. Inevitably, girls from minority groups end up carrying a further stigma, rather than being encouraged to emancipate themselves.

In their evaluation of the Dutch emancipation policy, Keuzenkamp and Teunissen (1990, pp. 158-76) have argued that the policy on girls is implicitly founded on the idea that girls have to become like boys in order to participate in society. In the Girls' Memo socialisation (in the family) is seen as a crucial element in the understanding of how girls come to adopt the 'wrong' female behaviour and embody the 'undesirable' type of girlhood. According to Keuzenkamp and Teunissen this observation presents the government with a serious problem so long as the development of the personal (gender) identity is seen as the private responsibility of parents and educators. The policies on girls, therefore, cannot be directed at the earliest stages of identity building, but have to be restricted to the social construction of girlhood in the public sphere. As a result state policies are restricted to various attempts to change public mentality, whereas interventions in the private sphere of raising children and educating them are taboo. In this respect van der Zande and Hoogeveen (1991, pp. 131-2) have also made a plea for a 'political choice' from the Dutch government, which, in their opinion, can no longer only pay lip-service to the views and the knowledge acquired by the women's movement and women's studies without taking into account all the possible consequences, including those pertaining to the private sphere.

The social construction of girlhood

What is the cultural and political background of this social policy on girls and young women and why is this policy so well elaborated in the Netherlands, as compared to other European countries (Waal 1990)? Answers can be found in the ideological and political situation in the Netherlands, especially the tradition of pillarisation (cf. Bussemaker in this volume). Within this tradition, citizenship has always been linked with the right to participate in society on the basis of social and political organisation in the pillar of one's own 'choice'. Religious and denominational freedom, founded on a political consensus between the Catholic and Protestant movements, was for decades the remedy against state policies intended to break down a family ideology which continually reproduced the notions of the male breadwinner and the female caregiver (Bussemaker 1993).

Residues of pillarisation can still be found in the positions taken on women's issues by the different political parties within the Dutch parliament. In their examination of the views on the state policy on girls held by each of these parties, Hoogeveen and van de Velde (1992) have shown that in the last two decades agreement was reached (although 'unwillingly' on the part of the Christian Democrats) on the importance of a social policy on women's emancipation. Only small, right wing Christian members of parliament contested the very idea of women's emancipation on the grounds that it contravened divine laws. In their opinion women's central position in the home and in family life is intended by God, and can therefore not be changed by men, let alone by women. Until recently this view was shared by the large, more moderate Christian Democrat party. Nowadays they have altered their position, mainly under pressure from feminists in their own ranks as well as from Liberal and Social Democratic members, with whom the Christian Democrats have shared power in several governments in the recent past.

Thus, the policy on women's emancipation that developed from the 1970s onwards, was mainly due to the persistent political pressure exerted by women of the Social Democratic and the Liberal party. 'State feminists' and 'femocrats' like those responsible for the bureaucratic machinery that has laid the basis for the social policy on women are left wing in orientation (Outshoorn 1994). It is important, however, to recognise that, in the past, the political situation often obliged femocrats to moderate radical options for (structural) change. Political negotiations between the Social Democrats and citizens with the same rights as men to full participation in society. A political compromise was the inevitable result. The Christian Democrats emphasised that women would now be given opportunities to participate in paid labour. The Social Democrats, and the femocrats in 'The Hague', reconciled themselves to a policy that mainly concerned changes in mentality. The social policy on girls and women thus became a policy of persuasion. Instead of being forced to participate in society, women and girls had to be convinced of new opportunities outside the home. Only very recently, since the Christian Democrats have lost their political dominance, has the idea of the duty for (young) women to be economically independent gained real significance.

Not only in the present but also in the recent past, the pillarised Dutch welfare state has been split between the denominational views on the one hand and the those of the left and liberal wings on the other. For a long time one of the key issues was that citizens should be free to determine their 'private lives'. Political decisions have had and still have great impact on the personal lives of citizens. Yet the prevailing orthodoxy has been that politics should never interfere in the private domain. In their pleas in favour of the family ideology, which was in fact hegemonical, and in their political practices, denominational parties have succeeded in using the concept of 'private life' in the limited sense of 'individual freedom'. This freedom could be insulated from political action if the state was prevented from interfering on 'private' issues (cf. Bussemaker in this volume). This has not only been the case in matters of education, in which the social construction of girlhood in the past mainly took place, but also in the sphere of non-state public initiatives aimed at the upbringing of girls. From the Second World War onwards the Dutch welfare state has upheld an important tradition of youth work and youth care. Welfare work for youths was pillarised and markedly segregated along gender lines, particularly in the denominational organisations. Girls and boys participated in large numbers in youth clubs, Sunday schools and youth movements. After school time or working hours it was common for many youngsters to remain under the surveillance of a whole army of denominational reformers and pedagogues, who educated them in the traditions and convictions of the relevant pillar. Their 'caring power', directed towards the well-being of individuals and the construction of their identity (Drenth 1991), had a strong influence on the social construction of girlhood by which many girls were guided into a future as mother and housewife (Essen 1990). After the Second World War, when youth organizations were at their most successful, the aims of youth work for girls started to change. Besides underlining the future female duties in the family, youth workers stressed the importance of a fine feminine personality and thus gave girlhood a more personal content (Drenth 1993a 1993b; Drenth and Poel 1992). They prepared the way for a development that would ultimately give girls and women more opportunities to participate in social life. Changes were, however, very slow. Whereas the duties to take care of others and to be 'the angel of the house' (Woolf 1995) were still very well-defined, no notion of citizenship in terms of rights to participate in public life played any role in youth work and youth care at that time.

It is safe to say that until the 1960s the Dutch welfare state was made up of a pillarised network of non-state based organizations that supervised youth life and influenced the (future) private relations of Dutch citizens. Traditional youth care, indeed most aspects of private care, in the hands of these pillarised private organizations, confirmed the idea of personal life as a 'free' domain, although the private sphere was certainly invaded and this not without success. When women, from the left wing as well as liberals, initiated early forms of state feminism in the 1970s, based on the feminist slogan 'the personal is the political', a new dimension in political struggle became possible. Now femocrats, of Liberal as well as Social Democratic origin, voiced the opinion that policies aimed at women's emancipation needed state intervention in private life. In fact, up till the present day their success in creating a basis for such a policy has been but partial. Notions of structural change (in terms of power relations) never gained real significance, for example in the social policy on girls (Keuzenkamp and Teunissen (1990, pp. 175-6).

Citizenship and friction

What has been the situation of girls in the Netherlands in the recent past and how did a social policy on girls, mainly directed at showing them that they might participate in the work force 'like the boys', work out? If we consider the lives of Dutch girls in the last two decades we can notice considerable changes, in particular as regards the customary length of full-time education. Education has been seen as increasingly important for both girls and boys, while the option of participating in the labour market is now seen as more or less self-evident by many girls. The following table not only shows that youngsters in general go to school longer than ever before, but also that the gap between the participation by boys and girls is gradually closing.

Table 6.1
Participation in full-time education for age group and gender (in percentages)

	Ages 16-18		Ages 19-23	
	Male	Female	Male	Female
1971	53.7	36.7	18.1	7.1
1974	63.0	47.8	21.2	9.0
1980	70.8	65.1	25.1	13.8
1985	78.1	75.6	29.6	19.9
1988	77.7	75.7	31.6	23.6

Source: M. Niphuis-Nell 1992, p. 211.

Young men and women have become more equal, not only in the duration but also in the level of their schooling (Dam 1991). Although there still is some underrepresentation of specific groups of girls, for example from ethnic minorities, there is good reason to be optimistic about the future. In her evaluation report on the social policy on girls Niphuis-Nell (1992) concluded that the final level of schooling of girls from the '1990 generation' will probably not be too different from that of their male peers in the near future. At the same time, however, she has also noticed that girls' school results today still decline at the age of 14 or 15. Furthermore, not too much has changed in the strongly gendered character of the choices girls (and boys) make for vocational training. The stereotypes of female and male options - the 'soft and caring' ones for girls and the 'hard and technical' ones for boys - are as popular as ever before. In particular girls are limited by this sex segregation in their opportunities to establish a successful career (Niphuis-Nell 1992, p. 38). This, however, is not only the case in vocational schooling at different levels, but also in higher education, where, for example, students in pedagogy are mainly female and those in mathematics are almost exclusively male (Arends 1988, p. 33).

Research among youngsters has made clear that it is not only socialisation by parents and other educators such as teachers and youth leaders which leads to sex segregation. Peers also play a significant role in the construction of gender, in male and female lifestyles, cultures and in personal identities. Taking her findings from participant observations among girls of secondary schools Waal (1989) discovered that girls have relationships amongst each other in the course of which they develop their feeling for a gendered identity. In order to understand the meaning of femininity they force each other to evaluate the femininity of other girls. The notion of 'a nice girl', which consists of a stereotype of femininity as being altruistic, modest, friendly, good looking and, last but not least, spontaneous and clever although never at the cost of others, stands as the ideal. According to Waal the ideal of the nice girl is so important in the girls' school culture that it dominates other issues. Relating to one another and establishing a sphere of cosiness gradually become the girls' priorities, undoubtedly affecting their results at school. Notwithstanding the fact that girls are still very active in school, their performance drops to a lower level because they put in just enough effort to satisfy the (not too high) expectations of their parents and teachers.

Boys also play a role in the process of constructing a feminine identity. The expectations boys have of girls and their future partners can be very influential, as Naber and Peters (1991) have shown. As girls grow older a decline in their professional ambitions is often apparent, together with a decreasing enthusiasm for adding a future career to what for many has become the primary goal of motherhood. Although girls nowadays seem to be more aware of the importance of economic independence, they also show a willingness to quit their jobs in order to take care of children. It looks as if girls anticipate working in paid labour as well as the attitudes of boys which are often more traditional when it comes to gender roles. In spite of the changes in the expectations girls undoubtedly show in comparison to their mothers' generation, the progress that has actually been made is still limited. Girls tend to modify their initially rather emancipated ideas on combining paid work with care for children as soon as they become older and more 'realistic' because of a relationship with a male partner. Furthermore, research has shown that class differences and the girl's final level of education play significant roles in the Netherlands in this respect. Girls from lower social classes, and girls with little or no education, more often opt for a traditional two phase model: having a job, often a specific 'women's job' before marriage and leaving paid labour when the first child comes (Naber 1992; Peters 1992).

In general one could say that girls share a notion of citizenship based on the right and the duty to be economically independent in the future. In this respect they agree with femocrats. The problem is, however, that they do not seem to be fully aware of all the consequences of this conviction, and a certain degree of friction results. This becomes clear when we consider the results of a study by den Uyl and Cornelissen (1991) on the provisions needed by girls in order to help them realise their new responsibility. Girls do not have a lot of expectations in this respect. In addition, they do not relate to feminism and the women's movement, let alone to the claims that are made for more rights and support for women. Instead girls show an easy optimism that they will secure their own emancipation. Illustrative examples of this are the quite assertive statements often made by girls along the lines of 'our child will also be his child', as if a supportive husband is the norm in everyday life. They simply consider what might be possible as what is most likely to happen in the future or even what will inevitably happen. In reality, however, (young) women are almost always the ones who are responsible for the care-giving in the family. Remarkably missing in the girls' various expressions of self-confidence is any awareness that child-care facilities, mentioned by 51 per cent of the girls as a solution to any practical problems, are still lagging behind in the Netherlands. Add to this the fact that girls hardly express any need for support in the sphere of the labour market, and we can reasonably conclude that friction between the notion of citizenship in the policy on girls and their daily lives, now and in the future, abounds. In general, girls are too optimistic about the possibilities of combining raising children with having a (full-time) job, which provides them with real economic independence.

Girls' citizenship and participation: conclusion

Although girls generally do not want to align themselves with any professedly feminist position, they have actually adopted the view of femocrats. They regard economic independence as normal for every citizen in the welfare state, including women. They accept a notion of citizenship in which one is responsible for one's own income. It has become self-evident to them that they will participate in the work force, although it is not clear for how long. They tend to hang on to the idea of 'individual freedom' that is also given to them in the policy. If their autonomy is stressed by this policy, emancipation can only mean making your own choices as an independent woman. They thus feel free to think and act as they like, irrespective of what is stated by the feminist movement or the government. As individuals they make their own choices and it is exactly this choice-making that they consider to be the heart of women's emancipation. Consequently, when teachers and television experts tell them to make other choices, as for example to take up 'hard sciences' or 'technical professions', the girls brush this advice aside as 'nagging' (Uyl and Cornelissen 1991, p. 60).

The femocrat notion of citizenship that stresses one's responsibility to participate in the labour market without positing a social policy that affords girls more opportunities so as to resist the entrenched privileges of boys, does not really question a traditional model of femininity that is synonymous with care-giving. Moreover, the absence of a notion of inclusive citizenship in the social policy on girls leaves the stereotype of the male breadwinner unaffected too. In an article on 'the disintegration of policy relating to girls and the absence of policy relating to boys' Hoogeveen and van der Zande (1993) are quite right to ask 'nothing wrong with the boys?'. Neither girls, nor boys or men are confronted with a concept of citizenship that includes care-giving responsibilities as incumbent upon every citizen. Boys are not bothered, and girls feel the friction. After all, their (new) duty to participate in society is not accompanied by any intention on the part of men to share the duty of taking care or caring. Women are still held solely responsible for the caring role, both in the sense of caring for the opinions of their (future) partner and taking care for the well-being of man and children in the future. As a result girls tend to react by escaping into an ideology of emancipation as the freedom to make one's own choices in life. They show an optimism towards the future, as they are convinced that they will be able to do things however they like. Girls regard themselves as already 'emancipated', which encourages them to ignore the problems they have to face in combining the duties of paid work and private care. As a result we should not be surprised that gender relations do not rapidly change in the Netherlands. Research in other European countries confirms that the persistence of gender structures among youngsters in modern welfare states is strong (Peters and Chisholm 1991).

What would a notion of inclusive citizenship based on the rights of receiving care as well as the duties of giving care mean for a social policy that really wants to change the situation of girls? Firstly, a policy on girls and women which is founded on this inclusive model of citizenship should be more than mainly symbolic legislation. If the policy is only focusing on changes in ideas and mentalities, however important they may be, the effects of such a policy will be disastrous. Telling girls and women that they have to make new choices and that participation in society as full citizens is necessary, without at the same time providing them with better opportunities to participate, forces them back into traditional attitudes. Girls and women will find themselves obliged to take what is their 'true feminine' responsibility: they will be readier to give care to others close to them than they will be to participate in the world outside the home, as their 'own' social duty demands.

Secondly, inclusive citizenship also implies that a social policy on boys and men has to be developed. The traditional dislike of many Dutch politicians for intervening in personal relations as far as they concern the sexes and gender identities, makes it difficult to develop policies that will be accepted. The duty to be a 'caring citizen' could, however, be realised by a careful consideration of the development of gender identities, for example in schooling, vocational training and even leisure activities. Furthermore, the duty to care can be included in the approach of employers towards their employees, of politicians and the state towards citizens, and of people towards each other. The state and its femocrats have the duty to develop a policy which really recognises inclusive citizenship.

Acknowledgments

1.   This article is based on a paper entitled 'Girlhood and the Politics of Everyday Life. Citizenship and Social Policy on Girls in the Netherlands' which was presented at the international conference, 'Crossing Borders: International Dialogues on Gender, Social Politics and Citizenship' in Stockholm, Sweden, in May 1994. I am grateful to Rian Voet for her constructive criticism of this earlier version and to Marjolein Moreé for her support in rewriting it.

7 Political empowerment of women in the Netherlands

Monique Leijenaar

Apart from wooden clogs and tulips, the Netherlands is perhaps best known for having been ruled - since 1890 - by a queen, even if her duties are largely ceremonial. The real political decision-makers are the politicians: the cabinet ministers, the MPs, the local and provincial councillors, mayors and state-commissioners. Politics, however, also takes place outside the institutes of the state, and includes (sometimes formally but often informally) all kinds of special interest organisations.

This chapter looks at the participation of women in political decision-making. I will first provide a brief outline of the Dutch political system as the specific context within which this decision-making takes place. In the section that follows I will describe the changing political representation of women over four periods. Next, I will place the findings in an international context: is the Dutch situation unique or does it reflect a European trend? Then I will focus on women's participation in social organisations. The results of a large survey of 4200 national organisations will give a clear picture of the participation of women in this area of power. In the final section of this chapter I will discuss some future developments in the empowerment of women.

The Dutch political system

The Dutch are often described as 'nuchter', a term meaning cool, not easily aroused and rational. This phlegmatic approach is reflected in the political system. Dutch politics allows even the smallest party some parliamentary representation and every interest group to have its say. Moreover, the system is based on the principle of compromise, since no one party can ever have a majority.

The constitutional monarchy was established in 1814 under a multi-party parliamentary system, with a monarch as the formal head of state and a prime minister as head of government. Cabinet ministers are responsible to a bicameral parliament, the 'Staten General'. The cabinet and the individual ministers need the confidence of the majority of the Second Chamber. It is not the queen, but the parliament that has the power to 'fire' a minister or a cabinet. Two Chambers make up the parliament: in the Second Chamber, the Lower House, there are 150 representatives who are directly elected. Elections take place every four years or whenever the cabinet resigns. The 75 representatives of the First Chamber are elected indirectly by the members of the provincial councils. Often the First Chamber, or Senate, is referred to as the Chamber of Reflection, because its main task is to review the details of laws as well as establishing whether or not they are constitutional; there is no separate Constitutional Court in the Netherlands. Unlike the 'Bundesrat' in Germany or the House of Lords in Great Britain, the Senate in the Netherlands does not represent regions, or certain classes of people.

Apart from choosing the members of the Lower House, Dutch citizens have the task of directly electing representatives of the 600 municipal councils as well as the members of the 12 provincial councils. This happens every four years. Since 1917, when universal suffrage for men was introduced, the representatives have been elected by a system of proportional representation. Before then, only men with a certain income were allowed to vote and a 'first past the post' system was used.

The current electoral system works quite simply. All citizens 18 years and older are eligible to vote. They do not have to register. Each voter casts one vote and for all practical purposes the country as a whole forms one constituency. The ballot contains the names of all candidates competing for seats, grouped by party. It is the political party that decides on the order of its candidates. Although citizens may vote for any candidate on the list, most people choose to support candidates at the top of the list.

Given the low threshold for gaining representation, about 0.67 per cent of the total valid vote, there has always been a relatively large number of parties winning seats in parliament. Three parties have dominated parliamentary politics and the formation of coalitions from the post-war period until the 1980s. The 'Christelijk Democratisch Appel' (Christian Democratic Appeal, CDA) was founded in 1980 out of a merger of three religious parties. The second party, the 'Partij van de Arbeid' (Labour Party, PvdA), is the only mass-based, left wing party in the Netherlands. The third party is 'Volkspartij voor Vrijheid en Democratie' (Liberal Party, VVD), which contains strong conservative overtones reminiscent of the British Conservative Party. Since the 1980s another more leftist-liberal party, called Democrats '66, has gained much electoral support. Between five and ten additional parties can be found in parliament. Some of these have occupied seats long before World War Two, but most of them sprung up since the late 1950s.

The origins of the Dutch party system are usually traced back to mass emancipation movements during the second half of the nineteenth century. These movements were shaped not only by class conflict, as was the case in all European countries, but even more markedly by religious divisions between Calvinist, Catholic and Dutch Reformed segments of the population. The dominant issues of the end of the nineteenth century reflected and subsequently reinforced the religious and class cleavages in Dutch society.

Conflict centred on government funding for private (religiously oriented) schools and the extension of suffrage. These issues were resolved in 1917 in a major compromise between the political groups which had already been formed. This so-called 'pacification' of 1917 established equal state funding for private and public schools and universal suffrage, first for men and then, in 1919, for women too.

The various emancipatory movements had also given rise not only to political parties, but also to a wide array of other social institutions, organised along denominational and class lines (cf. Bussemaker this volume). This process, generally known as 'verzuiling' or the pillarisation of Dutch society, began to break down in the 1960s as religion became less important.

Another important characteristic of Dutch political development is the extension of the corporate sector after the Second World War. In the 1950s and 1960s a highly institutionalised network of interest groups was formed, the majority of these oriented towards ministries, such as the Ministry of Social Affairs, Internal Affairs, Culture and Agriculture. In the neocorporatist political system, group interests were represented on all kind of advisory boards (Andeweg 1995, p. 355).

Context of women's political involvement

These characteristic features of Dutch society, 'verzuiling' and neocorporatism, are important in explaining women's political involvement in the Netherlands. First, strong religious pressures reduced the possibilities for women to participate. In general the practice of religion encouraged and strengthened the de facto inequality of women in the family and in society by promoting the idea that women's proper role was at home. The hostility of many religions, especially the Catholic Church, towards birth control, also limited women's advancement, as did the reluctance of the religious parties to welcome women in their midst. It took the Protestant Party, for example, until 1953 to allow its women members to stand for election.

Another consequence of 'verzuiling' was the pillarisation of women's organisations. Prior to the new women's movement of the 1960s, women were organised in so-called 'traditional' women's organisations. Examples of these traditional organisations include the Catholic Women's Club ('Katholiek Vrouwen Dispuut'), Dutch Organisation of Housewives ('Nederlandse Vereniging van Huisvrouwen'), Dutch Organisation of Farmers Wives ('Nederlandse Bond voor Boerinnen'), and the Dutch Catholic Organisation of Farmers Wives ('de Nederlandse Katholieke Boerinnenbond'). Besides these organisations there existed - and still do - separate women's wings in many labour unions and political parties. Most of the traditional women's organisations viewed themselves as politically neutral and they were not bothered with questions of gender inequality or the oppression of women. It was left to the women's wings of the parties and trade-unions to lobby on behalf of greater female representation in the political decision-making bodies.

The system of neocorporatism also restricted women's political involvement. Swiebel and Outshoorn (1991, p. 6) note that for newcomers to the political arena, such as the organisations of the women's movement, it was hard to get into the system of close-knit policy networks, often formally institutionalised in official advisory bodies. Moreover, the corporatist network is heavily dominated by economic interests and women's interests tend to be ignored (Hernes and Hänninen 1985, p. 122; Lovenduski 1986a, p. 166; Oldersma 1990).

It is in this context of a pillarised and corporatist political structure that women had to fight for their political rights. Their first goal was to win the right to vote and to stand for election.

Political participation of women

1917-1946 : the pioneers

Women have been allowed to stand for election since 1917. Two years later, in 1919, women were also allowed to vote. The parliamentary election of 1922 was the first election in which women cast their votes. Gaining these formal political rights did not happen overnight, however. At first the debate on suffrage, mainly led by adherents of the socialist and liberal parties, focused on suffrage for men only.

Until 1887 there was no explicit constitutional prohibition barring women from the vote. It was a woman, Aletta Jacobs, who pointed out the discrepancy between the constitution and the actual practice. Being well-off herself (the first woman allowed to go to university and, subsequently, a medical practitioner), she used the parliamentary elections of 1883 in an attempt to assert her rights:

> When the lists with the names of the voters were published in 1883, I looked at whether my name was included. Of course I knew my name would not be there, but I wanted to do everything right. When I did not find my name on the list, I sent a letter dated March 22 1883 to the Mayor of Amsterdam, requesting to be placed on the voters' list, since I answered all conditions for eligibility. I included written proof of this. The Mayor and aldermen thought my letter to be very entertaining. To great laughter my letter was read out loud and nobody really understood the meaning of its content (Jacobs [1924] 1978, p. 94).

Her request was denied, since:

> ...the author may refer to the Law, but according to the Spirit of our Political Institutions, women do not have the right to vote. And even, if one denounces the Sprit of our Laws, one should question whether women should possess all the rights of citizenship. Looking at civil laws, women are barred from custody with the exception of the custody of their children. (ibidem, p. 95)

Appeal to the Higher Court did not help. The Higher Court ruled that when the constitution refers to an 'inhabitant of the Netherlands' it is referring to men, since 'otherwise this would have been explicitly stated'. Moreover, it was argued that since it is the husband and father who pays taxes for his wife and children, it is logical that women should not be allowed to vote. Rather conveniently, those women, such as widows and unmarried women, who also payed taxes were not taken into account. The result of Jacobs' action was that in 1887, when the constitution was renewed, the word 'male' was added to 'inhabitant of the Netherlands'. The publicity around this case raised interest in the issue of female suffrage, and led to the establishment of the 'Vereeniging voor Vrouwenkiesrecht' (Organisation for Women's Suffrage) in 1894.

In the end, women got the vote as part of the 'pacification' deal, rather than because of any mass support from male MPs. From this time on, however, women became important targets as potential voters. There was no conscious policy to nominate women for political positions, even though parties had women's wings whose main task was to educate women voters and mobilise them into becoming party members. Women entered parliament only very slowly and during this period their representation was never higher than seven per cent.

Who were these pioneers in Dutch politics? Some background characteristics are shown in Table 7.1.

The few women in the Parliament at that time were most respectable. They were often from an upper (middle) class family, with a university degree, unmarried, and childless. For the party élite which nominated the parliamentary candidates, mothers were unacceptable choices; this was especially true of the religious parties. The majority of the women MPs were lawyers or teachers before becoming a parliamentarian. Only two women are represented in the Senate and no women are to be found in the pre-war cabinets.

Table 7.1
Background characteristics of male and female MPs, 1918-1946

	Men		Women	
	%	N	%	N
Social Class (profession father) : high	47.5	295	76.9	13
Mother Member of a political party : yes	57.3	124	66.7	12
Mean age when entering*	45.4	216	46.6	13
Education : university	44.6	303	53.8	13
Marital Status : married	100.0	5†	50.0	6
Children : yes	100.0	3	16.7	6

* in years
† only in a few instances do we know whether MPs were married or had children
Source: Leijenaar, 1989, pp. 142-52.

1946-mid-seventies: the tokens

The first change in attitude towards the political integration of women occurred immediately after the Second World War, mainly inside the religious parties. Traditionally these parties had criticised women's participation in the public sphere more than the other parties had. Because of the duties many women had performed during the war, when most men were absent, and also because of their role in the resistance, their exclusion from political office became a source of some embarrassment. Besides, the (Catholic) women themselves took a firm stand against being relegated back to the kitchen. In 1946 they established the Catholic Women's Group ('Katholiek Vrouwen Dispuut') with strong ties to the Catholic Party and petitioned the party to select women for the representative bodies.

In this second period the representation of women did not rise above ten per cent, but more parties felt obliged to nominate at least one woman. The practice of appointing a token woman became even more apparent In the cabinets of the time. The first woman ever appointed was a Catholic junior minister, Mrs. Anna de Waal in 1953. In seven of the eight cabinets formed between 1953 and 1972 there was always one woman acting as a minister or junior minister. In the cabinet governing from 1956-1958 there were two women.

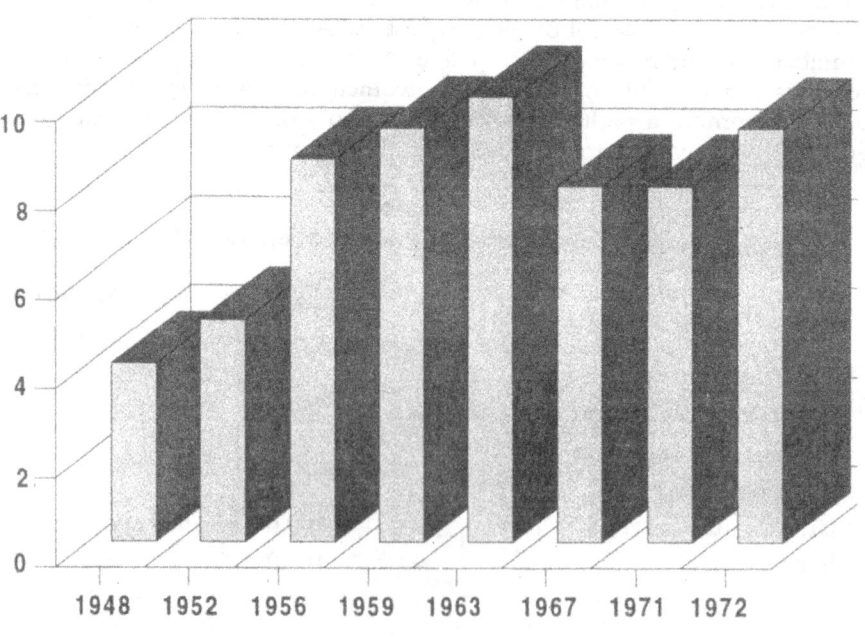

Figure 7.1
Percentage of women in Parliament, 1946-1975

As in the first period, although the parties regarded the generality of women as housewives and mothers, they preferred their female MPs to be unmarried and childless.

Women were present within the parties and representative bodies on the basis of a very restricted gender-identity (Velde 1994, p. 374). In 1956, for example, 4 of the 13 women MPs participated in the committee for Social Work and Culture and 3 of them in the committee for Justice. The other committees in which women took part were those for Education and Social Affairs (Leijenaar 1989, p. 171).

1977-1990 : the group representatives

The mid-seventies mark a turning point in the political representation of women in the Netherlands. The Dutch political system had been confronted in the 1960s with developments such as depillarisation and secularisation, as well as with a growing demand for more political influence and a less paternalistic, more open, attitude on the part of the political elite. In the late sixties women's groups were also emerging, pursuing equal rights for men and women. The combination of these demands for more participation and for equal rights turned out to be a strong catalyst in the fight for equal political representation. After the elections in 1977, for example, the percentage of women MPs increased from 9 per cent to 14 per cent and four women junior ministers and one woman minister were appointed in the cabinet formed in 1977. From that time on the debate focused primarily on the question of how - not whether - to increase the participation of women in politics.

How can we explain this change in attitude, the fact that within political parties, women's organisations and within the government the political representation of women by women became more and more an issue?

From the late 1960s on the new women's movement gave rise to many different organisations. On the one hand there were the traditional women's organisations which regarded themselves as non-political; on the other hand, there were the feminist groups more concerned with defining a woman's world. This pattern changed in the late eighties. More women's groups became involved with increasing the numbers of women in politics, realising the need for governmental and parliamentary support to their cause. Many activists worked in the women's wings of the political parties and participated in the internal party discussions on gender equality. At the end of the seventies and beginning of the eighties the women's wings in PvdA, CDA and in the smaller left-wing parties were active pressure groups. In general they assumed a much more radical stance than their parties on issues regarding women, which on some occasions brought the women's wing into conflict with the other party bodies.

Outside the formal political arena, there was the Dutch Association for Women's Interests ('Nederlandse Vereniging voor Vrouwenbelangen') which, since its founding in 1894, has argued for the political empowerment of women. In the 1980s they started a campaign 'M/V - 50/50' mobilising voters to vote for women candidates and lobbying parties to nominate more women for the electoral bodies. But it took until the 1990s before all the different women's groups that were actively striving for a gender balance in political decision making combined their efforts.

In the Netherlands the government has played a crucial role in creating the present positive attitude towards the political integration of women. As part of its overall policy on women, the government has worked to increase female political participation. A committee was installed in 1982, consisting of women from the women's movement as well as civil servants from several ministries, whose task was to draw up an Emancipation Policy Programme for 1985-1990. This Programme has formed the touchstone for all subsequent government emancipation policies.

The Policy Programme recognises that there is a structural imbalance of power relations between women and men, which is rooted in Dutch society. Women have fewer opportunities than men do. The Programme is meant to prepare for a plural society in which everyone has the opportunity to lead an independent existence irrespective of their sex or marital status and in which women and men have equal rights, opportunities, freedom and responsibilities.

From the mid-1980s the advancement of women in politics and public administration has been one of the main aims of the governments' emancipation policy. Successive governments have financed large research projects, both quantitative and qualitative, that try to account for the limited political representation of women. On the basis of these results it has been possible to outline concrete strategies. At the same time, the government has put pressure on the parties to nominate more women. Because of the constitutional autonomy of political parties, the government has hesitated to interfere directly, but they offered financial support to each political party represented in Parliament, under the condition the money was used for activities aiming to increase the number of women in the electoral bodies. All parties, with the exception of a small orthodox Calvinist party, accepted the money and most parties used it to hire someone for three years in charge of formulating affirmative action strategies. Two other orthodox parties, who do not subscribe to the governments' policies on gender equality, used the money for training (Leijenaar 1993, p. 226).

Thanks to this governmental initiative, the main parties now have so-called Positive Action Plans, which carry facts and figures about the participation of women in the party, as well as many concrete recommendations for increasing this participation.

Within the parties the women's wings put a lot of pressure on the party leadership to nominate women both for the representative bodies and for internal party bodies. Several women's wings were able to persuade the party to accept quotas. In 1977, for example, the Labour Party adopted a recommendation to appoint at least 25 per cent women to all the party boards and on the candidate lists. Some small left wing parties also flirted with quotas. In short, the women's wings have kept the issue of the under-representation of women on the agenda of the national executives of the parties (Velde 1994, pp. 314-22).

In this period the emphasis has been less on gender differences than on the premise that sex should no longer be grounds for differentiation. Equality policies as well as those aimed at increasing women's political participation, all start from the position that women are currently discriminated against and neglected, but not that they are different.

The main arguments for a more balanced participation between women and men in political decision-making refer to equality between the sexes as a founding principle of Dutch law, to the democratic principle which recognises women's rights to full citizenship, and to the notion that these rights must be reflected in the effective participation of women at all levels of political life. It was also argued that there cannot be a true democracy if women are excluded from positions of power (Ministerie van BiZ. 1992, p. 5). The affirmative action policies show that women politicians are viewed as representatives of their group: the other half of the population. Although scholars of gender studies were involved in debates about the definition of women's interests and argued that these interests should be defended and articulated by women politicians, political parties and the government were mostly concerned with statistics.[1]

1990s : the players

A group becomes significant when it reaches a critical mass of 30-35 per cent. In 1990 the percentage of women MPs was 28 and with the elections of 1994 it increased to 32 per cent (see Figure 7.2). In the 1990s, women are no longer treated as victims, as neglected human beings in need of special treatment. More and more political parties and policy makers are recognising that having more women in their midst may be an asset for the organisation. Taking ideas from management and organisation studies, the selectors of political personnel assume that having more women will bring about a different atmosphere and a change in focus, in short, give a fresh perspective to politics and decision-making at a time of a declining interest in (party) politics.

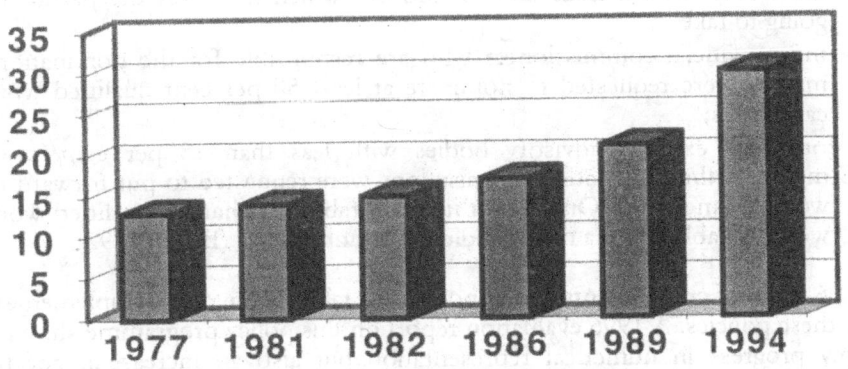

Figure 7.2
Percentage of women in Parliament, 1977-1994

This change in attitude among party leaders can be seen from the selection criteria that parties now use to choose their candidates. In the past a common route to political office was to gain experience through working (voluntarily) for the party. A long period of party service and party activism used to be essential steps on the road to the legislature (Hillebrand 1992, p. 290; Koole 1992, p. 306). However, with the election of 1994 coming up, the larger parties explicitly acknowledged the need to look for more women and younger candidates. Long and faithful party service no longer guarantees selection and there seems to be more room for political amateurs. Ties with interest organisations or specific professional experience have become more important attributes for office-seeking candidates. All these changes in the selection criteria have facilitated the nomination of women. An illustrative example is the reform the D'66 party introduced in the 1994 election. Regardless of a candidate's place on the D'66-list, if he or she gets at least 25 per cent of the votes one needs for election (0.67 per cent of the total valid vote) this person will be automatically become part of the parliamentary party.[2] Again, this regulation will be favourable to the election of women candidates, because in general they get more preference votes than do male candidates (Leijenaar 1989, p. 42).

In 1992 the Dutch government decided to take additional measures to raise the percentage of women in politics and public office. In a specific policy programme submitted by the cabinet and accepted by parliament, targets were set for increasing the relative number of women in the representative bodies, as well as advisory bodies, and for an absolute increase of the number of women mayors. To reach these targets 19 concrete measures were set out. To name a few:

- the Ministry of Internal Affairs would monitor the participation of women in politics and public administration. Every year statistics would be published and sent to the parliament, together with an analysis of the progress made;
- regular talks with the party leaderships were announced to discuss the importance of the issue and to find out which measures the parties were going to take;
- the provincial commissioners who are responsible for the nomination of mayors were requested to nominate at least 50 per cent qualified women candidates;
- for those external advisory bodies with less than 15 per cent women members the nominating organisations were requested to put forward only women candidates. Only when it was established that no qualified women were available could a male candidate be nominated. (Bi.Zn. 1992).

A team of civil servants was appointed to take charge of the implementation of these policies. A 1996 evaluation report on this policy programme shows not only progress in numerical representation, but also an increase in 'goodwill' with regard to the empowerment of women (Leijenaar 1996a). In 1996 a second policy programme was published by the Ministry of Internal Affairs announcing further measures and new targets for the years 1996-2000 (Ministerie van Bi. Zn. 1996).

Immediately after the disappointing outcome of the municipal elections of 1990, when the percentage of female candidates increased by only three per cent, some regional women's bureaus and the Netherlands Association for Women's Interests decided to found an association for Women in Politics ('Vrouwen in de Politiek, VIP'), which would coordinate all future activities. A total of 29 organisations joined the Association including five women's wings, three black and migrant organisations, the regional women's bureaus and several training institutes. In the three years of their existence many activities were arranged, from training sessions for women interested in becoming a local councillor, to seminars explaining the objective of the campaign. They have also published a good deal - two booklets, for example, one about equality policy at the local level and one with facts and figures about the political participation of women and interviews with women councillors. Three of these activities have been subsidised by the government: the launch of the campaign, the publications and a theatre play on the subject.

All these activities helped to keep the issue on the political agenda, but the campaign did not lead to an increase in the local representation of women, partly because the Labour Party and the Christian Democratic Party, large parties which do take the selection of women candidates seriously, lost in many municipalities. Many seats went to so-called local lists, parties without a national organisation and therefore without any policy obligation to select women. The comparison with the national level, where an increase of more than six per cent women MPs took place in the same year, shows that in this period, when it is no longer necessary to convince people of the right of women to get elected, actions of governments and party leadership directed to influence the selection procedures are more effective than awareness-raising campaigns by women's organisations.

Overview

In each period different reasons have been given for selecting women to political positions. In the first period there was no conscious activity to select women as MPs. Only 'acceptable' women were chosen by the party leadership, which meant unmarried, upper-class and highly educated women. In the second period parties accepted that they should select at least one woman in the parliamentary party or cabinet. Those women were expected to defend and articulate women's interests, then defined as the interests of mothers and housewives. From the mid-seventies on, the under-representation of women in political decision-making became an issue on the agenda of parties, women's organisations and the government. When half of the population is consistently underrepresented, the legitimacy of existing political structures might very well be called into question. Women's organisations insisted that women are more aware of their own needs and interests and are therefore better able to press for them. In the final period, the 1990s, many have argued that any gender imbalance in political decision-making is an inefficient use of human resources. Women comprise half the world's pool of potential talent and ability and their participation in politics would maximise the human and material resources of the state, for the common good. Alternatively, it is said that women will bring a fresh perspective to politics and decision-making (Leijenaar 1996; Outshoorn 1984; Sapiro 1981).

The Netherlands in comparative perspective

Are the trends described here for the Netherlands unique, or are they part of a common pattern in the European Union? Across the European Union national governments as well as of inter- and transnational organisations are reaching consensus on the need for equity. In most of the 14 other EU countries there is a certain willingness in both state and society to promote and implement policy initiatives that would allow a more equitable distribution of economic, social and political resources between men and women. Concern about the persistent low representation of women in politics can be found in many documents as well as in policy programmes Of the European Union. Two other EU countries (Sweden and Belgium) have their own explicit policy plans which aim to achieve a more balanced representation of women in political decision-making. Sweden is a front runner not only with respect to the numerical representation of women in politics, but also in mainstreaming, that is, integrating a gender perspective in general (mainstream) policies and activities. An example is a course on the importance and meaning of gender in Swedish society which all Swedish ministers and junior ministers are compelled to take. Belgium is the only country with legislation demanding that by 1999 parties have 33 per cent female representation in the parliament.[3]

Figures from 1997 show us (see Table 7.2) that the three Scandinavian countries Sweden, Finland and Denmark have the highest number of women in their parliaments at 33 per cent to 40 per cent, followed by the Netherlands, Austria, Germany and Spain. For the Upper Chamber we find the highest percentage in the Netherlands (23 per cent). In Belgium and Austria the proportion of women is 22 and 21 respectively.

Table 7.2
Women's participation in political decision making (in percentages)

Country	Date women won the right	Date of most recent election	% Women in Lower	% Women in Upper
Belgium	1948	1995	12	22
Denmark	1915	1994	33	-
Germany	1919	1994	26	19
Greece	1952	1996	25	-
Spain	1977	1993	16	13
France	1944	1997	11	6
Ireland	1922	1997	13	13
Italy	1945	1996	11	8
Luxembourg	1918	1994	20	-
Netherlands	1919	1994	31	23
Austria	1919	1995	27	21
Portugal	1975	1995	13	-
Finland	1906	1995	33	-
Sweden	1919	1994	40	-
United Kingdom	1928	1997	18	7

Table 7.3
Women's participation in European Cabinets, European Parliament, Regions and Local Councils (in percentages)

Country	Date of formation	Govt	European Parliament	Regional Parliame	Local Counci
Belgium	1995	12	32	18	20
Denmark	1994	35	44	31	28
Germany	1994	16	36	26	22
Greece	1995	4	16	‡	4
Spain	1994	18	33	16	11
France	1995	13	30	12	17
Ireland	1994	17	27	*	14
Italy	1995	8	13	7	22
Luxembourg	1994	17	33	*	10
Netherlands	1994	35	32	*	22
Austria	1994	24		20	‡
Portugal	1991	10	8	9	11
Finland	1995	39		*	30
Sweden	1994	50		48	41
United Kingdom	1992	7	18	*	‡

Sources: Panorama: European Network Women in Decision-making, European Commission 1995; IPU: Parline, Inter Parlementarian Union, source: Internet, 15 June 1997.

‡ : no data available
* : no regional government

The average proportion of women cabinet ministers in the 15 Member States is 16 per cent; of the 537 members of government (figures are from 1996) there are 84 women. There are four front runners: Sweden has a balanced government of 50 per cent men and 50 per cent women and in Finland, Denmark and the Netherlands, more than a third of cabinet members are women. There seems to be a correlation between a low percentage of women MPs and the number of women cabinet members: in Greece, Italy, Portugal and the United Kingdom less than ten per cent of government members are women. At this moment there is no woman prime minister in Europe, but there are four women heads of state: Ireland has an elected woman president while Denmark, the United Kingdom have, like the Netherlands, a queen as their hereditary head of state.

Interestingly enough, compared with the national parliaments, we find a far higher representation of women in the European Parliament. In nine of the 15 Member States one third of the Euro-delegation are women. Eleven Member States have elected more than 25 per cent women to the European Parliament. The differences are striking for countries such as Greece and France, where the representation of women in the European Parliament is double the figure for their national parliaments. The representation of women at the regional and local level fluctuates for most countries between 10-20 per cent. At one end of the scale is Sweden, with more than 40 per cent women in the regional and local councils; at the other, Greece with only 4 per cent women councillors. The suggestion that it is easier for women to enter local councils than the national assemblies, because eligibility criteria are less stringent and because, since these are not full-time jobs, council positions are easier to combine with rearing children, seems to be true for countries like Belgium and France. In the other Member States more women can be found at a higher level of political decision-making, perhaps because it is easier to use affirmative action policies given the more centralised candidate selection procedures used in these countries.

1990s : women in social organisations

There are several reasons why we should extend our analysis into this area of power. In the Netherlands decision-making structures are closely connected, consisting as they do not only of representative bodies, advisory committees and the bureaucracy, but also of all kinds of special interest organisations and voluntary groups. Social organisations influence policy by putting pressure on the government, but also because they help implement the policies themselves (Mierlo 1989, p. 127). Furthermore, now that political parties are less popular, social organisations have started to take over as intermediaries between politicians and citizens. In the Netherlands less than 3 per cent of the electorate are members of a party, while 30 per cent of those 18 years and older are involved in one way or another with a social or voluntary organisation (SCP 1988, 1989). Likewise, debate on the caring and responsible society now often centres on the role of voluntary organisations. According to, for example, the

Christian Democratic Party, a large number of caring tasks, for example in the field of health, should not be provided by the state, but by society itself.

Regarding these three perspectives for looking at social organisations: the importance of social relations, the provision of care and services, and the representation of interests, the role of women in social organisations is most often mentioned in relation to care and services. Traditionally women have been very active in voluntary work, particularly in organisations linked to the service industry. Compared to the formal political institutions, other recruitment mechanisms are at work here. First of all social organisations, although they can represent certain groups of people, do not represent national, regional or local electorates with 50 per cent women among them. Second, the criteria for nominating people for the boards are often more specific than is the case with political posts. For certain organisations, knowledge about sea cargo or traffic flows (for example) may be necessary. Third, social organisations are even more autonomous than parties so that government cannot interfere so easily.

In this section I report on a study conducted in 1992, showing the relatively low number of women board members of social organisations (Leijenaar and Niemoller 1994). In the over 4100 nationally based social organisations, one fifth of the board members are women, a somewhat lower figure than in the political bodies. Large differences in the representation of women can be found between organisations:

- in 38 per cent of the organisations there are no women at all, while in 4 per cent we find only women in the board. Very few women can be found in organisations belonging to the economic sector, the military, transport and the agrarian sector. 'Women only' organisations have a specific feminist objective ;
- organisations with a commercial objective have fewer women in their boards (average of 3 per cent); the highest representation (23 per cent) can be find in idealistic and non-commercial organisations;
- religious organisations have, with an average of 25 per cent, more women in their boards;
- organisations with fewer members have relatively fewer women board members (11 per cent);
- organisations recruiting board members by open application have relatively more women board members: 35 per cent (Leijenaar and Niemoller 1994, p. 257).

Why so few?

Confronted with the question why there are only 20 per cent women in the boards of these organisations, the answers of the respondents of the social organisations are very similar to the answers given by politicians when they were asked the same questions ten years before (Leijenaar and Niemoller 1983). More than 50 per cent of the women refer to the gender division of labour: women take care of the children and the house and often have a part-time job outside the home, meaning there is hardly any time left for other social activities. A second barrier is that very few women can be found in high-level jobs and it is from these jobs that board members are often recruited. Thirty-five per cent of those asked think that women are too modest and do not stress their own distinctive assets. The other side of the story, according to 16 per cent of the interviewed women, is that men are more ambitious and accept a board membership because it furthers their career. According to 11 per cent of the respondents, men view women as different and will therefore not invite them to participate in these boards. Eighteen per cent remark that men look for successors in their own networks (Leijenaar and Niemoller 1994).

While the political sector has, at least since the 1980s, generally acknowledged that gender is one of the selection criteria, the majority of interviewed women stated they have been selected to the board because of their competence in the field of the organisation. It helps, though, when one has at one's disposal certain characteristics such as being enthusiastic, being a good communicator and being oriented towards problem solving. The majority of women say that gender has played no role at all, for or against their selection; three quarters claim that a woman can become a chair of a board as easily as a man (Leijenaar and Niemoller 1994).

It appears that the women interviewed do not think of themselves as representatives of their gender. They carry out these jobs because they are an expert in a certain field. As is the case with the formal political institutions, an important cause of the relatively low participation rate is the selection criteria. Selectors look around for their successors in their own networks and business circles, whether or not these contain any women.

Concluding remarks

Eighty years ago women in the Netherlands gained the right to be elected in the parliament. At the first elections for which women could stand, one woman was elected for the Labour Party but it was not until 1943 that party leaders appointed a woman as a junior minister. Now, after the 1994 elections, one-third of the cabinet and of the parliament are women. Thanks to the activities of women's organisations, women's wings and the government, the political parties, still the main selectors of political personnel, have acknowledged the demand for a gender balance in political decision-making and have acted accordingly, often with success.

We know much less, however, about the role of women in social organisations. Although these organisations have always played a very important role in Dutch politics, and should therefore be important objects of study, not much research is available. From a 1992 study we know that 20 per cent of those involved on the boards of social organisations are women.

What is the future of women's political participation? In politics, power relations are notoriously resistant to change. Getting more women into political decision-making entails a redistribution of power, and we have seen from past experience that men cannot be expected to give up their positions voluntarily and promptly. On the other hand, however, many policies to increase the number of women in politics and public administration have been implemented and gender is taken into account when recruiting officers for boards or other governing bodies. In the political bodies, women used to be selected because of the group they represented, while in the social organisations expertise was more important. In the future we can expect that two other arguments will encourage the hiring of women in decision-making positions. Demographic developments will increase the demand for female workers and at the same time there is greater acknowledgement about the distinctive contribution that women can make in leadership positions. Maybe soon enough women, for the first time in history, can be real players.

Notes

1. For a good overview of this debate, cf. Oldersma 1996, pp. 55-64; Leijenaar and Velde 1989.
2. The majority of votes (about 70-80 per cent) are cast for the first person on the list.
3. The Belgian law of 24 November 1994 imposes a minimum percentage of candidates of the same sex. For elections taking place between 1996 and 1999 party lists must have 25 per cent women candidates. After 1999 the percentage must be 33.

8 Furthering the 'cause': femocrat strategies in national government

Joyce Outshoorn

When interviewed on the major achievements of the women's public policy unit within the Dutch national government, shortly before the cabinet change of 1994, a senior femocrat reflected:

> Successes since 1978? [JO:yes] mmm ... that there's a decent bureaucratic network, with the effect that people who want to undertake action have access to do so ... it is important for the women's movement that it relies on institutions that others have made, such as women's education centres, funding, frames of reference ... the fact that we have done this groundwork and created an image of how things can be, means that any time there's an impetus to do something within the bureaucracy, people have some sort of lever.

Setting up a nationwide apparatus for change, institutionalising women's groups, providing subsidies for feminist projects, and altering the accepted frames of reference ... in a nutshell this quotation sums up the directions taken by what Australian feminists have dubbed the 'femocrat strategy', namely, the system by which feminists enter government in order to further the cause of equity for women. This phenomenon has occurred in many of the post-industrial democracies of the western world. 'Femocrats' were by-products of the rise of 'state feminism' in the seventies, as governments tried to meet the challenges posed by the resurgent women's movement. In the Netherlands, the government even developed a 'national machinery' (the term coined by the UN to designate institutions charged with the betterment of women's status, cf. Stetson and Mazur 1995a, p. 3) to accommodate the demands women articulated. Initially, this 'machinery' lacked personnel, and many feminists entered government bureaucracy precisely to fill the gap. For the purposes of my research I have used the term 'femocrat' for all those civil servants working within the government to develop and implement policies advancing women's demands. Whether they identified themselves as feminists was one of the central questions I sought to answer in the course of my research (Outshoorn 1994).

The rise of 'state feminism' has raised a series of questions about whether the state can in fact be used as an instrument of feminist activism, through the inclusion of gender issues in national policy agendas and by the access to public power it allows feminist advocates. If the apparatus of government can be so used, it would seem to open up new possibilities for women to participate fully as citizens of modern welfare states. State 'femocracy' has the potential of enhancing participation in a double sense. Not only can femocrats advance the cause of women's participation in politics by pressing for more balanced representation of women in public life (as, for example, through sponsoring female appointments or supporting female lobby groups), but they can also expand the very arena of women's participation by making a range of general policy issues gender issues. In other words, several existing issues can be redefined in terms of gender, thereby giving women's advocacy groups access to government and justifying their inclusion in policy decisions from which they would formerly have been excluded (Stetson and Mazur 1995b).

This line of inquiry differs from the customary approaches in political science to the 'women and politics' issue, and is to be distinguished from the research on the presence of women in representative bodies or on their political participation and electoral behaviour. It should be distinguished, likewise, from the matter of women in organisations or feminist discussions of bureaucracies - although we cannot ignore these facts and theories when we come to consider just how femocrats operate within bureaucratic contexts such as national government. Through my analysis of the state feminist or femocrat phenomenon, I hope to establish that femocrats have succeeded in expanding the scope for women's participation. They have done so by creating spaces in which women's issues can be addressed, by providing the skills necessary for getting women's issues addressed, and by attempting to take gender issues into (or sometimes out of) policy debates.

Recent scholarship is agreed that the femocrats have shaped the course of contemporary Dutch society in several crucial respects (Eisenstein 1990, 1991a, 1991b; Franzway, Court and Connell, 1989; Outshoorn 1994, 1995, 1996a; Sawer 1990; Sawer and Groves 1994). Not only have the femocrats been exemplary for the degree of motivation and expertise they have brought to their own work, but they are also the major actors linking the women's movement organisations to parts of the government bureaucracy. Femocrats can signal wants and demands, and play a crucial role in their articulation. They can define issues in such a way that other civil servants will pay attention to them and act. In an earlier article on Dutch femocrats I showed that most femocrats working at the national level thought of themselves as allies to the women's movement, identified their own position as feminist, and often described themselves as brokers, missionaries or teachers who mediated between the movement and the government (Outshoorn 1994).

In this chapter I shall analyse how national femocrats and their policy unit, the 'Directorate for the Co-ordination of Equality Policy' (Directie Coordinatie Emancipatiebeleid - DCE), have developed strategies for enhancing the scope of women's politics, thus making for increased participation. In order to do so, I shall first explain how the 'national machinery' runs, and describe the three major strategies the DCE has deployed in its work: providing the basic philosophy and tenets of women's equality policy, developing intersectoral policy and setting up a strong women's movement network. Then I shall turn to the femocrats themselves and consider their thoughts on the directions being taken by the DCE. What has been effective - in their opinion? What are the problems of intersectoral policy? How do they envisage future femocrat strategies?

The context: the national machinery

The history of women's public policy in the Netherlands dates back to 1975, when the Emancipation Commission ('Emancipatiekommissie') was established by a national coalition cabinet in which the Social Democrat party dominated (Outshoorn 1995). It was formed to answer some the demands of Men-Women-Society, (MVM) the group at the forefront of the second wave of Dutch feminism, and, in part, to recognise (albeit tardily) the course set by the UN International Women's Year. The Emancipation Commission laid down the premises for future government policies on gender and set up the state 'machinery' to develop them. It translated the major feminist demands into moderate and comprehensible terms for civil servants, thereby providing the core of the first government 'White Paper' on women's equality, *Emancipation: Process of Change and Growth* (Handelingen, 1977). Men and women were to be free to shape their lives as they chose. To this end, femocrats promoted policies that would allow women to make up for lost opportunities, they widened the range of options open to both sexes and restated the importance of so-called feminist values and activities. It is a sign of the Commission's importance that the cabinet should have let outsiders - the majority of the Commission consisted of representatives of the women's movement and some feminist experts - develop policy instead of its own civil servants. One unintended and unwelcome consequence of this accommodation, however, was that the legitimacy of the enterprise was undermined in the first few years of its existence (Dijkstra and Swiebel 1982). Weakening too was the lack of any retraining programme among incumbent civil servants that might have guided them in devising policies for women.

As part of the new national machinery, a central policy unit within the Ministry of Culture, Recreation and Welfare was formed in 1978 - the Directorate for the Co-ordination of Equality Policy. As women's policy by definition overlapped several other policy areas the DCE was intended from the start to be intersectoral, that is, to co-ordinate, activate and monitor policy in other departments. It was to be headed by a state secretary at cabinet level, the first of whom was appointed in 1977. In later years a cabinet minister sometimes took over the reins. In 1981 the DCE was relocated to the Ministry of Social Affairs, reflecting a shift in basic tenets of its policy, which now held economic independence to be the central issue for women. Later that year the

Emancipation Commission was succeeded by the Emancipation Council ('Emancipatieraad'), the official advisory body to government on women's issue, which was to be consulted on major policy issues concerning women. The national machinery reached its apex in 1986 with the establishment of a Cabinet Committee for women's policy, chaired by the prime minister and functioning as a gatekeeper to the cabinet itself. This achievement, however, concealed a number of problems. From the late seventies it had become government policy that the principles of gender equality should be integrated into the practices of all its departments. This process sooner or later was bound to call into question the existence of the DCE itself, as what was left to them when other departments and ministries assumed their responsibilities? Fierce debates were held within the department and the ministry. An outside consultancy firm was called in to resolve them and in 1993-4 a new set of objectives were drawn up. I interviewed femocrats from the unit over this period. The changes that were taking place made them keenly aware of the link between the women's movement and the unit, the strategy of the unit and its achievements. In the meantime the Cabinet Committee had been abolished in 1989 and the Parliamentary Standing Committee disappeared after the last elections in 1994. Moreover, the Emancipation Council was dissolved in 1997.

After the national elections of 1994, the new Socialist Minister of Social Affairs and Employment took charge of women's policy himself. One of his first deeds was to appoint an outsider as the new head of the DCE, a former parliamentary leader of the Green Left party who had no previous involvement with the women's movement or indeed with the civil service. At the end of 1995 a new policy 'White Paper' was produced which signalled a shift in DCE strategy that affects both the femocrats working there and the network of women's movement groups the DCE has helped to develop in the past. I shall return to this point later.

In the course of its existence the DCE developed three major strategies for attaining its policy aims. First of all, it produced regular policy papers which laid out the groundwork for women's equality in the Netherlands. Various cabinets have based all of their women's policy on these papers. In the early years the papers emphasised freedom of choice, changing mentalities and consciousness-raising. When the DCE was relocated within the Ministry of Social Affairs and Employment, the emphasis of its policy shifted to economic independence for women, making entitlement to social security and access to paid employment the primary issues. At the same time the issue of sexual violence took on a new prominence. The landmark 1985 'White Paper' (Beleidsplan 1985) argued that equality could only come about through structural change, both of the traditional division of labour between men and women and of received notions of femininity and masculinity. More recently, however, as cabinets have sought to cut welfare costs, women's policy has effectively been reduced to labour market policy. This shift is compatible with the social democratic analysis of women's status, which locates inequality within the division of labour between the sexes (Outshoorn 1996b).

Secondly, the DCE endeavoured to implement intersectoral policy. Unfortunately, it has not always proved easy to convince other departments of the need to address women's issues. However, the DCE's work has not been wholly ineffective, for they have been able to influence a considerable number of debates and have convinced some departments to devise policies that take women's needs and demands into account. Success has been most apparent in the areas of education, health, sexual violence and equal rights (Outshoorn 1995). The DCE has managed to set the agenda on migrant women's issues and on the vexed topic of sexual harassment. On the debit side of the ledger, they have failed to shape debates on socio-economic policy, in particular as regards women's rights to social security. In later years, when the difficulties of intersectoral policy have been most apparent, many feminists have criticised the decision to be intersectoral at all. But it followed naturally from the definition of 'women's policy' as something that impinged on all other policy areas, and, in any case, the dominant government approach to all complex issues at this time was almost always intersectoral.

Thirdly, the DCE has given the women's movement a strong institutional backbone by funding a huge variety of women's initiatives and groups. Even during the substantial budgetary cuts of the eighties and early nineties, the DCE finances have remained relatively stable. The unit has provided about forty million guilders each year in setting up and maintaining what in policy jargon is called the 'women's public policy support structure': the network of women's service centres, policy bureaus and funded women's groups. This strategy was launched in the late seventies through the formation of a number of provincial and local women's bureaus intended to support women's groups at the grass roots level. Criticised at first by many feminists as examples of 'co-optation', they were later embraced enthusiastically when the advantages of providing money for new initiatives, such as lobbying for women's issues, setting up new networks, continuity and better services became apparent. The DCE also provided many subsidies for women's projects aimed at a national audience. These included women's cinema, women's publishing, dozens of conferences and small businesses. One of the most effective innovations has been the 'emancipation worker', an equal-rights officer working on women's issues in non-governmental organisations funded by the DCE, who raises consciousness about women's position and develops women's equality projects within these organisations. Women have done this work in organisations as diverse as the National Sports Federation and the national broadcasting company. The DCE has also been very effective in helping to establish women's studies within the universities by means of an independent grants commission that funds research projects for 800,000 guilders per annum over a period of six years.

One of the DCE's most valuable functions has been to back women's groups which set up feminist service projects. Rape crisis centres, women's health groups, women's adult education centres, projects for women returning to the labour market and migrant women's groups all received strong financial support in the eighties. As career feminists have increasingly taken over from volunteers, there has been a greater degree of professionalisation, and a sharper division of labour among the various groups. One drawback, however, has been the decline of debate within the women's movement; there no longer is a common platform, both metaphorically and organisationally, on which pressing women's issues can be discussed. Over the last years the DCE has followed a policy of concentrating its numerous subsidised ventures into a limited number of institutions and persuading other ministries to provide the funding. Thus the women's legal centre is now funded by the Ministry of Justice, the women's health institute by the Ministry of Health, Welfare and Sports.

State provision of funding has made for continuity in organisation and the institutionalisation of new initiatives. In this way the DCE created its own clientele and its own legitimacy (Outshoorn 1995, p. 177). It has unquestionably cultivated feminist expertise and given feminists access to a number of policy areas where they have been increasingly accepted by the 'normal' experts in the field. Inevitably, however, this elaborate network remains dependent on the state. Although the DCE has not hitherto suffered much from budgetary cuts, the process of concentrating the network has sped up recently, making for more state interference and control as well as the loss of feminist expertise in the policy areas involved.

The femocrats

When the DCE was set up in 1978, new staff members had to be recruited. They were initially selected from the staff of the Emancipation Commission or from its original base - the Ministry of Culture, Recreation and Welfare and its family policy unit. Over the years femocrats have come and gone, but two striking aspects of recruitment have remained quite constant. First of all, the number of self-professed feminists has been high. Many of the femocrats whom I interviewed two years ago mentioned that they had a background in the women's movement and that their views and relation to the women's movement were discussed during their job interview (Outshoorn 1994). According to several of the longer time employees, this has always been the case. Secondly, many of the femocrats did not have a civil service background prior to entering the DCE. Many came in by way of the feminist service projects or a women's bureau; only a handful were recruited from other departments. This recruitment policy was possible as the Dutch national bureaucracy allows for decentralised recruitment by departments. It meant that while femocrats were often unacquainted with bureaucratic procedure, they did have a definite 'feminist spirit'. Within the agency this spirit waxed and waned, as one of the senior civil servants who has been at the DCE from its early beginnings remarks:

> [Feminism] fluctuates here. We used to have a strong culture that you had to be really feminist, against compulsory heterosexuality and such ... and a number of people really wanted everything to be terribly ideologically correct, and then you see a stage when that recedes, that people come in who see their work here as part of their career, and then a generation walks in who seems to know all the basic feminist things by nature and you don't have to explain anything.

Most of the civil servants working within the unit would agree that feminism itself no longer leads to vehement debates among the staff. Some of the femocrats contend that this is because too few femocrats can debate on a high ideological level, and they ascribe the disappearance of major disagreement to the club being 'so fixated on practical action' that there is no longer any reason to discuss feminism. Others point out that debate usually focuses on very concrete issues which do not require ideological reflection. According to some, debate has become less attractive as by now everybody knows everybody else's point of view, so discussion has become boring. The 'state of the women's movement', however, is still a major topic, with very different opinions concerning its 'health'. Some maintain the movement is 'dead'; others are more optimistic. As one 'veteran' femocrat comments:

> The story about the movement being dead - no movement has been declared dead so often as the women's movement. I'd say it apparently has the capacity of a Lazarus!

In recent years methods of recruitment have changed. This is partly due to cuts in government spending which have limited external recruitment and encouraged internal mobility within the departments; but this has led to fewer feminists getting in. Some of my informants maintain that this effect is intentional, with the ministry trying to 'mainstream DCE'. Indeed, one of the leading senior civil servants in the unit explicitly told me that, 'naturally', she wants her civil servants to be able to read policy documents with a feminist eye on the consequences for women, but, 'first and foremost', she wants them to be 'just normal civil servants'. Even though the DCE has become more hierarchical that in former years, it is still characterised by an informal culture, with frequent contacts between junior and senior staff and direct access to the minister or state secretary in charge of women's equality policy. Juniors also have access to the minister when their particular policy area is under discussion. The unit was divided into three sections in the early nineties (for socio-cultural affairs, socio-economic policy and legal policy); their superiors and the heads of the department constitute the management team. Each staff member is also responsible for one ministry or sector, labelled by some as 'being the watchdog of the ministry of X' or by others, more neutrally, as being 'the contact'.

Reflections on strategies

As mentioned above, the position of the DCE and its femocrats became less secure in the early nineties as a result of the ongoing integration policies in other ministries. In the beginning, the DCE had been designed as a body that would encourage other departments to develop policy in their areas, and that would co-ordinate these policies and supervise future initiatives. Not having many formal powers of its own, the DCE was heavily dependent for its success on strong political leadership and a clear vision of what had to be done. No ministers or civil servants attached to other departments welcome trespassers on their own turf unless a more powerful colleague has the clout to coerce or convince them to carry out a certain policy. As one senior femocrat remarked:

> We're a small unit, but we have always been relatively powerful. Why? Because we knew what our political boss wanted. If you are aware of that, you can do a lot as a civil servant.

She goes on to point out that if the political bosses, who come and go, do not have any clear goals, others immediately divine this, and the influence of the unit is drastically curtailed. All senior femocrats subscribe to the view that political support is crucial, the more so when the policy is controversial, which many women's issues were. One's own minister can be used to tackle unwilling fellow ministers and senior civil servants, but only as a last resort. It has to be done subtly; it is seldom possible to give an ultimatum along the lines of 'well, it's cabinet policy so if your permanent secretary is obstructing, I'll let my minister know and then yours will have some explaining to do!'

To counter the dangers of total integration, the DCE came up with two counter-strategies. First, there are now bilateral talks at the ministerial level aimed at monitoring how effectively integrative policy in other departments is being carried out. Second, when a new policy is being developed, there is now a standard procedure for assessing its effect on gender issues. Later in this chapter I shall return to examine how far the position of the DCE, and thus a major part of the femocrat strategy, has been safeguarded.

How do the femocrats themselves feel about these various strategies? What do they consider their own 'success stories'. When I put these questions to them, nearly all came up with a number of examples, both positive and negative, of how these strategies have worked in practice. Many needed no prompting on this score, although a couple started sighing:

> Pfff, those aren't things I have prepared and ready. That's difficult [JO: you've been around for some time] Civil servant: Yeah, you have to be able to line up a whole row of successes, sure, what did others say? [JO: others came with long lists] Civil servant (sighing): They would.

Roughly speaking, the successes fell into two categories: substantive issues and the institutionalisation of the policy network. Sexual violence was the most outstanding example of the substantive issues, being mentioned by nearly everybody. The DCE picked up various aspects of this issue, which had been politicised by the feminist movement in the late seventies, at a very early stage, organising a high-level conference on the topic in 1982, and establishing it as a fundamental issue of women's equal rights policy in several policy papers, including the landmark one of 1985, which set the political agenda for the next ten years (Handelingen 1985). The role of the DCE in keeping the issue of sexual harassment before the public eye was especially important. Thanks to the strong ties between the women's movement and a number of its civil servants (Outshoorn 1994), the DCE was able to take the lead in bringing this issue into the government arena and implementing an effective policy for the government bureaucracy itself. Later, the DCE financed the first large-scale Dutch survey on the prevalence of both incest and violence against women in the home. From 1982 the issue of the traffic in women became part of the government agenda; the DCE has financed women's support groups on this issue and has been able to influence Dutch policy on it (Outshoorn 1996a).

Among the other substantive issues mentioned in the course of the interviews, civil servants emphasised affirmative action within the civil service itself, and changes in child-care policy, as well as less prominent issues such as women in technology and projects for black and migrant women. Many civil servants recalled various acts of equal rights legislation, although the length of time it took to have the bills made into law was often criticised. And several suspected that these reforms would have come about anyway, with or without their efforts, given the guidelines on equal treatment laid down by the EC (Outshoorn 1995). The first bill was passed into law in 1981; only in 1994 was a revision passed by Parliament which added a ban on discrimination on the grounds of sexual orientation, an amendment the women's movement and the DCE had always supported.

The other major achievements of the unit have undoubtedly been its success in creating a policy network, and setting the administrative machinery in motion. In this regard, the assessment of the senior femocrat quoted at the beginning of this chapter is quite typical. Basic policy documents are also said to have been crucial to the success of the DCE:

> Already the fact there's a policy paper, it's not being implemented everywhere, but it's there. It gives you something at hand, you can do something with it...It sounds a bit weird, but the production of policy papers has also been important. The 1985 Policy Plan, the 1992 Policy Programme, have been important steps forward. The fact we now have targets means you can hold others accountable. It's been toil and tears, but we've made progress across the whole range of government.

The building of the women's movement network in the areas of women's adult education, women's employment, women's health and women's shelters also figure prominently in the accounts given by the femocrats. They are well aware of the importance of the feminist expertise thus created. The relationship of the DCE to these projects is, however, often ambivalent. One civil servant, who herself worked in one of these service projects for some time, recalls that during the negotiations on funding 'they're always complaining about it not being enough, that it's too little'.

Now that the projects are being centralised and brought under the control of various government departments or integrated into other social services, the relationship has deteriorated further, creating an uncomfortable situation for a number of femocrats who fear the loss of feminist expertise but feel powerless to turn the tide. They regard the other ministries taking over the funding from the DCE as a victory for the feminist cause, but at the same time they know that in the future they will be powerless to intervene directly.

One pattern which emerged from the interviews is that while the younger femocrats were readier to mention concrete issues, the older and more senior ones tended rather to stress the importance of the national machinery and the policy network. All but one of the 'veterans' held forth on this issue. Some of the younger ones pointed to the policy programmes and the use they could make of these in their day-to-day work, and a couple of the senior ones still took great satisfaction in having been able to influence the Equal Treatment Bill and having taken the lead in the sexual harassment issue. From their responses, it is not possible to say whether the femocrats who considered themselves allies to the movement perceived 'success' in their work differently from the smaller group of 'regular civil servants'. Both groups acknowledged that it was of the first importance to have a properly institutionalised policy network, they agreed on the importance of funding women's projects, and they regarded the role taken by the unit in tackling the problem of sexual violence to have been a success story.

The debate on intersectoral policy

Over the years, then, the DCE has put equality issues into specific policies and set up a national apparatus to assist the women's cause in general, largely through its use of an intersectoral approach. As mentioned earlier, intersectoral strategies were adopted from the beginning to enhance women's status, because it was taken for granted that the 'woman question' impinged in some degree on all other policy areas. In practice this has meant that the DCE has acted as a central steering unit to co-ordinate policy across the various departments, while at the same time staying in contact with the rest of the national machinery such as the Emancipation Council, the women's movement and parliament when necessary. Like a spider in the web, the DCE lies at the centre of an elaborate network, exchanging information, guiding, co-ordinating and initiating policy. It provides a sort of 'helicopter view', in the words of one younger civil servant. Many feminists see their unit either as a 'motor', which gets things started in the bureaucracy and keeps business going or as a 'conscience', a reminder to others about women's issues:

> If you mean does it make a difference we are there, yes, because we function as a conscience. Like you just have to show your face and people immediately realise oh yeah, we have to do something about women. Often one doesn't have to do more than that.

This idea of a 'motor' or 'conscience' is linked to the assumption that other parts of government take little independent initiative, but that these can be encouraged or prodded into action by conversion and persuasion by the civil servants of the DCE. Femocrats subscribing to this view point out that in other departments the conditions for successful integration are lacking:

> If we weren't here any longer ... it would depend very much on coincidental situations or the right people on the right spot if something is to happen. Taking new initiatives ... departments do things because they have to, but really new things, building up contacts with the grass roots, that sort of thing, that would evaporate. I don't believe it is an autonomous process with its own dynamic that would go on, not at all.

In their opinion, the other departments lack the appropriate expertise:

> (In other departments) you meet enthusiastic people but often they don't know what you're talking about. And they don't have any vision how to anchor equality policy within their policy area.

Others point out that there has been an increase in the number of people in other departments and ministries who have shown themselves willing to take initiatives, or have worked out their own ideas on equality policy:

> One notices that in the department I watch there are really people by now, men too, who are prepared to pull their weight, and don't say 'you tell us', but who have their own ideas and back these with good arguments, now then I think what on earth can I still offer?

But the pessimist might observe that these people are often scattered across different organisations and areas, making it difficult to set up informal networks. Also, despite the cuts in government personnel, mobility is still common in the civil service, and staff regularly come and go, so that their successors must often be convinced or 'converted' from scratch.

For these reasons intersectoral policy has become a topic of much heated debate within the DCE. Letting go of the achievements of intersectoral policy would be a loss in the eyes of some:

> ...we worked really hard to break into that arena [of socio-economic policy - JO], now we have a position to ensure that all policy papers pass our way and we can place commas and sentences etc etc .... If we let go of intersectoral policy what will remain of the real gritty work ... one loses one's expertise, it's often about policies which are real brainteasers ... if you lose the insight into the process, then there's nothing one can do except give a yell from the outside, which then just will not be heard.

If intersectoral policy were to be given up, this kind of practical expertise, learned on the job, would simply wither away. At the same time she - like several others - believes that continuing the strategy of intersectoral policy is so over-stretching the capacities of the unit that new priorities are now inevitable. Seeing the unit as a motor or a conscience, metaphors often used by the older members of the DCE, is by this reckoning at once outdated and over-ambitious. Others, although highly critical of other departments and convinced that many of these continue to resist women's issues, feel that DCE policy should remain intersectoral. This brings us to the debate on the future of the femocrat strategy and of the DCE itself.

Future strategies

With the onset of integration, the position of the DCE had to be reconsidered. After an attempt by the permanent secretary of the Ministry to abolish the unit just before the 1994 elections, an enquiry was held on what the future of the DCE should be. It was decided that the DCE should be kept, but that some changes needed to be made. First and foremost, the unit had a public relations problem in that too few people were aware of its work and its value. It was recommended that in future the DCE should try to enhance its reputation through a different, more co-operative approach to interdepartmental politics. The present Minister of Social Affairs and Employment, who also is in charge of women's equality policy, is currently giving open support to the unit, and his choice for a new chief of the unit in 1994 is in line with the chosen strategy; the new head has a high public profile, if not a reputation as a feminist.

Less emphasis is now placed on intersectoral strategy. Instead, the unit is trying to make itself more 'visible' in order to increase its support within the bureaucracy and among those members of the political elite outside government. As is to be expected, several of the femocrats I interviewed are sceptical of this shift. Many are reluctant to relinquish the hard-fought positions of influence within other departments. In the words of one femocrat:

> The DCE is to become less threatening and to work more as a salesman ... (JO: which means?) A bit of a softer approach, a lot of information in brochures, lots of symposia, bringing people together, but less participation in formal negotiations in the decision-making structures ...

The changes call for a more 'market-oriented approach', with other civil servants (and perhaps women's groups) as the target groups. This is anathema to the critics of the new approach:

> Policy is not a product ... it's a lengthy process, waiting to see if you score if you didn't last time, it's often not very visible. But the priorities of the DCE have changed, and it no longer pays to work in this fashion anymore, now you have to adopt a high profile.

But others maintain that the DCE has to reset its priorities. By involving itself in all issues touching on women - an inevitable consequence of intersectoral policy - the DCE has reached saturation point. Quite simply, under the previous system the workload had become unmanageable. Some femocrats believe that higher visibility and a more diplomatic approach to other departments would in fact make the DCE and its policies more effective. As one remarked:

> we've made a real change in culture, from an approach accentuating ideology and activating to how we can convince others in their own terms and interests ... as the DCE we are now operating as a provider of services, like this is what we have to offer: we've got a suitcase, a toolkit, a lot of practical advice and sometimes some money.

Among the femocrats I interviewed, opinion was not strictly divided along generational lines. The most important factor seems to be how femocrats define what a professional civil servant is and what kind of expertise a femocrat needs. Whether a femocrat considers herself an ally of the women's movement or just a regular civil servant is beside the point. Tenure in the job, however, does seem to influence opinion; that is, the longer a femocrat has been a civil servant, the more likely she is to subscribe to the old ideal of a professional civil service creed with its distinctive ethos of expertise, perseverance, hard work, and keeping a low profile. It is not surprising that those who subscribe to this ideal, are the most opposed to a policy change which calls for a more flamboyant and public style. The most immediate effect of the debate has been a very high turnover since 1994; of the original group of fifteen senior femocrats I interviewed, nearly two-thirds have since left.

Conclusions

From the analysis of 'the femocrat strategy' in the Netherlands, we can conclude that it has been relatively successful compared to other nations (Stetson and Mazur 1995). But it would also appear that the foundations of this strategy have been seriously eroded in recent years. Its strength originally lay in its ability to utilise state subsidies for the development of strong feminist groups and services. The women's movement was thereby given a highly institutionalised network, co-ordinated by a unit that could, through its intersectoral approach, powerfully influence government policy making. Both the women's movement and the DCE were able to keep the women's issue on the political agenda and ensure that a number of substantive policy areas were addressed. The DCE's policy White

Papers set the standard for other ministries and although a number of these have been very slow in addressing women's status in their own sectors, the White Papers have provided the necessary support for those civil servants who were willing and able to take up the challenge. Government funding has allowed for the cultivation of feminist expertise and given access to women at many levels and sectors in society. The numbers and scope of women now participating in policy making have significantly increased.

But as we have seen, these achievements are now under threat because of the new policies of integration, which are bringing many femocrat initiatives under government control. As this process continues, feminist expertise may well be lost, and women may find it harder to get direct access to policy-making the loss of autonomy or to articulate new political demands. Moreover, the national machinery itself has already been partly dismantled. The Emancipation Council, the Ministerial Committee and the Parliamentary Standing Group for women's affairs have all been abolished. It remains to be seen if ministries will continue to take on many women's issues if there is no longer a 'watchdog' DCE. On the positive side, the unit has the support of a strong minister so that it is itself less at risk, but it is too early to say if the new strategy of higher visibility and new alliances will lead to more satisfactory outputs.

Of major importance for the future of the femocrat strategy are two current issues on the political agenda involving women's status and rights. First, labour policy being the top priority of the incumbent government, the issue of women's participation in the work force has taken on a new urgency (cf. Plantenga in this volume). When it was still labelled women's policy the opposition would always claim the state had no right to intervene in the private sphere and should not interfere with the division of labour in the family (Outshoorn 1996b). Now matters such as flexible working hours, part-time work and more liberal shopping hours - all matters many feminists have been demanding for years - have become defined as labour issues in which the state traditionally has a strong role, policies and laws that would have been unthinkable a few years ago have been out into practice. Secondly, family politics is back on the political agenda, thanks to the efforts of the Christian Democrats (cf. Bussemaker in this volume). Feminists were quick to point out that much of current family policy simply follows what they themselves had been recommending for years, above all the need to improve caring arrangements through the redistribution of paid and unpaid work among women and men. In this way the present government has been taking up femocrat issues. So it may well be that with the 'mainstreaming' of women's issues into all policy areas, women's status is now more firmly on the agenda than ever before. With the access for women in relevant policy arenas created by the femocrat strategies of the past and the now widely available feminist expertise, new windows of opportunity have opened which might well ensure further gains for women in the near future.

9 Can a woman be just like a man? The representation of women in the corporatist world in the Netherlands

Jantine Oldersma

For two generations after the introduction of passive and active voting rights for women in the Netherlands, in 1917 and 1919, only a small minority of women entered politics. From the 1970s onward, this situation has changed dramatically; women now make up around 25-40 per cent of most elected bodies. Progress has been slower in appointed positions. Advisory bodies are a case in point. In 1976, women accounted for only 5 per cent; by 1995 the figure was 16 per cent - a much smaller increase than in the elected bodies (cf. Leijenaar in this volume).

In these matters, the Netherlands still lags well behind the Scandinavian countries, Norway in particular. By the early seventies, for example, the Norwegian authorities were already implementing policies to get more women in committees and councils. Guidelines to ensure equal representation for men and women were brought out by the Netherlands in 1987 - Norway had adopted these as early as 1976. In 1981 and 1985 respectively, Norway and Denmark legislated that at least 40 per cent of council and committee members must be female. These policies have clearly been successful. Comparing the Scandinavian countries in 1984, Helga Maria Hernes found Norway to have the highest representation of women on committees, followed closely by Sweden and Denmark, while Finland and Iceland lag behind (Hernes 1984). Even the United Kingdom had an unexpectedly large number of women in its committees and councils by 1986, although the numbers of women parliamentarians continued to be very low (Lovenduski 1986b). Reports from Belgium indicate that there are still few women on its committees, in spite of a law introduced in 1990, compelling all organisations to propose a male and a female candidate for every vacant position. In 1996 an attempt was made to give this law more force (BKV. 1996-7).

Why should there be so few women in advisory bodies in The Netherlands? What kind of people are politicians looking for when they appoint advisers? What do persons who hold the positions stand for? To answer these questions, studies of women in the corporatist world initially relied on theorists of 'neocorporatism' to analyse the place of women in committee systems.[1] This led to the important insight that it is not only necessary to look at the position of women in organisations but also at the kinds of organisations that are invited to advise government. Theorists of 'neocorporatism', however, tend to overlook that governments can always wield their own power by choosing just which organisations get to be represented. Instead of problematising the relationship between social and political citizenship, theorists of 'neocorporatism' have sometimes obscured the dynamics of politics itself (cf. Siim 1994).

To broaden the scope of analysis I took a closer look at the central concepts governing the composition of advisory bodies and at the interplay of gender with these central concepts (cf. Bergquist 1995). Here I will briefly summarise discussions about the Dutch political system from an international perspective, and debates among Dutch politicians on the corporatist world. A survey of feminist research on key concepts of the corporatist system, namely, 'representation', 'expertise' and 'problem definition', will follow. Having outlined the theoretical considerations basic to my study, I will proceed to lay out my results and conclusions.

Consociationalism or corporatism

The network of councils to be consulted in different stages of the process of making and implementing policy in The Netherlands has been extensively studied and commented upon. The distinct characteristics of small European states had been largely neglected in the writings of political scientists, until, in the course of the 1970s and 1980s, they became the focus of two lines of analysis: the theme of 'consociational democracy' and that of 'neo-corporatism'. In both research traditions the involvement of voluntary associations in policy making has been seen as crucial. Nevertheless, the two traditions have largely evolved in isolation, and only of late have attempts been made to combine the insights of both (Cawson 1986; Lijphart and Crepaz 1991; Williamson 1989;.

The model of consociational democracy was developed to explain what appeared to be a paradox: how can polities divided by distinct ideological cleavages produce stable democracies? The answer was found in a complex system of give and take bargained for by the élites from each ideological 'block'. Compromise was made easier by the depoliticisation of policy issues, and widespread political apathy among the common people. The élites who worked out the 'balance of power' between the various blocks were drawn not only from the top level of the political parties, but also from leaders of voluntary organisations belonging to the different ideological 'families'. Councils and commissions, containing representatives of many interest groups, played an important part in building the necessary consensus and served as 'refrigerators' when policy issues became too hot to handle. Two political 'cleavages', class and religion, were bridged by this Dutch practice of consociationalism (Daalder 1964; Bussemaker in this volume; cf. Daalder 1984; Lehmbruch 1967; Lijphart 1968).

In the latter half of the 1970s a new interest in corporatism appeared, signalled by Schmitter and Lehmbruch's famous volume (1979) which gave rise to the so-called 'neocorporatism' debate. The main thrust of the argument of these authors was that a new type of political system had evolved, in which what are considered to be the major interest groups in society, business and unions, enjoy a monopoly of interest representation in government sponsored bodies. This new type of political system has become necessary to give capitalism a chance to survive in polities with extensive unionisation and with a strong social democratic influence. The ensuing literature on neocorporatism is mainly concerned with comparing socio-economic policy in different countries. The benefits of neocorporatist arrangements to the performance of economies are studied in depth. Many of the 1970s studies applauded the virtues of the system for lowering inflation and unemployment rates, spurring economic growth and lowering strike activity, but by the 1980s the tone was less enthusiastic. Some publications even suggested that corporatism might hamper economic growth (cf. Lijphart and Crepaz 1991, pp. 236-7; Smith 1993, pp. 36-7; Woldendorp 1995, pp. 122-3).

The British theorist Cawson (1986) has tried to find a middle ground. In his design of a 'dual state theory', 'pluralism' and 'corporatism' are thought of as coexisting forces. Pluralism is defined as a relationship between the state and interest organisations characterised by freedom. Citizens organise themselves and try under conditions of free competition to influence the state to adhere to their wishes. Under corporatism, interest organisations will bargain with the state over policy. The state gains co-operation from organisations essential to the maintenance of the economic order; those organisations can bargain for better deals for their members, but are also bound to discipline their members to a certain degree. States might differ in the extent to which corporatism has spread. There might also be differences, from state to state, in the relative importance of pluralist versus corporatist arrangements between central and local government. (Cawson 1986, pp. 145-7)

In trying to incorporate it into a unified theory of the state, Cawson neatly illustrates the weakness of corporatist theorising: its economistic and deterministic bias. Economic interest organisations are seen as 'naturally' powerful.[2] This view of politics might indeed look 'natural' from a Scandinavian vantage point. As in other Central European countries, however, advisory bodies in The Netherlands have always had to deal with religious as well as class-based antagonisms.

Advice in Dutch politics

In and between Dutch political parties, opinions have differed as to whether a separate representation of interests is compatible with the idea of a governing body - parliament - that represents 'the common good'. Dutch Liberals have been of the opinion that parliament is the sole representative of the people. Christian Democrats, both Catholic and Protestant, have valued the participation of voluntary groups in society and in politics and have maintained that central government should complement and not replace them in the arrangements for the modern welfare state (Klink 1991). Social Democrats have been divided on this issue, some stressing the independent responsibilities of trade unions, and their right to have a say in politics, some stressing the right of parliament to reign supreme (Lehning 1989).

With no consensus on their legitimacy within the state system, the power of the advisory bodies has ebbed and flowed with the prevailing political currents. Changes have been drastic. In the sixties and seventies the system grew explosively; in the nineties many councils have been abolished and there is a plan to prune the system even more severely. In the seventies interest representation was prevalent; in the nineties expert advice is more sought after (Oldersma 1996).

Advisory bodies should be 'representative' (Ministerie AZ 1987; SER 1975). How this concept can be applied in the context I have described is not very clear. It is problematic at the level of the system as a whole, as well as at the level of individual committees and councils. The term 'representation' is usually applied to a polity as a whole, but since advisory councils are installed to advise on a well-defined policy area or a specific political problem, does that mean that the concept of representation does not apply? It would seem that the notion of representation is bounded by the special function of advisory bodies, to advise on the basis of expertise or to represent interests. Which organisations ought to be represented, which kinds of expertise consulted? Now that new political cleavages, such as women's issues, environmental concerns etc., have opened up, it is no longer self-evident how 'representation' must be interpreted. New rules have yet to be established. Political science offers no guidance on these questions and Dutch politicians are only beginning to address them in a systematic way (Handelingen 1992-93).

I borrowed the term 'functional representation', to designate the relationship between political problems and membership of committees, from the political scientist Anderson (1979). In introducing this term, he aimed to 'open up an arena of reasoned argument' within which the notion of 'representation' could be rethought. That modifier 'functional', however, raises more questions than it answers. When advising on social policy, do we need the organised interests of workers and employers only? Or do we also need consumers organisations, organisations of welfare dependents and housewives' organisations? When talking about economic policy, do we need experts on finance and economics only, or do we also need ecological expertise? In my opinion, the system of advisory bodies lacks a firm basis of normative insights, at the level of both system and committee. At the system level there is no agreement about the legitimacy of advice nor about the kind of advice that is needed or allowed. On the level of committees there are no guidelines on what 'functional representation' might imply. Where to look for gender in this complex of criteria? What is to be said about representation, expertise and problem definition, when we look at them through the prism of gender?

Gender in the process

Representation of women has been argued for along three lines: that it 'mirrors' the population, that it represents 'women's interests' and that it represents 'women's special view' (Leijenaar, Ch. 10). The demand that a governing body should mirror the whole population, and not exclude women, seems self-evident, but two important objections have been made against it. In the first place, not every personal aspect merits political representation. A certain variable, like sex, has to be 'politicised' to become a politically meaningful distinction. Secondly, to what extent does mirroring imply that women's interests and viewpoints will be represented (Leijenaar 1989; Phillips 1991; Sapiro 1981)?

The notion of 'mirroring' presupposes equality between women and men. If women are not present in governing bodies, then that is a problem to be explained. Can the discrepancy be explained simply by the 'fact' of sexual difference? The notions of both 'women's interests' and the 'women's special viewpoint' work from the assumption that women are different. Interests must be constructed, argued for and organised to become politically relevant (Jónasdóttir 1988; Phillips 1991; Voet 1995). As it applies to women, the concept of representation thus entails both arguments derived from a presupposition of equality, i.e. 'mirroring', and arguments based on a presupposition of difference, i.e. 'women's interests' or 'women's views'. In Dutch debates about the lack of women in politics and in public administration, the demand for 'mirroring' has been most prominent. This demand has also been made of advisory bodies, 50 per cent of whose members should be women, if a government guideline is to be followed. Yet virtually no attention has been paid to the incorporation of women's interests in committees and councils.

If 'representation' needs to be reviewed through the perspectives of gender, the same is true of the concept of 'expertise'. Lloyd (1984) argues that in western culture scientific knowledge has been constructed in such a way that it excludes women and the qualities attributed to them. Women have been equated with feelings, emotions, empathy. Scientific knowledge is seen as antithetical to these qualities; ideally it should be detached, not tainted by emotions or feelings. Expertise, furthermore, is supposed to be the property of the 'professional', someone who is academically trained and belongs to a group that has managed to attain a certain social status. Becoming a professional and maintaining that status demands not only a prolonged training period. Once admitted to the profession, long hours of work and dedication are expected. Being a professional also entails subscribing to a set of norms and a certain view of the world, and forming part of a 'brotherhood' of people who know how to behave. For a woman, to become a professional is difficult on a number of counts. The training and the long working hours make it hard to incorporate pregnancies and its consequences for the life cycle. But time is not the only problem: having been brought up to 'care', many women find it difficult to refashion themselves as detached and 'objective' (Stivers 1993; cf. Knijn in this volume).

The critique of expertise has in Dutch feminist politics resulted in pleas for affirmative action policies. Demands to incorporate expertise on gender issues into politics or public administration have been few, and hesitant. When policies for women were first being formulated, feminist activists regarded 'expertise' with suspicion, as a concept that belonged to the enemy, not to themselves (Outshoorn 1994). Only recently, in a recommendation by the 'Emancipation Council' on changes to the structure of the system of advisory bodies, was any stress laid on the need for advisory councils to have expertise on gender issues (Emancipatieraad 1994).

A recent trend in Dutch political analysis points to the importance of the definition of political problems for the representation of women in politics. In the course of policy making processes, the gender aspects of political problems tend to disappear, or they become reworked so as to fit neatly into the explanatory framework current in other policy fields (Keuzenkamp and Teunissen 1990; Mossink and Nederland 1993). Obviously, this is a subject relevant to the problem of the representation of women in the corporatist system. If women are not seen as relevant to the problem, they will probably have less of a chance to be properly represented. This possibility inspired me to explore the relationship between the definition of the political problem and representation.

Gender might be relevant at different stages of forming a council: it might be a factor at work in the definition of the problem, it might be relevant when it comes to representing particular interests and it might be pertinent to selecting experts for a committee. Last but not least, when the council composition as 'mirroring' the general sex-ratio is made an issue, this too may prove relevant for the choice of council members.

Looking for 'the same' woman

To explore the role of gender in the formation of advisory bodies, I started with a 'qualitative' research model. I analysed the link between problem definition and the choice of council members by means of case studies. Between January 1991 and November 1993 I conducted four case studies, taking as my samples two expert committees and two committees largely made up of representatives. The areas of concern of the expert committees were urban renewal and the costs of health care; the representative committees handled social security arrangements and unemployed teachers. These policy areas were chosen because they are 'gendered' areas in Dutch politics, i.e. politicised by the women's movement and subsequently adopted by government as 'women's issues' in the context of policies for women. Only in those areas where women's issues had clearly been at stake for some time, I argued, was it reasonable to expect to find all forms of representation: 'mirroring' the population, the representation of interests and the incorporation of expertise on 'women's issues'. To analyse the political problem the council was formed to solve, I studied government memoranda. To find out how and why the actual members of the committee had been selected, I interviewed civil servants, politicians, committee members themselves and prominent spokespeople in the organisations they represented.

In the memoranda and other documents stating the nature of the problem in 'mainstream' politics, the issue of gender was not highlighted. Outside the field of policies specifically for women, political problems were defined in gender neutral terms. Of course, that does not mean that all political actors necessarily perceive them as such. Surprisingly, most politicians and civil servants showed themselves sensitive to women's issues. On the whole, representatives of trade unions and organisations of small employers were readier to see a 'gendered' edge to the problem at hand; representatives of 'big business' were more inclined to see the problem as gender neutral. In most interviews, however, women were portrayed as victims in the context of the political problem. Any suggestions that women's groups or expertise on women's issues might help to solve the problem were rare.

Although the problems of women were certainly borne in mind, women were never seen as possible political actors in their own right, only victims of unjust policies. Consequently, no-one recognised the need to have women represented for their 'functional' relationship to the problem at hand. In the committees based on expertise the choice of expertise seemed to be rather haphazard. Juridical and financial, and sometimes medical, expertise are believed to be essential and the five major political parties all require an equal quota of such experts. These aside, the field is largely open to the preferences of ministers or sometimes the chairman of the committee. Specific expertise on women's issues was never wanted. Further questions on this matter drew a variety of responses: expertise on gender issues was synonymous with 'experience' or with interest representation; such expertise did not really exist; gender expertise was only a rag-bag of ideology - or it was derived from a nonsensical demarcation of research fields. 'One can be a jurist or a sociologist, but not an expert on women', commented one sceptic.

In the case of committees based on interest representation the situation was more complex. The choice of organisations was always traditional. Employers' organisations and trade unions had worked closely for many years with the home ministry of the committees under study, and although the propriety of this arrangement was sometimes discussed, change was never seriously considered. As a result, representation of other types of interests, such as that of the unemployed, beneficiaries, the handicapped, and housewives was not considered.[3] It would not be right to conclude at this point that women's interests are not represented. The largest trade union and organisations of small employers all have been persuaded by female members to form advisory centres on women's issues like social security arrangements, wage and workplace discrimination, sexual harassment, etc.. In the case of the smaller employers, the problems of the 'working wife' demand attention. These advisory centres were expected to brief representatives of their organisations in committees. Thus, women's interests have certainly been represented in some cases; mostly, however, by men.

Representation of women in the sense of 'mirroring' - the requirement of 50 per cent female membership - proved to be very popular. Most spokespeople were very concerned to have more women either in their committees or their organisations. Attaining this ideal, however, was not easy. In the case of experts, informers stated that they had been searching for women, but were very wary of the lowering of standards that this might involve. Women must be 'women of quality'. One obvious way to find such women would be to look for experts on women's issues; but as we have seen, that avenue of expertise is held in low regard. Instead, selectors have tried to find women who possessed all the qualities of desirable male candidates, but were women as well. Such persons were hard to find. In one case a woman accountant was wanted, but there are only a very limited number of these currently available in the Netherlands, and all of them work for the same firm. Unfortunately, working for that firm was incompatible with membership of the intended committee! Luckily, a female doctor could be found for another position, so that the accountant could be a man.

In the case of the committee on social security the committee members were either functionaries or employees of the organisations they represented. There were few women among them. This might in part be attributed to the 'professional' nature of the job. Most members were recruited from within the organisation, which until recently consisted mainly of men.

Women were even more scarce in the fourth case, that of unemployed teachers, where 'specialists' - experts selected by organisations, but not involved in the daily activities of these organisations - were wanted as council members. The people needed for this committee also had to be professionals and a number of organisations had chosen a retired member of their organisation. Among these 'wise old men' was only one woman. She stressed that she was chosen for her wealth of experience (which was indeed impressive). According to her, being a woman neither helped nor hindered her selection. Organisations in this case consisted of employers and employees working in the field of education. Though 62 per cent of elementary school employees are women, as are 26 per cent of secondary school employees, the employees and functionaries of intermediate organisations in education are mainly men. Spokespeople for these organisations said they were interested in attracting more women as employees, but did not consider the sex of a candidate when it came to choosing members for committees. Being a member was simply part of the job or a consequence of being suited, and available, for the position. It would appear, then, that the notion that women must be represented in advisory bodies has taken root, but that this consensus applies only to representation based on equality. The women wanted are those who are 'the same' as the men they must replace. Such women are hard to find, for women tend to cluster in some kinds of expertise and to shun others. I concluded that the kind of representation that results is a 'socratic' representation: women are represented, but only when they have become the same as men (cf. Elshtain 1981; Hernes and Voje 1980).

The council member

To find out what kind of men and women become council members, my colleague and I conducted a survey among all members of councils and committees advising central government in the Netherlands.[4] Council members, according to our data, are on average 53 years old, 77 per cent are academically educated, mostly in law (22 per cent), science and technology (16 per cent) or economics (15 per cent). More than half of the members had parents who were not academically trained. Nearly a quarter of all council members earn their daily bread in education (many are full professors), another 16 per cent are employed in other branches of the public sector. Half of the members spend considerably more than 40 hours a week in paid employment. They work for the council (or councils) during their regular working hours, but keep the financial remunerations of this extra activity for themselves. In their religious allegiances, council members largely resemble the general population, though Protestants are slightly over-represented. In voting behaviour, members largely mirror the Dutch voters.

Council members are very active in voluntary associations. The majority were members of sports and other youth clubs in their early years - scouting was very popular among both boys and girls. About a third of the council members became members of the board of a youth organisation before they were eighteen years old. This active organisational life was prolonged by men and women over their student and adult years. When interviewed, in 1993, about half of the members still performed tasks in a diverse array of organisations. Two out of every five council members are active members of political parties; many are active in the new social movements, in schools and neighbourhood organisations (Oldersma 1997).

Little difference was found between members recruited to their committee as experts, and members recruited as representatives of a special interest organisation. Both kinds of members appear to belong to the class of 'professionals': they are highly educated, have demanding jobs and are very active in social life. The percentage of women among experts and among representatives was exactly the same. As for religion and political allegiances, both types of members largely resemble the Dutch population and the Dutch voters at large. Council members see their position in the organisation they work for as important to their career as members; scientific accomplishments and experience in an executive function are also highly valued. Networks, contacts, commitment and personal qualities are rarely mentioned.

Women formed 18 per cent of the respondents, slightly more than the apparent proportion of female council members during the period under study (15.5 per cent, Oldersma 1993). All in all, they closely fit the usual image of 'professionals'; and there are no housewives among them. Although most of them have jobs no less demanding than the men's, the women are more active in voluntary associations. They further differ from the men in ways that might be expected: on average the men are older, more often have partners, more often have children (and more of them), work part-time less, earn more and have better jobs. The male council members appear to be considerably more successful on the marriage market and have more children than the average Dutch male. Female members resemble their average Dutch sisters in having partners, but have fewer children. While most male members have partners who stay at home or have part-time jobs, most female members have partners with jobs as demanding as their own. For women in politics nowadays, it seems that a career can very well be combined with a partner, but children still are a handicap (cf. Hernes and Voje 1980).

Although women tend to have less prestigious positions than men, their fathers and mothers were better educated and had better positions than those of the men. Taking into account that the women are more active in voluntary associations than the men, this leads us to the conclusion that women 'earn' their position by bringing more 'cultural' and 'social capital' to their positions.

The policy fields in which council members are asked to advise can be divided into 'men's' and 'women's' interests according to the relative numbers of women and men active in the different fields. This division parallels the interest of male and female students in universities: technology and economics are typically 'male' subjects; language, culture and social affairs are 'female' subjects. Women might be disadvantaged for a career in councils if the typically 'female' areas of knowledge were seen as less relevant by the governmental agencies that set up the councils. This does not seem to have happened, however, since both types of knowledge are about equally represented in councils.

Only a third of all members represented an organisation. Of those, a further 15 per cent represented other levels of government and public companies. In the corporatist system only a small space is open to the concerns of voluntary associations. What is left is still dominated by economic interests: more than a quarter of all representative council members represented trade unions (11 per cent) and employers' organisations (17 per cent). Only one per cent of members represented a women's organisation. The dominant position enjoyed by representatives of economic interest organisations becomes more striking when we compare the membership of trade unions - 1.8 million - to the membership of women's organisations, conservatively estimated at 1 million. The door between central government and voluntary associations has been slowly closing during the past decade; for women's interests it has never been open.

Finding 'different' women?

If the object of selection procedures was to find 'the same' women, they have to a certain extent failed. To begin with, the women are younger, less religious and vote more often for left wing parties than the men. The women are educated in medicine, language and cultural studies more often than are the men, and they are more likely to be members of organisations of 'do-gooders' - third world or peace organisations, for example. Thus, they may be expected to bring different interests to their committees. A third of the women indicate that they have expertise on women's issues and a third of the women are members of women's organisations, both assets that were virtually non-existent among the men.

Do council members attribute special qualities to women functioning in the corporatist world and will more women change the daily workings of the system? We tried to find out council members' opinions on these matters. The proposition that women's interests would be looked after better if more women entered the system did appeal to many women (41 per cent in agreement) and a substantial amount of men (31 per cent). A significant minority of women described themselves as practical problem-solvers (38 per cent), but fewer men were prepared to do so (only 10 per cent). Not many women or men were convinced that women were usually egalitarian or prone to compromise. About

75 per cent (men and women) refused to believe that having more women in councils would change the advice given.

We asked our respondents not only to describe advisory life as they saw it, but also to suggest how they thought women should be represented in politics. We formulated six propositions based largely on Sapiro's article on the representation of women and presented these to the respondents. The idea that women are best represented by their husbands because spouses have the same interests, popular among men in debates about voting rights for women around the turn of the century, was rejected by a majority of the women and nearly half the men. Two propositions considered whether women in fact constitute a distinct category in politics. Half of the women did see 'women' as distinctly 'different' in politics, but 41 per cent saw differences between women as more important than whatever might unite them. Most men and women alike rejected biological differences as a basis for political interests, but half of the men and nearly three-quarters of women agreed that women are set apart from men in politics due to their different social positions. 'Mirroring', i.e. reserving half of all political positions for women, was favoured by a majority of women (54 per cent) but only a quarter of the men. We might conclude that most council members believe that women need political representation, but what form that representation should take often leads to disagreement along gender lines.

Though only 25 per cent of the men thought that women should occupy half of all positions in politics, no less than 65 per cent of the men were of the opinion that women are underrepresented in advisory bodies, as compared to 72 per cent of women. Most men (58 per cent) attributed this to a lack of 'expertise' and 'ambition' on the part of women. Many respondents wrote in the margin that this problem would resolve itself in time. Most women (63 per cent) attributed the under-representation to discrimination, to the exclusion of some groups in the political system or to barriers in the career paths of female representatives. In other words, men, when confronted with the under-representation of women, tend to blame the women and are confident this gap will be bridged if women only try harder. Women, on the other hand, tend to find fault with the current system of democracy.

Conclusion

None of the adherents of the two strands of theorising that have been important to the analysis of the Dutch political system, 'consociationalism' and 'neocorporatism', have ever felt the need to explain why women and their movements have not been invited to take part in building the national consensus. Paraphrasing Schattschneider (1975, p. 35) we might say that the 'flaw in the pluralist heaven' that 'the heavenly chorus sings with a strong male accent' went unnoticed by pluralists. Neocorporatism could be used to provide a 'natural' cause for the exclusion of women: as outsiders in the world of economic interest organisations they need not be 'pacified'. Only the demystification of the power of economic interest organisations could provide an opportunity for the dynamics of politics to be put on the research agenda.

In this article, I have analysed the definition of political problems to find out where the 'gendering' of politics takes place or disappears and whether the gendering of problems leads to adequate representation for women. Dutch politics seems divided into two still often exclusive camps: politics for women and mainstream politics. Memoranda on politics for women analyse political problems and point out where women's interests are at stake; mainstream politics seems to be completely unaffected by this activity. Political actors have heard of 'women's problems', but prefer to think of women as victims, not as political actors in their own right.

In the Dutch corporatist world, women are selected on the basis of equality, which means in practice that they are supposed to be 'the same' as the men they are to replace. In the selection process forms of representation based on 'difference' are virtually non-existent. Nevertheless, the women who are selected are different from the men: they do represent women in the sense that they have affiliations with women's organisations and have expertise on women's issues. They also represent more 'feminine' interests in voluntary associations. Most interestingly however, they have a different viewpoint from men on matters concerning the representation of women. They see women as a category in need of representation which has been unjustly denied them. An encouraging number of women in the corporatist channel are fully equipped to bring women's politics to politics at large.

Notes

1. Hernes (1984) and Hernes and Hänninen-Salmelin (1985) use Schmitter; Lovenduski was inspired by Schmitter (1986a) and Cawson (Lovenduski 1986b).
2. Both Smith (1993, pp.36-37) and Hemerijck (1992, p.352) stress the contingent nature of corporatism.
3. I consider both 'traditional' and 'feminist' groups as possibly representative of 'women's interests'. On a number of issues, like work and social security, traditional and feminist women's groups in The Netherlands have joined forces. The top levels of 'old' and 'new' organisations have converged ideologically in the past twenty years.
4. The survey was carried out in spring 1993 by my colleague Mia Janzen-Marquard and myself and was partly modelled on Hernes and Voje's survey of Norwegian council members (1980). In total 53 per cent of the members answered our questionnaire; the following characteristics are based on 1198 respondents, 981 men and 212 women. Five members did not state their sex.

Bibliography

Akkerman, T. (1985), 'Inleiding', in T. Akkerman and S. Stuurman (eds), *De zondige rivièra van het katholicisme. Een lokale studie over feminisme en ontzuiling 1950-1975*, SUA, Amsterdam, pp. 11-38.

Akkerman, T. (1997, forthcoming), 'Liberalism and Feminism in England, 1860-1914', in T. Akkerman and S. Stuurman (eds), *Feminist Political Thought in European History. From the Medieval to the present*, Routledge, London.

Akkerman, T. and Stuurman, S. (1997, forthcoming), 'Introduction', in T. Akkerman and S. Stuurman (eds), *Feminist Political Thought in European History. From the Middle Ages to the Present*, Routledge, London.

Anderson, C.W. (1979), 'Political Design and the Representation of Interests', in P. Schmitter and G. Lehmbruch (eds), *Trends toward Corporatist Intermediation*, Sage, London, pp. 271-98.

Andeweg, R.B. (1995), 'Beleidsvorming', in J.Th.J. van den Berg et al. (eds), *Inleiding Staatkunde*, Deventer, Kluwer, pp. 355-69.

Andeweg, R.B. and Irwin, G.A. (1993), *Dutch Government and Politics*, Macmillan Press, Houndsmills.

Arends, J. (1988), *Sociale atlas van meisjes. Een inventarisatie van de maatschappelijke positie van meisjes in Nederland*, Raad voor het Jeugdbeleid, Amsterdam.

Arendt, H. (1958), *The Human Condition*, University of Chicago Press, Chicago.

Arons, G. (1981), 'Collectivering van huishoudelijke arbeid', *Socialisties-feministiese teksten* 6, Sara, Amsterdam, pp. 111-37.

Barbalet, J.M. (1988), *Citizenship, Rights, Struggle and Class Inequality*, Open University Press, Milton Keynes.

Barber, B. (1984), *Strong Democracy: Participatory Democracy for a New Age*, University of California Press, Berkeley.

Barrett, M. (1980), *Women's Oppression Today: Problems in Marxist Feminist Analysis*, NLB, London.

Belgische Kamer van Volksvertegenwoordigers (BKV) (1996-1997), *Wetsontwerp tot wijziging van de wet van 20 juli 1990 ter bevordering van de evenwichtige aanwezigheid van mannen en vrouwen in organen met adviserende bevoegdheid*, B.K.V. 860/1-96/97.

Bergquist, C. (1995), 'Changing the Institutions - State Feminism in Sweden', Paper presented at the ECPR Joint Sessions Workshop on State Feminism, Bordeaux, France, 27 April-2 May.
Bervoets, L. (1994), *Opvoeden tot sociale verantwoordelijkheid. De verzoening van wetenschap, ethiek en sekse in het sociaal werk in Nederland rond de eeuwwisseling*, IISG, Amsterdam.
Biagini, E.F. and Reid, A.J. (eds) (1991), *Currents Of Radicalism. Popular Radicalism, Organized Labour and Party Politics in Britain 1850-1914*, Cambridge University Press, Cambridge.
Bock G. and James, S. (eds) (1992), *Beyond Equality and Difference. Citizenship, Feminist Politics and Female Subjectivity*, Routledge, London and New York.
Bock, G. and Thane, P. (eds) (1990), *Women, the State and Welfare*, University of Wisconsin Press, Madison.
Boer, A. de (1994), *Informele zorg: een verkenning van huidige en toekomstige ontwikkelingen*, Sociaal Cultureel Planbureau, The Hague / VUGA, Rijswijk.
Boissevain-Pijnappel, M. (1921), 'Bijzondere kinderzorg. Rijkskindertoeslagfonds' in *Verzamelde referaten. Congres voor sociale verzekering*, Vereeniging van Raden van Arbeid, Amsterdam, pp. 159-70.
Borkus, M. et al. (1994), *Vrouwenstemmen; 100 jaar vrouwenbelangen: 75 jaar vrouwenkiesrecht*, Walburg pers, Zutphen.
Bosmans, J. (1989), 'De politiek en de arbeid van de gehuwde vrouw in Nederland', *Spiegel Historiae*, vol. 24., no. 11, pp. 468-74.
Bosmans, J. (1991), *Romme. Biografie 1896-1946*, Spectrum, Utrecht.
Bovens, M.A.P. (1990), *Verantwoordelijkheid en Organisatie. Beschouwingen over aansprakelijkheid. Institutioneel burgerschap en ambtelijke ongehoorzaamheid*, Tjeenk Willink, Zwolle.
Braun, M. (1992), *De prijs van de liefde. De eerste feministische golf, het huwelijksrecht en de vaderlandse geschiedenis*, Spinhuis, Amsterdam.
Brinkler-Gabler, G. (ed.) (1979), *Frauenarbeit und Beruf* (Die Frau in der Gesellschaft, frühe Texte), Fischer Tachenbuch Verlag, Frankfurt am Main.
Brubaker, R. (1992), *Citizenship and Nationhood in France and Germany*. Harvard University Press, Cambridge.
Bruijn, J. de (1989), *Haar werk. Vrouwenarbeid en arbeidssociologie in historisch en emancipatorisch perspectief*, SUA, Amsterdam.
Bussemaker, J. (1991), 'Equality, Autonomy and Feminist Politics', in E. Meehan and S. Sevenhuijsen (eds), *Equality Politics and Gender*, Sage, London, pp. 52-70.
Bussemaker, J. (1993), *Betwiste zelfstandigheid. Individualisering, sekse en verzorgingsstaat*, SUA, Amsterdam.
Bussemaker, J. (1994), 'Tussen zelfopoffering en eigenbelang: de civil society in relatie tot de prive- en publieke sfeer', in P. Dekker (ed.), *Civil Society*, Sociaal en Cultureel Planbureau, Rijswijk, pp. 163-83.

Bussemaker, J. (1997, forthcoming), 'Equality and Anti-hierarchy: the Language of Feminism in Modern Welfare States', in T. Akkerman and S. Stuurman (eds), *Six Feminist Waves*, Routledge, London.

Bussemaker, J. , Drenth, A. van, Knijn, T. and Plantenga, J. (1997, forthcoming), 'Welfare Structures and the Position of Lone Parents in the Netherlands', in J. Lewis (ed.), *Social Policy, Labour Market Participation and Care in Europe: the Case of Lone Parents*, London, Kingsley Publishers.

Bussemaker, J. and Kersbergen, K. van (1994), 'Gender and Welfare States: some Theoretical Reflections', in D. Sainsbury (ed.), *Gendering Welfare States*, Sage, London, pp. 8-25.

Bussemaker, J. and Kersbergen, K. van (1996), 'Gender Inequality and Conservative Welfare States. A Four-nation Comparison', Paper prepared for the 1996 Annual Meeting of the American Political Science Association, San Francisco August 29 - September 1, 1996.

Carter, A. (1988), *The Politics of Women's Rights*, Longman, London.

Cawson, A. (1985), *Organised Interests and the State; studies in meso-corporatism*, Sage, London.

Cawson, A. (1986), *Corporatism and Political Theory*, Blackwell, Oxford.

Collini, S. (1991), *Public Moralists. Political Thought and Intellectual Life in Britain 1850-1930*, Clarendon Press, Oxford.

Commissie ingesteld bij beschikking van de minister van Binnenlandse Zaken van 11 juni 1949 No 15792/R afdeling ambtenarenzaken (1952), *Het vraagstuk van de gehuwde ambtenares*, report, Staatsdrukkerij, The Hague.

Commissie ingesteld door den Nationalen Vrouwenraad van Nederland ter bestudering van het vraagstuk der moederschapszorg (1925), *Rapport*, report, Nationale Vrouwenraad van Nederland, n.p.

Commissie ingesteld door het bestuur van den R.K. Centrale Raad van Bedrijven tot het ontwerpen van een modelkindertoeslagregeling (1920), *Kindertoeslag*, report, R.K. Centrale Raad van Bedrijven, Utrecht.

Commissie inzake moederschapszorg van de Algemeene Nederlandsche Vrouwen-Organisatie (1921), *Rapport*, report, Algemene Nederlandse Vrouwen-Organisatie, n.p.

Commissie Toekomstscenario's Herverdeling Onbetaalde Arbeid (1995), *Onbetaalde zorg gelijk verdeeld*, VUGA, The Hague.

Coole, D.H. (1988), *Women in Political Theory. From Ancient Misogyny to Contemporary Feminism*, Wheatsheaf, Brighton.

Cott, N. (1987), *The Grounding of Modern Feminism*, Yale University Press, New Haven.

Cox, R. (1993), *The Development of the Dutch Welfare State: From Workers' Insurance to Universal Entitlement*, University of Pittsburgh Press, Pittsburgh.

Culpitt, I. (1992), *Welfare and Citizenship. Beyond the Crisis of the Welfare State?* Sage, London.

Daal, H.J. van (1990), *Vrijwilligerswerk en informele hulp in Nederland*, NIMAWO, The Hague.

Daal, H.J. van (1993), 'Vrijwilligerswerk in een veranderend zorg- en arbeidsbestel', *Tijdschrift voor Arbeid en Bewustzijn*, pp. 185-95.

Daal, H.J. van and Willems, L. (1993), 'Volunteering in the Netherlands', in J.Davis Smith (ed.), *Volunteering in Europe: Opportunities and Challanges for the 90s*, The Volunteer Centre, UK, Berkahmsted.

Daalder, H. (1964), *Leiding en lijdelijkheid in de Nederlandse politiek*. Assen, Van Gorcum.

Daalder, H. (1984), 'On the Origins of the Consociational Democracy Model', *Acta Politica* 1984, vol. 1, pp. 97-115.

Daalder, H. (1989), *Ancient and Modern Pluralism in the Netherlands*, The 1989 Erasmus Lecture at Harvard University (Centre for European Studies Working Paper Series).

Dam, G. ten et al. (eds) (1991), *Sekseverschillen in het onderwijs. Curriculum, didaktiek en organisatie*, Wolters-Noordhoff, Groningen.

Damsma, D. (1986), 'Van hoeksteen tot fundament. Het gezin in Nederland 1850-1960', in H. Peeters, L. Dresen-Coenders and T. Brandenbarg (eds), *Vijf eeuwen gezinsleven*, SUN: Nijmegen, pp. 209-247.

Damsma, D. (1994), 'Family Wages or Family Allowances? Debates in the Dutch Labour Movement, 1890-1920', in *Economic and social history in the Netherlands. Family strategies and changing labour relations*, vol. 6, NEHA, Amsterdam, pp. 169-83.

Dekker, P. (1994), *Civil Society. Civil Society en vrijwilligerswerk 1*, Sociaal en Cultureel Planbureau, Rijswijk.

Dietz, M.G. (1985), 'Citizenship with a Feminist Face: The Problem with Maternal Thinking', *Political Theory*, vol. 13, no. 1, pp. 19-39.

Dietz, M.G. (1987), 'Context is All: Feminism and Theories of Citizenship', *Daedalus*, vol. 116, no. 4, pp. 1-25.

Dijkstra, T. and Swiebel, J. (1982), 'De overheid en het vrouwenvraagstuk: emancipatie als mode en taboe', *Socialisties-Feministiese Teksten*, vol. 7, Feministiese Uitgeverij Sara, Amsterdam, pp. 42-64.

Dijsselbloem, J.J. (1937), *De gezinstoeslag en zijn toepassing in Nederland*, Brussel: Standaard-Boekhandel.

Dorp, E.C. (1910), *Prae-adviezen over de maatschappelijke betekenis van den arbeid der gehuwde vrouw, en de houding, door de overheid aan te nemen tegenover dat vraagstuk*, M. Nijhoff, The Hague.

Drenth, A. van (1991), *De zorg om het Philipsmeisje. Meisjes in de elektrotechnische industrie in Eindhoven 1900-1960*, Walburg Pers, Zutphen.

Drenth, A. van (1992), *State Policy on Girls. The Implications of Government Feminism in the Netherlands*, Paper prepared for the First European Conference of Sociology, University of Vienna (Austria).

Drenth, A. van (1993a), ' "Philips Wants Men And Girls". The Unattainable Adulthood of Factory Girls in the Technical Industry in the Netherlands (1891-1960)', *Paedagogica Historica*, vol. 29, no. 1, pp. 189-203.

Drenth, A. van (1993b), 'From Future Womanhood to Actual Girlhood: the History of Discourse and Social Policy on Factory Girls', in M. De Ras and M. Lunenberg (eds), *Girls, Girlhood And Girls' Studies In Transition*, Het Spinhuis, Amsterdam, pp. 190-206.

Drenth, A. van and Poel, J. te (1992), '"Samen-meisje-zijn". Constanten en veranderingen in jeugdwerk en meisjescultuur van de jaren vijftig en zestig', *Tijdschrift voor Vrouwenstudies*, vol. 13, no. 2, pp. 183-99.

Duyvendak, J.W. (1994), *De verzuiling van de homobeweging*, SUA, Amsterdam.

Eijl, C. van (1994), *Het werkzame verschil. Vrouwen in de slag om arbeid 1898-1940*, Verloren: Hilversum.

Eijl, C. van (1994), *Het werkzame verschil. Vrouwen in de slag om arbeid 1989-1940*, Verloren, Hilversum.

Einhorn, B. (1993), *Cinderella Goes to Market: Citizenship, Gender and Women's Movements in East Central Europe*, Verso, London.

Eisenstein, H. (1990), 'Femocrats, Official Feminism and the Uses of Power', in S. Watson (ed.), *Playing the State. Australian Feminist Interventions,,* Verso, London and New York, pp. 87-103.

Eisenstein, H. (1991a), 'Feminism and Femocrats', in H. Eisenstein (ed.), *Gender Shock. Practising Feminism on Two Continents*, Allen and Unwin, Sydney, pp. 19-26.

Eisenstein, H. (1991b), 'Women, the State and your Complexion', in H. Eisenstein (ed.), *Gender shock. Practising Feminism on Two Continents*, Allen and Unwin, Sydney, pp. 27-39.

Elshtain, J.B. (1981), *Public Man, Private Woman, Women in Social and Political Thought*, Princeton University Press, Princeton.

Emancipatieraad (1987), *Meisjes en jonge vrouwen. Advies*, report, Emancipatieraad, The Hague.

Emancipatieraad (1994), *Met het oog op mei 1997. Toekomstige advisering met betrekking tot het emancipatiebeleid*, report, Emancipatieraad, The Hague, February.

Emancipatieraad (1996), *Met zorg naar een nieuwe zekerheid. Advies over een geëmancipeerd inkomens- en sociale zekerheid*, report, Emancipatieraad, The Hague.

Engbersen, G., Schuyt, K. Timmer, J. and Waarden, F. van (1993), *Cultures of Unemployment. A Comparative Look at Long-Term Unemployment and Urban Poverty*, Westview Press, Boulder.

Esping-Andersen, G. (1990), *The Three Worlds of Welfare Capitalism*, Polity Press, Cambridge.

Essen, M. van (1990), *Opvoeden met een dubbel doel. Twee eeuwen meisjesopvoeding in Nederland*, SUA, Amsterdam.

European Network 'Women in Decision-Making'(1996), *Panorama of Activities 1992-1996*, report, Brussels, European Commission DG V, V/1205/96/EN.

European Network on Child Care Provisions (1996), *A Review of Services for Young Children in the European Union, 1990-1995*, report, n.p., Bruxelles.

Evans R. (1977), *The Feminists*, Croom Helm, London.

Foucault, M. (1982), 'The Subject and Power', in H.L. Dreyfus and P. Rabinow, *Michel Foucault: Beyond Structuralism and Hermeneutics*, Harvester, New York

Frader, L. (1996), 'Social Citizens without Citizenship: Working-Class Women and Social Policy in Interwar France', in *Social Politics*, Summer-Fall, pp. 111-35.

Franzway, S. , Court, D. and Connell, R.W. (1989), *Staking a Claim. Feminism, Bureaucracy and the State*, Polity Press and Blackwell, Oxford.

Fraser N. (1989), *Unruly Practices. Power, Discourse and Gender in Contemporary Social Theory*, Polity Press, Cambridge.

Fraser, N. (1994), 'After the Family wage. Gender Equity and the Welfare State', in *Political Theory*, vol. 22, no. 4, pp. 591-618.

Frazer, E. and Lacey, N. (1993), *The Politics of Community: A Feminist Critique of the Liberal-Communitarian Debate*, Harvester Wheatsheaf, Brighton.

Gastelaars, M. (1985), *Een geregeld leven*, SUA, Amsterdam.

Gelder, M. van (ed.) (1993), *The Dutch Revolt*, Cambridge University Press, Cambridge.

George, V. and Taylor-Gooby, P. (eds) (1996), *European Welfare Policy. Squaring the Welfare Circle*, Houndsmill, Macmillan.

Geyl, P. (1963), *History of the Low Countries: Episodes and Problems. The Trevelyn lectures 1963 with four additional essays*, MacMillan, London.

Giele, J.J. (1981), De arbeidsenquête van 1887: een kwaad leven, Link, Nijmegen.

Gosker, R. (1970), 'Geschiedenis van de kinderbijslagverzekering', in *De groei van de sociale verzekering in Nederland*, Vereeniging van Raden van Arbeid, Amsterdam, pp. 79-104.

Goudt, M. and Hartman, I. (1995), 'Politieke eisen in plaats van vernieuwingsrethoriek', in M. de Wit (ed.), *Politieke Vernieuwing & Sekse*, Amsterdam, Instituut voor Publiek en Politiek, pp. 46-71.

Guéhenno, J.-M. (1995), *The End of the Nation-State*, University of Minnesota Press, Minneapolis and London.

Gunsteren, H.R. van (1992), *Eigentijds burgerschap/WRR publicatie*, report, Wetenschappelijke Raad voor het Regeringsbeleid, The Hague.

Haan, I. de (1992), 'De lachspiegel van het burgerschap', in: J.B.D. Simonis, A.C. Hemerijck and P.B. Lehning (eds), *De staat van de burger. Beschouwingen over hedendaags burgerschap*, Boom, Amsterdam/Meppel, pp. 161-80.

Handelingen Tweede Kamer [NL] (1977) *Emancipatie. Proces van verandering en groei*, report, zitting 1976-1977, vol. 14496, nos. 1-2.

Handelingen Tweede Kamer [NL] (1985), *Beleidsplan Emancipatie*, report, zitting 1984-1984, vol. 19502, nos. 1-19.

Handelingen Tweede Kamer [NL] (1988), *Maatschappelijke positie van meisjes en jonge vrouwen*, Memorandum of the Ministeries van SZW, WVS en O&W, zitting 1988-1989, vol. 20939, no. 1.

Handelingen Tweede Kamer [NL] (1992-1993), *Raad op maat. Rapport van de bijzondere commissie Vraagpunten Adviesorganen*, Commissie-de Jong, zitting 1992-1993, Vol 21427, no. 29.

Harris, J. (1992), 'Political Thought and the Welfare State 1870-1940; an Intellectual Framework for British Social Policy', *Past & Present*, no. 135, pp. 116-42.

Hart, J. de (1995), *Tijdopnamen*, Sociale en Culturele Studies, no. 22, Sociaal en Cultureel Planbureau, Rijswijk.

Hausen, K. (1976) 'Die Polarisierung der "Geschlechtscharaktere", Eine Spiegelung der Dissoziation von Erwerbs- und Familienleben', in W. Conze (ed.), *Sozialgeschichte der Familie in der Neuzeit Europas*, Ernst Klett Verlag, Stuttgart, pp. 363-393.

Heater, D. (1990), *Citizenship. The Civic Ideal in World History, Politics and Education*, Longman, London and New York.

Heek, F. van (1973), Van hoogkapitalisme naar verzorgingsstaat; een halve eeuw sociale verandering, 1920-1970, Boom, Meppel.

Hemerijck, A. (1992), *The historical contingencies of Dutch corporatism*, Ph.D at Balliol College, Oxford.

Hernes, H.M. (1984), *The situation of women in the political process in Europe. part III. The role of women in voluntary associations and organisations*, Council of Europe, Directorate of Human Rights, Strassbourg.

Hernes, H.M. (1987), 'Women and the Welfare State: the Transition from Private to Public Dependence', in A. Showstack Sassoon (ed.), *Women and the State; the Shifting Boundaries of Public and Private*, Hutchinson, London, pp. 72-91.

Hernes, H.M. and Hänninen-Salmelin, E. (1985), 'Women in the Corporate System', in E. Haavio-Mannila et al. (eds), *Unfinished Democracy; Women in Nordic Politics*, Pergamon Press, Oxford, pp. 106-34.

Hernes, H.M. and Voje, K. (1980), 'Women in the Corporate Channel: a Process of Natural Exclusion?' in *Scandinavian Political Studies* N.S., vol. 3, no. 2, pp. 163-86.

Hillebrand, R. (1992), *De Antichambre van het parlement*, DSWO Press Leiden.

Hobson, B. (1990), 'No Exit, No Voice: Women's Economic Dependency and the Welfare State', *Acta Sociologica*, vol. 33, no. 3., pp. 235-50.

Hobson, B. (1994). 'Solo Mothers, Social Policy Regimes, and the Logics of Gender', in D. Sainsbury (ed.), *Gendering Welfare States*, Sage, London, pp. 170-187.

Hollis, P. (1987), *Ladies Elect. Women in English Local Government 1865-1914*, Clarendon Press, Oxford.

Holton, S.S. (1986), *Feminism and Democracy. Women's Suffrage and Reform Politics in Britain 1900-1918*, Cambridge University Press, Cambridge.

Hoogeveen, K. and Velde, H. van de (1992), *Girls as a Subject of Political Debate in the Netherlands*, Paper for 'Alice in Wonderland', First International Conference on girls and girlhood, Section 'Policy-making and the state', Amsterdam.

Hoogeveen, K. and Zande, I. van der (1993), 'Nothing Wrong with the Boys? On the Disintegration of Girls Policy Relating to Girls and the Absence of Policy Relating to Boys', in M. de Ras and M. Lunenberg (eds), *Girls, Girlhood and Girls' Studies in Transition*, Het Spinhuis, Amsterdam, pp. 247-75.

Hoogeveen, K. and Zande, I. van der (1995), 'Women's Emancipation and Girls' Policy', in M. du Bois-Reymond and P. van Lieshout (eds), *The Dutch Welfare System*, Schäuble, Rheinfelden/Berlin, pp. 51-87.

Hooghiemstra, B.T.J and Niphuis-Nell, M. (1993), *Sociale atlas van de vrouw. Deel 2. Arbeid, inkomen and faciliteiten om werken en de zorg voor kinderen te combineren*, Sociaal en Cultureel Planbureau, Rijswijk.

Huizinga, J. (1968), *Dutch Civilization in the Seventeenth Century: and Other Essays*, F. Ungar, New York.

Israel, J.I. (1995), *The Dutch Republic: Its Rise, Greatness, and Fall, 1477-180x*, Clarendon Press, Oxford.

Jacobs, A. (1922/23), 'De taak der vrouw in het politieke leven', *De Opbouw*, no. 5, pp. 60-73.

Jacobs, A. (1978 [1924]), *Herinneringen*, Sun reprint, Nijmegen.

Jager, R. de (1988), *Kruis of munt. Christelijk-sociale ideeen aangaande het gezinsloon 1891-1919*, Unpubl. paper, Amsterdam.

Jaggar, A. (1983), *Feminist Politics and Human Nature*, Harvester Press, Sussex.

James, S. (1992), 'The Good-Enough Citizen: Citizenship and Independence', in G. Bock and S. James (eds), *Beyond Equality & Difference. Citizenship, Feminist Politics and Female Subjectivity*, Routledge, London and New York, pp. 48-68.

Jansweijer, R. (1989),'1990 begint nog lang niet', *Jeugd en Samenleving*, vol. 19, nos. 6-7.

Jansz, U. (1983), *Vrouwen Ontwaakt!*, Amsterdam, Bert Bakker.

Jansz, U. (1990), *Denken over sekse in de eerste feministische golf*, Sara/Van Gennep, Amsterdam.

Jansz, U. (1991), 'Sociale kwestie en sekse in de politieke geschiedenis. De Arbeidswet van 1889', in M. Schwegman et al. (eds), *Op het strijdtoneel van de politiek. Twaalfde jaarboek voor vrouwengeschiedenis*, SUN, Nijmegen, pp. 70-90.

Jónasdóttir, A.G. (1988), 'On the Concept of Interests, Women's Interests, and the Limitations of Interest Theory', in K.B. Jones and A.G. Jónasdóttir (eds), *The Political Interests of Gender*, Sage, London, pp. 33-58.

Jones, K.B. (1990), 'Citizenship in a Woman-friendly Polity', *Signs*, vol. 15, no. 4, pp. 781-812.

Kant, I. (1991), 'On the Common Saying: "This May be True in Theory, But it Does not Apply in Practice" '1793], in I. Kant, *Political Writings*, Cambridge University Press, Cambridge, pp. 61-92.

Kanter, R.M. (1972), *Commitment and Community*, Harvard University Press, Cambridge.
Katzenstein, P.J. (1985), *Small States in World Markets: Industrial Policy in Europe*, Cornell University Press, Ithaca.
Kersbergen, K. van (1995), *Social Capitalism. A Study of Christian Democracy and the Welfare State*, Routledge, London.
Keuzenkamp, S. and Outshoorn, J. (1992), 'Emancipatiebeleid. Een pas op de plaats', *Beleidswetenschap*, vol. 6, no. 4, pp. 353-69.
Keuzenkamp, S. and Teunissen, A. (1990), *Emancipatie ten halve geregeld. Continuïteit en inenging in het emancipatiebeleid*, report, Ministerie van Sociale Zaken en Werkgelegenheid, The Hague.
Klandemans, P.G. (1983), *Participatie in een sociale beweging: een mobilisatiecampagne onderzocht*, Vrije Universiteit, Amsterdam.
Klink, A. (1991), *Christen-democratie en overheid, De christen-democratische politieke filosofie en enige staats- en bestuurrechtelijke implicaties*, W.D. Meinema BV, Delft.
Knijn, T. (1994a), 'Social Dilemmas in Images of Motherhood in the Netherlands,' *The European Journal of Women's Studies*, vol. 1, no. 2, pp. 183-206.
Knijn, T. (1994b), 'Fish without bikes: Revision of the Dutch Welfare state and its Consequences for the (In)dependence of Single Mothers', *Social Politics, International Studies in Gender, State & Society*, vol. 1, no. 1, pp. 83-105.
Knijn, T. and Kremer, M. (1997, forthcoming), 'Gender and the Caring Dimension of Welfare States: Towards Inclusive Citizenship', *Social Politics*, vol. 4, no. 3.
Knijn, T. and Verheijen, C. (1988), *Tussen plicht en ontplooiing. Het welbevinden van moeders van jonge kinderen in een veranderende cultuur*, ITS, Nijmegen.
Koch, K. and Scheffer, P. (eds) (1996), *Het nut van Nederland. Opstellen over soevereiniteit en identiteit*, Bert Bakker, Amsterdam.
Komter, A. (1985), *De macht van de vanzelfsprekendheid in relaties tussen vrouwen en mannen*, VUGA, The Hague.
Koole, R. (1992), *De opkomst van de moderne kaderpartij*, Het Spectrum, Utrecht.
Kortbeek, L. (1995), *Zusters weest bereid! Het gemeenschapsdenken van Esther Welmoet Wijnaendts Francken-Dijserinck (1876-1956)*, Unpubl. paper, Nijmegen.
Kossmann, E.H. (1978), *The Low Countries 1780-1940*, Oxford University Press, Oxford.
Kremer, M. (1994), 'Interpretations of Citizenship. Gender, Care and the Obligation to Work in the British, Danish and Dutch Welfare State', unpublished doctoral thesis, University of Utrecht.
Kriesi, H.P. (1993), *Political Mobilization and Social Change: the Dutch case in comparative perspective*, Avebury, Aldershot, Brookfield, Vt.
Kuyper, A. (1914), *De eerepositie der vrouw*, J.H. Kok, Kampen.
Kymlicka, W. (1995), *Multicultural Citizenship: A Liberal Theory of Minority Rights*, Clarendon Press and Oxford University Press, Oxford.

Lehning, P.B. (1989), 'Socialisten tussen plan en macht', in J.W. De Beus, J.A.A. Van Doorn and P.B. Lehning, *De ideologische driehoek, Nederlandse politiek in historisch perspectief*, Boom, Meppel.

Leijenaar M.H. and Velde, H. van de (1989), 'Belangenbehartiging door vrouwen: vrouwenpartijen', in *Acta Politica*, vol.24, no.1, pp. 3-29.

Leijenaar, M.H. (1989), *De geschade herlijkheid*. Politiek gedrag van vrouwen en mannen in Nederland, 1918-1988, SDU, The Hague.

Leijenaar, M.H. (1996a), *Vrouwen in Politiek en Openbaar Bestuur: Een evaluatie van de maatregelen verwoord in het kabinetsstandpunt 1992*, Ministerie van Binnenlandse Zaken, Den Haag.

Leijenaar, M.H. (1996b), *How to create a gender balance in political decision making. A guide to implementing the participation of women in political decision making*, European Commission, Brussels.

Leijenaar, M.H. and Niemoller, B. (1993), *De helft als minderheid, verslag van een onderzoek naar vrouwen in politieke functies*. VNG, Den Haag.

Leijenaar, M.H. and Niemoller, B. (1994), *Het maatschappelijk tekort. Vrouwen in besturen van maatschappelijke organisaties*, Vuga, Den Haag.

Leijenaar, M.H. and Verloo, M. (1996), *Kiesstelsel in Nederland. Een emancipatie effect rapportage*, Ministerie van Binnenlandse Zaken, Den Haag.

Lewis, J. (1984), *Women in England 1870-1950; Sexual Division and Social Change*, Wheatsheaf Books, Sussex.

Lewis, J. (1991), *Women and Social Action in Victorian and Edwardian England*, Edward Elgar, Aldershot.

Lewis, J. (ed.) (1993), *Women and Social Policies in Europe. Work, Family and the State*, Edward Elgar, Aldershot.

Lijphart, A (1968). *Verzuiling, pacificatie en kentering in de Nederlandse politiek*, De Bussy, Amsterdam.

Lijphart, A. (1968), *The Politics of Accommodation. Pluralism and Democracy in the Netherlands*, University of California Press (2nd), Berkeley.

Lijphart, A. (1985), *Power-sharing in South Africa*, Institute of International Studies, University of California, Berkeley.

Lijphart, A. and Crepaz, M.M.L. (1991), 'Notes and comments. Corporatism and Consensus Democracy in Eighteen Countries: Conceptual and Empirical Linkages', *British Journal of Political Science*, vol. 21, pp. 235-56.

Lister, R. (1990), 'Women, Economic Dependency and Citizenship', *Journal for Social Policy*, vol. 19, no. 4, pp. 445-467.

Lloyd, G. (1984), *The Man of Reason. 'Male' and 'Female' in Western Philosophy*, Methuen, London.

Lovenduski, J. (1986a), *Women and European Politics, Contemporary Feminism and Public Policy*, Harvester Wheatsheaf, Brighton.

Lovenduski, J. (1986b), 'Beyond the Welfare State: Women and Corporatism in Britain', Paper prepared for the ECPR Joint Sessions of Workshops, Göteborg, April.

Lovenduski, J. (1993a), 'Introduction', in J. Lovenduski and P. Norris (eds), pp. 1-15.
Lovenduski, J. and P. Norris (1993b), *Gender and Party Politics*, Sage, London.
Luykx, K. and Versloot, A. (1994), *Zorgverlening binnen familieverbanden: vrouwen en mannen in Nederland vergeleken*, Verslag Stageonderzoek Rijksuniversiteit Utrecht, Utrecht.
Maandblad Nederlandsche Vereeniging voor Staatsburgeressen, Amsterdam.
MacIntyre, A. (1985), *After Virtue. A Study in Moral Theory*, Duckworth, London.
Maddison, A. (1991), *Dynamic Forces in Capitalist Development. A Long-run Comparative View*, Oxford University Press, Oxford.
Mansbridge, J. (1993),' Feminism and Democratic Community', in J.W. Chapman and I. Shapiro (eds), *Democratic Community, NOMOS XXXV*, N.Y.U. Press, New York, pp. 339-95.
Marshall, T.H. (1965), 'Citizenship and Social Class', in T.H. Marshall, *Class, Citizenship and Social Development*, Anchor, New York.
Mead, L. (1986), *Beyond Entitlement: The Social Obligations of Citizenship*, Free Press, New York.
Meehan, E. (1993) *Citizenship and the European Community*, Sage, London.
Michel, S. and Koven, S. (eds) (1993), *Mothers of a New World. Maternalist Policies and the Origins of the Welfare State*, Routledge, New York,
Mierlo, J. van (1989), *Pressiegroepen in de Nederlandse politiek*, SMO, Den Haag.
Ministerie van Algemene Zaken [NL] (1987), *Algemene aanwijzingen voor de Rijksdienst inzake externe adviesorganen en inzake interdepartementale commissies*, vastgesteld bij besluit van de Minister-President handelend in overeenstemming met het gevoelen van de Ministerraad, 11 maart, no. 375699, report, Staatsuitgeverij, The Hague.
Ministerie van Binnenlandse Zaken (1992, 1996), *Kabinetsstandpunt vrouwen in politiek en openbaar bestuur*, Ministerie van Binnenlandse Zaken, Den Haag.
Ministerie van Sociale Zaken en Werkgelegenheid [NL](1995), *From Nairobi to Beijing. Report of the Measures Taken in the Netherlands to Implement the Nairobi Forward Looking Strategies (1985-1995)*, report, Ministerie van SZW, The Hague.
Morée, M. (1992) *Mijn kinderen hebben er niets van gemerkt*, Jan van Arkel, Utrecht.
Morée, M. and Vliet, I. van (1989), 'Economische zelfstandigheid: van Aletta Jacobs tot heden', in *Jeugd en Samenleving*, vol. 19, nos. 6-7, pp. 341-59.
Mossink, M. and Nederland, T. (1993), *Beeldvorming in beleid. Een analyse van vrouwelijkheid en mannelijkheid in beleidsstukken van de rijksoverheid*, VUGA/ The Hague and Free University Amsterdam/ Amsterdam.
Mouffe, C. (1992), 'Feminism, Citizenship and Radical Democratic Politics', in J. Butler and C. Mouffe, *Dimensions of Radical Democracy. Pluralism, Citizenship, Community*, Verso, London/New York, pp. 225-39.
Mozes, M. and Wester, F. (1993), *Zorgen voor de toekomst. Een onderzoek naar de carrièreperspectieven van verzorgende vaders*, VUGA, The Hague.

Naber, J. (1920), *Mag het huwelijk gelden als factor bij de bepaling van den loonstandaard?*, Publ. Comité van Actie tegen Gezinsloon.

Naber, P. (1992), *Vriendschap onder jonge vrouwen*, Acco, Amersfoort/Leuven.

Naber, P. and Peters, E. (1991), 'Een baan of een carrière? Jonge vrouwen tussen wens en werkelijkheid', in I. van der Zande (ed.), *Het is meisjes menens. Inleiding meisjesstudies*, Acco, Amersfoort/Leuven, pp. 67-80.

Niphuis-Nell, M. (1992), *De emancipatie van meisjes en jonge vrouwen: Rapportage the behoeve van een evaluatie van het meisjesbeleid*, The Hague, VUGA.

Niphuis-Nell, M. (1997, forthcoming), 'Eenoudergezinnen, stiefgezinnen en uitwonende ouders', in M. Niphuis-Nell (ed.), *Sociale Atlas van de vrouw 4*, Sociaal en Cultureel Planbureau, Rijswijk.

Noordenbos, G. (1995), 'Positie van vrouwen in de universiteit in internationaal perspectief', in *Universiteit en Hogeschool*, vol. 41, April, pp. 105-20.

Noordman, J. (1989), *Om de Kwaliteit van het nageslacht: eugenetica in Nederland, 1900-1950*, SUN, Nijmegen.

O'Connor, J. (1996), 'From Women in the Welfare State to Gendering Welfare State Regimes', in *Current Sociology* (special issue), vol. 44, no. 2, pp. 1-130.

OECD (1992), *Economic Outlook, Historical Statistics 1960-1990*, OECD, Paris.

Okin, S.M. (1989), *Justice, Gender and the Family*, Basic Books, New York.

Oldersma, J. (1990), 'Vrouwen in Adviesraden', in *Acta Politica*, vol. 25, no. 4, October, pp. 467-84.

Oldersma, J. (1993), '*Welfare State and the Feminisation of the Dutch Elite*', Paper prepared for the workshop 'Welfare States and Gender', Joint sessions of workshops of the ECPR, 2-8 April, University of Leyden.

Oldersma, J. (1996), *De vrouw die vanzelf spreekt. Gender en representatie in het Nederlandse adviesradenstelsel*, DSWO-Press, Leyden.

Oldersma, J. (1997, forthcoming), 'The Corporatist Channel and Civil Society in The Netherlands', in J. Van Deth (ed.), *Private Groups and Public Life. Civil Society, Voluntary Involvement and Democratic Politics*, Routledge, London.

Orloff, A. (1993), 'Gender and the Social Rights of Citizenship: the Comparative Analysis of Gender Relations and Welfare States', *American Sociological Review*, vol. 58, no. 3, pp. 303-28.

Orloff, A. (1996), 'Motherhood, Work, and Welfare in the United States, Britain, Canada and Australia', Unpublished paper SSHAC, New Orleans.

Ostner, I. (1994), 'Back to the '50: Gender and Welfare in Unified Germany', in *Social Politics*, vol. 1, no. 1, pp. 32-59.

Ostner, I. and Lewis, J. (1995), 'Gender and the Evolution of European Social Policies', in S. Leibfried and P. Pierson (eds), *European Social Policy. Between Fragmentation and Integration*, The Brookings Institution Press, Washington D.C., pp. 159-93.

Oud, P.J. and Bosmans, J. (1990), *Staatkundige vormgeving in Nederland. I. 1840-1940*, Van Gorcum, Assen.

Outshoorn, J. (1973), *Vrouwenemancipatie en socialisme. De SDAP en het 'vrouwenvraagstuk' 1894-1919*, SUN, Nijmegen.

Outshoorn, J. and Lovenduski, J. (1986), *The New Politics of Abortion*, Sage, London.

Outshoorn, J.V. (1994), 'Between Movement and Government:'Femocrats' in the Netherlands', in H. Kreisi (ed.), *Schweizerisches Jahrbuch fur Politische Wissenschaften*, vol. 34, Haupt, Bern, pp. 141-65.

Outshoorn, J.V. (1995), 'Administrative Accommodation in the Netherlands. The Department for the Coordination of Equality Policy', in D. McBride Stetson and A. Mazur (eds), *Contemporary state feminism*, Sage, London, pp. 168-86.

Outshoorn, J.V. (1996a), 'Dealing in Sex. The Trafficking in Women in the Netherlands', Paper ECPR Joint Sessions of Workshops, Oslo, April.

Outshoorn, J.V. (1996b), 'Op naar de arbeidsmarkt. De cultuuromslag in het emancipatiebeleid', in O. Van Heffen, P.J. Klok and M. De Vries (eds), *Culturele dynamiek en beleidsontwikkeling*, Van Gorcum, Assen, pp. 132-47.

Outshoorn, J. (1984), 'Meer vrouwen in de politiek?', in *Vrouwen in politieke functies, verslag van een studiedag*, Ministerie van Binnenlandse Zaken, Den Haag.

Pateman, C. (1988a), *The Sexual Contract*, Polity Press, Cambridge.

Pateman, C. (1988b), 'The Patriarchal Welfare State', in A. Gutmann (ed.), *Democracy and the Welfare State*, Princeton University Press, Princeton, pp. 231-60.

Pateman, C. (1989), *The Disorder of Women. Democracy, Feminism and Political Theory*, Polity Press, Cambridge.

Pedersen, S. (1993), *Family, Dependence and the Origins of the Welfare State: Britain and France 1914-1945*, Cambridge University Press, Cambridge.

Peters, E. (1992), *Veranderingen in de jeugdfase van meisjes: generaties vergeleken*, DSWO Press, Leyden.

Peters, E. and Chisholm, L. (1991), 'Gendered Youth Transitions: Are Patterns Changing? A view from the Netherlands', *British Journal of Education and Work*, vol. 4, no. 3, pp. 39-51.

Phillips, A. (1987), *Divided Loyalties. Dilemmas of Sex and Class*, Virago Press, London.

Phillips, A. (1991), *Engendering Democracy*, Polity Press, Cambridge.

Phillips, A. (1993), *Democracy and Difference*, Polity Press, Cambridge.

Phillips, A. (1995), *The Politics of Presence*, Clarendon Press and Oxford University Press, Oxford.

Plantenga, J. (1992), 'De kantelende tijd. Opvattingen over vrouwenarbeid in de jaren vijftig', *Tijdschrift voor Vrouwenstudies*, vol. 13, pp. 140-61.

Plantenga, J. (1993), *Een afwijkend patroon. Honderd jaar vrouwenarbeid in Nederland en (West-) Duitsland*, SUA, Amsterdam.

Plantenga, J. (1996), 'For Women Only? The Rise of Part-time Work in the Netherlands', *Social Politics*, vol. 3, no. 1, pp. 57-71.

Plantenga, J. and Doorne-Huiskes, A. van (1992), 'Gender, Citizenship and Welfare: a European Perspective', Paper presented at the first European Conference of Sociology, Vienna.
Polak, A. (1917), 'Gelijk loon voor gelijken arbeid', *Onze Eeuw*, vol. 17, pp. 395-420.
Polak, A. (1920), *Het gezinsloon*, Publ. Comité van Actie tegen Gezinsloon, n.p.
Polak, A. (1921), 'Voorbarige wenschen', *Sociale Voorzorg*, vol. 3, pp. 108-27.
Polak, A. (1925), 'Het onterfde gezin', *De Economist*, vol. 74, pp. 358-83.
Posthumus - Van der Goot, W.H. (1938), 'Uitkomsten van een onderzoek naar den arbeid van de gehuwde vrouw in Nederland', in *Internationaal Archief voor de Vrouwenbeweging, Jaarboek II*, E.J. Brill, Leyden.
Raad voor het Jeugdbeleid [RJB] (1988), *Meisjes de helft van de jeugd. Advies over de maatschappelijke positie van meisjes: opvoeding, school, werk, hulpverlening en vrije tijd*, Ministerie van Welzijn, Volksgezondheid en Cultuur, Rijswijk.
Rang, B. (1986), 'Zur Geschichte des dualistischen Denkens über Mann und Frau. Kritische Anmerkungen zu den Thesen von Karin Hausen zur Herausbildung der Geschlechtscharaktere im 18. und 19. Jahrhundert', in J. Dalhoff, U. Frey and I. Schöll (eds), *Frauenmacht in der Geschichte*, Schwann, Düsseldorf, pp. 194-204.
Rawls, J. (1971), *A Theory of Justice*, Harvard University Press, Cambridge (Mass.).
Rendall, J. (1985), *The Origins of Modern Feminism: Women in Britain, France and the Unites States, 1780-1860*, Macmillan, London.
Rendall, J. (1994), 'Citizenship, Culture and Civilization: The Languages of British Suffragists, 1866-1874', in C. Daley and M. Nolan (eds), *Suffrage and Beyond*, Auckland University Press, Auckland, pp. 127-50.
Richards, J.R. (1980), *The Sceptical Feminist. A Philosophical Enquiry*, Penguin, Harmondsworth.
Rijswijk-Clerk, L. van (1981), *Moeders, kinderen en kinderopvang*, SUN, Nijmegen.
Roche, M. (1992), *Rethinking Citizenship. Welfare, Ideology and Change in Modern Society*, Polity Press, Cambridge.
Roebroek, J. (1993), *The Imprisoned State*, Tilburg University, Department of Social Security Studies, Tilburg.
Rooy, P. de (1987), *Darwin en strijd langs vaste lijnen*, SUN: Nijmegen.
Ruddick, S. (1983), *Mothering: Essays on Feminist Theory*, Littlefield Adams, Totowa.
Sainsbury, D. (1994), 'Women's and Men's Social Rights: Gendering Dimensions of Welfare States', in D. Sainsbury (ed.), *Gendering Welfare States*, Sage, London, pp. 150-70.
Sainsbury, D. (1996), *Gender, Equality and Welfare States*, Cambridge University Press: Cambridge.
Sandel, M. (1982), *Liberalism and the Limits of Justice*, Polity Press, Cambridge.
Sapiro, V. (1981), 'When Are Interests Interesting? The Problem of Political Representation of Women', *The American Political Science Review*, vol. 75, pp. 701-16.

Sarvasy W. and Siim, B. (eds) (1994), 'Introduction' to the Special Issue on 'Gender and the Transition to Democracy', *Social Politics. International Studies in Gender, State and Society*, vol. 1, no. 3, pp. 249-55.

Sawer, M. (1990), *Sisters in Suits. Women and Public Policy in Australia*, Allen and Unwin, Sydney.

Sawer, M. and Groves, A. (1994), *Working from Inside. Twenty Years of the Office of the Status of Women*, Australian Government Publishing Service, Canberra.

Schama, S. (1977), *Patriots and Liberators: Revolution in the Netherlands, 1780-1813*, Knopf, New York.

Schattschneider, E.E. (1975), *The Semi-sovereign People. A Realist's View of Democracy in America*, The Dryden Press, Hinsdale (Il.).

Schlozman K.L. et al. (1995),'Gender and Citizenship Participation - Is There a Different Voice', *American Journal of Political Science*, vol. 39, no. 2, pp. 267-93.

Schmitter, P. and Lehmbruch, G. (1979), *Trends Toward Corporatist Intermediation*, Sage, London.

Schoot Uiterkamp, A. (1978), 'Terug naar het paradijs? Acties tegen de beperking van vrouwenarbeid in de jaren dertig', in *Jaarboek voor de geschiedenis van socialisme en arbeidersbeweging in Nederland*, Sunschrift 135, pp. 182-244.

Schuler, M.A. (ed.) (1990), *Women, Law, and Development: Action for Change*, OEF International, Washington, D.C.

Sevenhuijsen, S. (1996), *Oordelen met zorg. Feministische beschouwingen over recht, moraal en politiek*, Boom, Meppel/Amsterdam.

Siim, B. (1994), 'Engendering Democracy: The Interplay Between Women's Citizenship and Political Participation in Scandinavia', *Social Politics. International Studies in Gender, State and Society*, vol. 1, no. 3, pp. 286-305.

Simonis, J.B.D., Hemerijck, A.C. and Lehning, P.B. (eds) (1992), *De staat van de burger. Beschouwingen over hedendaags burgerschap*, Boom, Meppel/Amsterdam.

Skocpol, T. (1992), *Protecting Mother and Soldiers. The Political Origins of Social Policy in the United States*, Belknap Press, Cambridge.

Skocpol, T. and Ritter, G. (1991), 'Gender and the origins of Modern Social Policies in Britain and the United States', *Studies in American Development*, Spring, pp. 36-93.

Smit, J. (1984), *Er is een land waar vrouwen willen wonen. Teksten 1967-1981*, Feministische Uitgeverij Sara, Amsterdam.

Smith, M.J. (1993), *Pressure, Power and Policy, State Autonomy and Policy Networks in Britain and the United States*, Harvester Wheatsheaf, New York.

Sociaal en Cultureel Planbureau (1988), *Sociaal en Cultureel Rapport 1988*, SCP/VUGA, Rijswijk.

Sociaal en Cultureel Planbureau (SCP) (1996), *Sociaal en Cultureel Rapport 1996*, Rijswijk.

Sociaal-Economische Raad [SER] (1976), *Advies betreffende de representativiteit van organisaties van ondernemers en van werknemers in verband met de samenstelling van publiekrechtelijke colleges*, no. 5, 19 December 1975, Sociaal-Economische Raad, The Hague.

Sociaal-Economische Raad [SER] (1988), *Advies maatschappelijke positie van meisjes en jonge vrouwen*, SER, The Hague.

Soysal, Y. (1993), *Limits of Citizenship: Migrants and Postnational Membership in Europe*. University of Chicago Press, Chicago.

Spaans, J. and Veldhoen, E. (1995), *Kinderopvanggebruik en arbeidsparticipatie van vrouwen met kinderen. Stand van zaken per 31-12-1993*, Research voor Beleid, Leyden.

Spoormans, H. (1988), *'Met uitsluiting van voorregt' Het ontstaan van liberale democratie in Nederland*, SUA, Amsterdam.

Steenbergen, B. van (1987), 'Vrijwilligerswerk in toekomstperspectief', in Kwant, R.C. (ed.), *Dat doe je gewoon*, De Balie, Amsterdam.

Stetson, McBride, D. and Mazur, A. (eds) (1995a), *Comparative State Feminism*, Sage, London.

Stetson, McBride, D. and Mazur, A. (eds) (1995b), *Women's Policy Offices, Representation, and Deficient Democracies: A Cross-National Project*, Draft Research Proposal Research Network on Gender and the State.

Stivers, C. (1993), *Gender Images in Public Administration. Legitimacy and the Adminitrative State*, Sage, London.

Stokkom, B.A.M. van (1992), *De Republiek der Weerbaren. Burgerschap, Publieke Actie en Sociaal-democratie*, Van Loghum, Houten.

Stolk, A. (1921), *Enkele beschouwingen over het gezinsloon*, Dissertation VU, Amsterdam.

Stuurman, S. (1983), *Verzuiling, kapitalisme en patriarchaat*, SUN, Nijmegen.

Stuurman, S. (1992), *Wacht op onze daden. Het liberalisme en de vernieuwing van de Nederlandse staat*, Bert Bakker, Amsterdam.

Sullivan B. and Whitehouse G. (eds) (1996), *Gender, Politics and Citizenship in the 1990s*, University of New South Wales Press, Sydney.

Swiebel, J. and J. Outshoorn (1991), 'Feminism and the State: The Case of the Netherlands', Paper presented at the Annual Meeting of the Dutch Political Science Association, Twente, 12-13 June.

Tash, R.C. (1991), *Dutch Pluralism: A Model in Tolerance for Developing Countries*, P. Lang, New York.

Taylor-Gooby, P. (1991), 'Welfare State Regimes and Welfare Citizenship', *Journal of European Social Policy*, vol. 1, no. 2, pp. 93-105.

The Economist (1996), 'Tomorrow's Second Sex', 28 September.

Therborn, G. (1993), '"Pillarization" and "Popular" Movements: Two Variants of Welfare State Capitalism: the Netherlands and Sweden', in F.G. Castles (ed.), *The Comparative History of Public Policy*, Polity Press, Cambridge, pp. 192-241.

Tiedemann, E. (1993), '"We hadden er een, maar ze ging weg". Vrouw, zeldzame verschijning in de top van het bedrijfsleven', *Elsevier*, vol. 20, no. 3, pp. 62-8.

Twine, F. (1994), *Citizenship and Social Rights*. Sage, London.

Uitterhoeve, W. (1990), *De staat der Nederlanden*, SUN, Nijmegen.
United Nations Development Programme (1995), *Human Development Report*, Oxford University Press, New York.
United Nations Development Programme (1996), *Human Development Report*, Oxford University Press, New York.
Uyl, R. den and Cornelissen, W. (1991), *Ondersteuningsvoorzieningen en -behoeften bij meisjes. Het derde spoor van het meisjesbeleid: beinvloeden van de sociale omgeving*, Ministerie van Sociale Zaken en Werkgelegenheid/VUGA, The Hague.
Velde, H. te (1992), *Gemeenschapszin en plichtsbesef. Liberalisme en nationalisme in Nederland, 1870-1918*, SDU, The Hague.
Velde, H. te (1993), 'How High did the Dutch Fly? Remarks on Stereotypes of Burger Mentality', in A. Galema et al. (eds), *Images of the Nation. Different Meanings of Dutchness*, Rodopi, Amsterdam.
Velde, H.L.J. van de (1994), *Vrouwen van de partij: de integratie van vrouwen in politieke partijen in Nederland (1919-1990)*, DSWO Press, Leyden.
Vereeniging van Raden van Arbeid (1922), *Verslag, Congres voor Sociale Verzekering, 11-12 October 1921*, report, vereeniging van Raden van Arbeid, Utrecht/Amsterdam.
Verloo, M. (1992), *Macht en gender in sociale bewegingen*, SUA, Amsterdam.
Voet, R. (1995), *Feminism and Citizenship. Feminist Critiques of the Concept of Social-Liberal Citizenship*, PhD, Leyden University. Forthcoming as *Feminism and Citizenship* (1997), Sage, London.
Vogel, U. (1991), 'Is Citizenship Gender-Specific?', in U. Vogel and M. Moran (eds), *The Frontiers of Citizenship*, Macmillan, Houndsmills, pp. 58-85.
Vogel, U. (1994), 'Marriage and the Boundaries of Citizenship', in B. Van Steenbergen (ed.), *The Condition of Citizenship*, Sage, London, pp. 76-89.
Vries-Bruins, A.E.J. de (1938), 'Het voorontwerp-Romme', *De Socialistische Gids*, vol. 23, no. 2, pp. 65-80.
Waal, M. de (1989), *Meisjes: een wereld apart. Een etnografie van meisjes op de middelbare school*, Boom, Amsterdam.
Waal, M. de (1990), *Met meisjes is niks mis: meisjebeleid in Europees perspectief*, Raad voor het Jeugdbeleid, Amsterdam.
Waaldijk, B. (1996), *Het Amerika der vrouw. Sekse en geschiedenis van maatschappelijk werk in Nederland en de Verenigde Staten*, Wolters Noordhoff, Amsterdam.
Walby, S. (1986), *Patriarchy at Work*, Polity Press, Cambridge.
Walby, S. (1994), 'Is Citizenship Gendered?', *Sociology - The Journal of the British Sociological Association*, vol. 28, no. 2. pp. 379-95.
Walzer, M. (1991), 'The idea of Civil Society', in *Dissent*, Spring, pp. 293-304.
Watson, S. (ed.) (1990), *Playing the State. Australian Feminist Interventions*, Verso, London.
Wetenschappelijke Raad voor het Regeringsbeleid (WRR) (1990), *Een werkend perspectief. Arbeidsparticipatie in de jaren '90*, report, SDU, The Hague.

Wijnaendts Francken-Dijserinck, W. (1920), 'Prae-advies Nationale Vrouwenraad', in *Orgaan NVR*, 15 March-15 April, pp. 1-7.
Wijnaendts Francken-Dijserinck, W. (1924), *Moederschapszorg*, Tjeenk Willink, Haarlem.
Williamson, P.J. (1989), *Corporatism in Perspective*, Sage, London.
Wittert Van Hoogland, E.B.B.F. (1940), *De parlementaire geschiedenis der sociale verzekering, 1890-1940*, Tjeenk Willink: Haarlem.
Woldendorp, J.J. (1995), 'Neo-corporatism as a Strategy for Conflict Regulation in the Netherlands', *Acta Politica* 1995, no. 2, 121-152.
Woolf, W. (1995), *Killing the Angel in the House*, Penguin, London.
Wuertz K. and Pennen, T. van der (1987), *Van regent tot manager*, NCIV, De Bildt.
Young, I.M. (1989), 'Polity and Group Difference. A Critique of the Ideal of Universal Citizenship', *Ethics*, vol. 99, pp. 250-274.
Young, I.M. (1990), *Justice and the Politics of Difference*, Princeton (N.J.), Princeton University Press.
Young, I.M. (1995), 'Communication and the Other: Beyond Deliberative Democracy', in M. Wilson and A. Yeatman (eds), *Justice & Identity. Antipodean Practices*, Bridget Williams Books, Wellington, pp. 134-152.
Zahn, E. (1984), *Das unbekannte Holland: Regenten, Rebellen und Reformatoren*, Siedler, Berlin.
Zande, I. van der and Hoogeveen, K. (1991), 'Meisjesbeleid: economische noodzaak of politieke keuze?', in I. van der Zande (ed.), *Het is meisjes menens. Inleiding meisjesstudies*, Acco, Amersfoort/Leuven, pp. 118-36.